How
Alcoholics Anonymous
Failed Me

How Alcoholics Anonymous Failed Me

MY PERSONAL JOURNEY TO SOBRIETY THROUGH SELF-EMPOWERMENT

Marianne W. Gilliam

EAGLE BROOK

AN IMPRINT OF WILLIAM MORROW AND COMPANY, INC.

New York

This book is dedicated to everyone who suffers from an addiction
and to their loved ones.

Copyright © 1998 by Marianne W. Gilliam
Published by Eagle Brook
An Imprint of William Morrow and Company, Inc.
1350 Avenue of the Americas, New York, N.Y. 10019

It is the policy of William Morrow and Company, Inc., and its imprints and affiliates, recognizing the importance of preserving what has been written, to print the books we publish on acid-free paper, and we exert our best efforts to that end.

The Library of Congress has cataloged a previous edition of this title.

Library of Congress Cataloging-in-Publication Data
Gilliam, Marianne W.
How Alcoholics Anonymous failed me : my personal journey to sobriety
through self-empowerment / by Marianne W. Gilliam.
p.   cm.
ISBN 0-688-15587-1
1. Gilliam, Marianne W.   2. Alcoholics—United States—Biography.
3. Alcoholics—Rehabilitation—United States—Case studies.
4. Alcoholics Anonymous.   I. Title.
HV5293.G55A3   1998
362.292'86'092—dc21
[b]   97-37092
                                                                   CIP

Paperback ISBN 0-688-17013-7

Printed in the United States of America

FIRST PAPERBACK EDITION 1999

1 2 3 4 5 6 7 8 9 10

BOOK DESIGN BY HELENE WALD BERINSKY

www.williammorrow.com

FOREWORD
by Charlotte Kasl, Ph.D.

THIS BOOK REPRESENTS the early stages of a paradigm shift in the addiction field, a shift desperately needed to alleviate the human suffering involved in all addictions. The concept of empowerment presented by Marianne Gilliam is holistic, deeply spiritual—though not necessarily religious—and represents the belief that people are born with a potential wellspring of strength, courage, and wisdom to guide them in growth and healing. The key is to tap their wisdom, listen to it, and find the courage to follow it. By nature, the path will vary with each individual. "I'm not recovering, I'm recovered," Marianne tells a friend. These words—blasphemous in traditional AA (Alcoholics Anonymous) circles, where addiction is a life sentence—represent the hope and courage that sing through these pages. Marianne wanted happiness, joy, and vitality that surpassed the narrow concepts of sobriety and abstinence. By exploring the underlying pain, guilt, shame, and physical imbalance that fueled her addictions, she was able to heal and shed such limiting labels as "alcoholic," codependent," and "bulimic." AA was a step in the path that helped her maintain sobriety for a while, but it was a sobriety laced with fear, a fear intrinsic to the twelve-step approach.

While the twelve steps of Alcoholics Anonymous have been presumed a panacea for recovery from addiction, for a majority of people they are not. "Only one in fifteen of you will stay sober" is a frequent component of introductory lectures in drug treatment programs and rehabilitation centers. Why, one might ask, if the treatment outcome is so poor, don't professionals consider changing their methods? Few of us would consider having a costly operation if the chances were one in fifteen that we would survive. The reasons are grounded in fear and caught in a system that perpetuates itself.

AA has become akin to a fundamentalist religion inculcated and maintained by fear. "If you don't go to AA you will relapse, end up in prison, the gutter, or dead." When people are vulnerable and desperate for sobriety, they are at high risk to be indoctrinated into a system that promises hope and, for many, life. Most addiction counselors are brought up through the ranks of addiction recovery, which, in the field, gives them credibility. If individuals resist the teachings, they are told they are *in their addiction*—"utilize, don't analyze." Counselors in training have been reprimanded for questioning: "Keep up that kind of questioning and you'll be out of our program." Thus, the very things that help people mature—thinking, exploring new ideas, and being flexible—are treated as heresy and leave people in a double bind. To be accepted means to suppress one's intellect and passion—a dangerous proposition.

This brings to mind a story I frequently tell at addiction conferences: "One day I walk into my twelve-step group and say, 'Hi, I'm Charlotte, I'm feeling good, my life is going well, and I don't think I'll be coming much longer.' I ask the audience to guess at the response. Invariably there is silence, followed by sprinkles of laughter. 'You are in your addiction,' 'You're denying your addiction,' 'You've relapsed,' 'You've lost your humility' are the common responses. 'Okay,' I continue. 'If feeling good means I've relapsed, what is the definition of a healthy person who has recovered?' Silence again. And more silence. *There is no model of a healthy recovered person in all of the approved twelve-step literature.*"

Because Marianne desired health, joy, and happiness, she sought the true roots of healing, which she found in philosophy, psychology, and the spiritual writings of Shakti Gawain, Deepak Chopra, Gerald Jampolsky, Wayne Dyer, Carolyn Myss, and others. She realized that AA focused on behavior—"act as if," "fake it till you make it"—while spiritual writers focused on an inward journey toward love and wisdom.

When Bill Wilson founded Alcoholics Anonymous more than

fifty years ago, he was in the late stages of alcoholism, desperate for sobriety. He was instrumental in transforming traditional stereotypes of alcoholics as moral misfits lacking willpower into people with a disease that possibly had genetic origins. His gift liberated countless people from alcoholism and other addictions. Unfortunately, instead of adopting it as a model, thankful loyalists, caught in their own narcissism, acclaimed it as *the* model—no questions allowed. This resulted in blind adherence, lack of scientific inquiry, and a grandiosity that shunned those who ventured outside its limiting belief system. Their myopia has caused suffering for many. In researching *Women, Sex, and Addiction,* I interviewed numerous women who repeatedly relapsed until they dealt with abuse, incest, and addictive sexual relationships. Even though people have failed to stay sober going through treatment as many as fourteen times (Kasl, 1991), the programs never questioned themselves. "If you relapsed it was because you did it wrong." This arrogant stance is not surprising, because, in many ways, the "rules"and philosophy of the twelve-step approach are embedded in the rules and philosophy of patriarchy and hierarchy. I cite two. There are many more.

AA and patriarchy are both dualistic and based on fear—fear that if we allow ourselves passion, pleasure, joy, love, connection, and happiness, we will go out of control: If we don't work compulsively we will become lazy slobs. If we savor food and relish its deliciousness, it will become the enemy and we'll gain a hundred pounds; if we enjoy and explore sexuality as a form of spiritual bonding, it will overtake and dominate our lives. The message is containment rather than harmony, balance, and trust. Likewise in AA, people are controlled by fear: If you don't go to meetings, you'll relapse, and if you relapse, you'll die. In both systems people are instucted to bridle their passions and limit their lives, when, in reality, blocking our creativity, joy, and natural desires is at the root of addiction because it creates inner warfare. People constantly focus on *not* doing something or doing it wrong.

AA and patriarchy are both based on obedience and conformity. We are taught from early childhood to pledge allegiance to authoritarian rules that remain outside us. If we question or attempt to think for ourselves, we are troublemakers, rebels to be shunned or brought back to the fold. "Love it or leave it." "You're with us or against us." In twelve-step groups (my research included hundreds of interviews with a cross section of races and religions, cultures and classes), when people question the philosophy and practices of AA—the concept of an all-powerful male God, saying the Lord's Prayer at the close of meetings, the need for moral inventories or lifelong attendance—they are routinely handed platitudes: "If it ain't broke, don't fix it." Blatantly missing is a comprehension of the developmental process of differentiation intrinsic to models of human spiritual growth as explored by Fromm, Maslow, Erickson, and Fowler. A high level of differentiation—the ability to retain one's self in close proximity to other people and other ideologies—is the basis of healthy intimate relationships, which is central to mental health and recovery.

If I learned one thing from countless interviews and research it is this: People become addicted for numerous reasons, their addictions take many forms, and their paths of healing vary immensely. We have much to learn from listening to one another. For people who have been marginalized in our society, exploring cultural roots, understanding internalized oppression, and having economic opportunity are important aspects of desiring and maintaining sobriety. We need a comprehensive approach that asks all people, What do you need? What is missing from your life? What feeds your soul?

Spiritual maturity and freedom come from internalizing our values and living in the center of our own lives. As Marianne Gilliam shows, experimentation, confusion, disillusionment, doubt, and questioning are inherent in the process of shedding rigid belief systems and finding our own truths. She asked: What do I see? What do I believe? feel? observe? What's right for me? Instead of being a candle in the wind, she learned to reside calmly in the center of her own life, learning through experience, and feeling the breath of spirit touching her heart.

Marianne Gilliam has given us the gift of her inspiring story— breathtakingly honest, beautifully written. By showing us *her* way, she invites all people to find *their* way. This is a book that every thinking person concerned with the overwhelming rates of relapse and the widespread proliferation of all addictions should read.

—Charlotte Kasl, Ph.D.
Lolo, Montana

Charlotte Kasl is the author of *Women, Sex, and Addiction* and *Many Roads, One Journey: Moving Beyond the Twelve Steps* and founder of the sixteen-step empowerment model for discovery and overcoming addiction.

ACKNOWLEDGMENTS

WRITING THIS BOOK has by no means been a solitary pursuit. Without the kind assistance and presence of many people, this book would not have evolved into its present form.

First and foremost, I would like to thank Joann Davis at William Morrow for deciding to take this book on. I am eternally grateful for the patient and gentle way she molded the book into a much more personal account than I would have ever envisioned, making it into, I believe, a much more powerful story. And becoming a friend in the process.

I would also like to thank Mary Mullinax, Jeff Mathews, and Stanley Quarles for their thoughtful feedback on early versions of the manuscript. Many thanks also to Mary for her friendship of twenty-plus years. She is the only one other than my family who witnessed my full descent from innocence into addiction and finally to freedom. To my sister, Miriam, for being a well of inspiration to me, whether she knows it or not, and the courageous way she faces her life with faith, hope, and kindness. Her ever-present love is a joy in my life.

To my father and mother, words cannot convey the depth of gratitude I have for them. The unswerving love and devotion they have always given me, even when I didn't even love myself, has saved my life. Their faith in me gave me the ability to have faith in myself.

To Victoria Palmer, whose daily presence in my life has kept me sane on more than one occasion. To Sandy Candler, for attentively caring for my son while I wrote much of this manuscript. To Carolyn Watts for her bright smile every morning while she worked at our office.

To Michelle Shinseki for always being a cheerful voice on the other end of the line.

To Bill Gilliam, my wonderful husband, for all his support and love. And to Alexander and Maxwell for being two bright and beautiful beacons of light and love in my life. They have forever changed my life in untold wonderful ways, making me a far better person than I would have been otherwise.

CONTENTS

INTRODUCTION

I AM NOT a medical expert on addiction. I do not have a medical degree. I am not an expert on the psychological causes behind addiction. I do not hold a degree in psychology. I know nothing about the sociological aspects of addiction. But I am an expert on addiction because I was an addict. For fourteen years I specialized in addiction. Alcohol and drug abuse marked my teenage years and almost all of my adult life. I developed bulimia at age twenty-three and was plagued by binge-purge behavior for nearly seven years. I smoked cigarettes between the ages of fourteen and twenty-eight. Today I have recovered completely from all my previous addictions. Not "in recovery," not one day at a time for the rest of my life. Today I live fully and completely, no longer seeking to escape from the painful parts that require me to feel real feelings. I still have problems and challenges in my life, but I have found the tools to deal with those problems without needing to hide behind addictive behavior. My life and my outlook are 180 degrees apart from what they were during my years of addiction.

For so many of those years of addiction, I wanted to end my self-destructive behavior but didn't know how. I attended Alcoholics Anonymous and other twelve-step groups off and on for ten years. I looked to all these "experts" to tell me what to do. The medical experts told me that I had a progressive disease. They taught me that

I was born with a genetic predisposition to alcoholic behavior. The disease theory, I learned, had gained widespread acceptance in the 1950s as the result of E. M. Jellinek's *The Disease Concept of Alcoholism*. It was his belief, along with that of many others, that categorizing alcoholism as a "disease" was crucial to increasing the availability of help for the suffering alcoholic within established medical facilities. In other words, labeling alcoholism as a disease would enable insurance companies to pay for medical help at treatment centers and hospitals. I found all this very interesting, but knowing I had a disease did little to help me stop drinking.

The psychological experts told me that I needed to examine my childhood and embrace my inner wounded child. I learned all about my "dysfunctional family" and the emotional abandonment of my childhood. I was free to blame my family of origin for my behavior. The sociologists told me that addiction was a societal ill. Addiction was the result of a patriarchal, male-dominated society that suppressed and repressed women and minorities; as a woman I was free to blame society for my tendency to destroy my life.

And Alcoholics Anonymous told me that I was powerless and that God was the answer.

All the experts were offering me were superficial facts and empty solutions. All the expert knowledge in the world failed when it came to healing my addictions. It seems that the storehouse of knowledge surrounding addiction increases as rapidly as does the preponderance of addiction in our society. And alcohol is no longer seen as the only form of addiction. We now have gambling addicts, sex addicts, shopping addicts, food addicts, people addicts, caffeine addicts, television addicts, narcotics addicts, religious addicts, etc., etc. All of our addiction studies are doing nothing to change the high rate of relapse, over 70 percent of those seeking to obtain sobriety, and the low rate of long-term success (between 2.4 and 4.8 percent of the addicted population). I was in desperate need of some real solutions to my miserable, addicted life.

Alcoholics Anonymous was the most successful program in treating alcoholism, so I went there first. A.A. told me that I had a disease, the disease of alcoholism, and said that my only options were jails, institutions, or death. A.A. taught me how to focus on my moral wrongs, defects of character, and shortcomings and said that complete reliance on a Higher Power who was outside myself could relieve me of alcoholism one day at a time as long as I continued to attend their meetings. I was strongly warned that if I stopped attending meetings I would surely drink again, and if I drank again I would die. I did, in fact, achieve sobriety by following their plan. But I lived in fear.

I was fearful that if I didn't attend enough meetings, I would relapse. I was fearful that I wasn't humble enough. I was fearful without even realizing I was fearful. Fear had become the basis of my sobriety. I was fearful that if I didn't believe in the requirements for powerlessness, I would jeopardize my hard-earned sobriety. In Overeaters Anonymous, which I attended for my bulimia, I was fearful that if I wasn't eating "abstinently,"* I wasn't as good a person. I came to believe that God liked me better when I was sober. And I became fearful of not living up to God's expectations of me. I was afraid to admit to the group how I really felt about some of the ideas taught in A.A. because I was shunned every time I did so. I resented being told I had to do for others. I wanted desperately to learn how to do for myself first. I felt as if I had been living my whole life for others and that this had, in part, contributed to my addictions. I wanted someone who could teach me how to do for myself and how to love myself. And then there were little things that I hated being told I *had* to do, as if my sobriety hinged upon my willingness to do these things. I was afraid to admit that I didn't really want to help clean up after meetings. And I didn't like making small talk after meetings if I was in a bad mood; I was ridiculed for always leaving right after a meeting. I was especially tired of having someone else dictate "the solution" to me and tell me how to live *my* life.

Dr. Deepak Chopra writes similarly in his book *Overcoming Addictions: A Spiritual Solution:* "Fear of the past, fear of the future, fear

---

*In Overeaters Anonymous, the goal is "abstinent eating," which is defined as three meals with nothing in between. Throughout the book I use the term "abstinence" and "food abstinence" to refer to this moderate form of eating.

of using the present moment for experiencing real joy—so many fears haunt the ways in which we become immersed in addictive behaviors. Fear is also a part of many treatment programs for addiction. Yet a fear-based approach cannot, in my opinion, be successful for the majority of people over an extended period of time."

So I abandoned A.A. and O.A. I wanted, I craved, a model of healing that validated *me*, and all of the things that were right about me, instead of asking me to continually focus on my wrongs and shortcomings. I was acutely aware of all my wrongs. I was acutely aware of the harm my horrible behavior had caused. I didn't need to be humbled anymore. Overwhelming guilt and humility only contributed to lowering my self-esteem and setting me up for further addictive episodes. I wanted a model of healing that taught me how to seize my inner power and use it as the basis for a new life. I wanted an intimate relationship with a God who was *inside* me and part of me, not outside me and judging me. I wanted to feel whole and complete for once in my life.

I did a bit of research into A.A. and other twelve-step groups and was startled by what I discovered. Although A.A. is the most successful program for achieving sobriety, its relapse rate shocked me. Let me give you some overall statistics about alcoholism. Of the estimated 14 million adult Americans who are deemed alcoholic, less than 10 percent of them will be seeking help at any given time. Of those 10 percent, 70 percent won't achieve lasting sobriety. Seventy percent of those who achieve sobriety in A.A. will relapse within five years. The relapse rates for one year are even higher. So for long-term sobriety, only *3 percent* of all adult alcoholics will successfully quit drinking by using A.A. Three percent! (Calculated as 30 percent of the 10 percent of the entire drinking population who are seeking help.) Why such high relapse rates and why such a disappointingly low number of people seeking treatment? What happened to the big recovery movement of the late seventies and early eighties? The numbers all went up when they were supposed to go down.

And what about the number of people who had achieved sobriety but were still not happy or satisfied with their lives? Was alcohol really the problem, or was there something deeper going on that was causing us to be dissatisfied and the alcohol was simply masking it? I found that I drank *for a reason*. My addictive behavior did not occur in a vacuum. I didn't drink, use cocaine, and binge and purge on food simply because I had the "disease of alcoholism." The genetic link was too simplistic. I had to go within myself, discover the root cause of *why* I drank, and heal those reasons, heal the pain I had been running from all my life.

At the height of my despair I would have done anything to be able to quit drinking and to end my binge-purge behavior. A.A. rescued me for a while but I felt I was unable to grow personally and spiritually until I moved beyond the parent-child relationship encouraged by A.A. When alcoholics are sick and in desperate need of direction and fellowship, A.A.'s open arms can be a wonderful respite from the stormy days and nights of addiction. But as I started attending A.A. meetings I witnessed the cultlike devotion given to the A.A. publication, *Alcoholics Anonymous* (known as the Big Book), and the expectation that it would provide people with the answers to all of life's problems. The Big Book meetings I attended were remarkably similar to Bible study groups I had gone to as a child, to my mind, a scary correlation.

But I could understand why A.A. members acted this way. It simply indicated how much we all want answers, solutions, and meaning in life. But in my opinion, the Big Book is not the place to look.

In fact, my experience underscored the whole dilemma I had with A.A., which was its tendency to put the responsibility for our problem, alcoholism, outside us by blaming our "disease" and then telling us that the solution lay outside us as well. A.A. requires members to admit that they are powerless over their disease. And then we are told to turn our will and our lives over to a Higher Power *outside ourselves* (in other words, don't even think about looking within ourselves for power). I had been weak all of my life and my addictions served only to weaken me further. Putting the solution for my healing outside myself weakened me even more. When I finally left A.A. I discovered that I had been looking in the wrong place. For long-term recovery, for long-term sobriety, for answers in life and the meaning of life, I needed to look within. As long as I believed in powerlessness, I would be powerless. I was now ready to carve out my own life, to embrace my own powerfulness, to awaken my own healing potential, and to connect with my internal spirituality and God consciousness.

I read everything I could about addiction and healing. Within months, I finally achieved sobriety, but my bulimia was still a noose around my neck that I couldn't seem to loosen. I attended more Overeaters Anonymous meetings hoping to discover something new; what I discovered was that I would have to find my own way. O.A.'s focus on food and on what everyone had eaten that day did nothing to heal my addiction, and instead implanted the message that the solution to my bulimic behavior lay in what I ate, which was not true. I prayed to God to help me but he seemed to be out of the office. I felt utterly alone.

I somehow, slowly and miraculously, began to learn to love myself and one day a light went on inside me. At the core of my healing was love, and at the root of my addiction was fear. I could heal with love and become empowered or I could heal with fear and remain powerless, prone to relapse and addiction.

I worked on nurturing my God within and I felt small, vague stirrings inside myself. I discovered that they were intuitive promptings trying to be heard and longing for expression. I slowly and hesitatingly began honoring my intuitive flashes; they were unerringly correct and remarkably astute. I found a wonderful, wise, patient, loving presence within me and I worked on releasing it. It took many years and countless struggles to dismantle the layers upon layers of limiting, fearful beliefs and I saw that the root of the problem was in my being all too willing to give away the power for my life. I saw the way I had been giving away my power for years—to parents, to schools, to religions, to institutions, to experts, all of whom wanted to tell me how to live and all purporting to know better than I did about my life.

When I stopped discounting myself and my own wisdom, for the first time I truly began to live. I truly began to heal.

It is still remarkable to me how quickly my addictions vanished as soon as I learned to take back the reins and the power for my life. As I resolved the internal struggles within myself, my addictions disappeared.

This book is my story. It is my hope that through my struggles others may be helped. There were seven components that were essential to my recovery. The first was to discover why I drank, why I acted self-destructively. The pat theory of my "disease" causing me to be powerless was no solution. I had to identify the root cause of my addiction and heal it. Second, I had to embrace my intuition, my wisdom within, and be the final authority for what was and wasn't right for me.

Along the way, I discovered how often I had let other people's experiences dictate my own, and how rampant fear and powerlessness were in my life. Third, I learned to honor and embrace my God within. Growing up, I had gotten all kinds of mixed messages about God. He's a male, external entity, in Heaven somewhere, watching over all of us, judging us. He likes us better when we are being good. We were born as hopeless sinners and only by His graciousness can we achieve salvation. I got just as many mixed messages about God in A.A. All we need is a belief in a Higher Power, we are told. But that power is repeatedly referred to as a male God. True empowerment for me came by recognizing that I wasn't some lowly sinner who had to adopt a stance of powerlessness and turn my will and my life over to someone or something else in order to heal. True empowerment came by affirming my belief in my goodness, affirming my belief in my own self-worth (whether I was drunk or sober), and especially by affirming my belief that the God who exists outside us and all around us also exists inside me and is part of me.

The fourth part was learning to trust again. I had developed so much doubt, cynicism, and despair about my life that I had become all too eager to turn the whole mess over to someone else. But true empowerment required me to start trusting that the Universe was a friendly place, that I knew what was best for me (and that sometimes includes asking for advice and assistance from others), and the expectation that hope would spring eternal in my life. The fifth part was learning acceptance in all areas of my life. The sixth part of my healing was a sort of conglomeration of all the rest and entailed my learning to be powerful in all areas of my life. I learned how to love and be loved and how to overcome fear when it was holding me back.

The final component ensured that I would stay centered on the healthy path I am now on. Creating a meaningful life has done more for me than I could ever have imagined. Before, I was always trying to live up to someone else's expectations of me and setting goals for what I thought I *should* be doing. I now allow my heart to dictate where I want to go and what I want to do. The first thing I wanted to create was a healthy, addiction-free body. I believe I have learned to do that. I now know how to create meaning in every area of my life—in my profession, with my husband, with my physical health, with my children, and with my emotional and spiritual life. If we have a real reason to live and are truly doing something meaningful, we are much less likely to crave addictive substances or to behave destructively toward ourselves and those around us.

I have divided this book into four sections. The first section, "When Your Twelve-Step Program Stops Working," begins with my own story of addiction, of my search for a real solution, and the shortcomings I found with the A.A. program. From the viewpoint that we become addicts for real reasons and not simply because of moral defects or disease, I address why A.A. is failing so many people and propose another way. The second section, "The Nature of Fear," outlines the many ways in which we unknowingly use fear as the motivation for change. While fear often works well for short-term change, long-term recovery and real personal growth require us to move forward using love as the basis for our thinking. We will forever remain mired in powerlessness if fear is our only instrument for change. One aspect of fear-based thinking suggests that if you heal the addictive behavior, you heal the problem. The problem with this type of thinking is that it doesn't address the root cause of the addiction. I could easily achieve sobriety in A.A. without ever scratching the surface of why I drank or used in the first place.

Section three, "The Nature of Love," outlines the predominate characteristics of love-based thinking. In today's world many of us operate from numerous limiting beliefs that are not only erroneous but unnecessary. I discovered that if I make the rules for my own life based on love and not fear, I will always be doing what is right for myself and for others. I was always taught that my true nature was sinful and selfish and not to be trusted, and that I therefore needed others to guide me. By living as my own authority, embracing my God within, I discovered that just the opposite is true. My true nature is love and my truest actions will always reflect that.

The fourth section is the seven components of my freedom, which I discussed earlier.

I conclude the book with some parting thoughts about going it alone and should you be interested, offer some alternatives to twelve-step programs.

Having said all of this, I cannot describe in concrete terms what Alcoholics Anonymous and other twelve-step programs are. Everyone's experience is based on different perceptions. I can, however, describe what I found twelve-step programs to be, and perhaps in doing so, others who feel the same way will be validated. If you disagree with any or all of what I have written here, you are entitled to that as fully and completely as everyone is entitled to his or her own opinion.

One final thought. My fondest hope is that my years and years of pain and struggle, and my incredible healing journey, will offer some help and insight into your own challenges or those of a loved one. Without the help of many others, this book would not have happened, and I hope you will feel free to share your own hopes, strengths, and struggles with me. We are all in this together and may my hope become yours and yours become mine.

Part One

WHEN YOUR TWELVE-STEP PROGRAM STOPS WORKING

1

Why Am I an Addict?

I WAS BORN in 1964, the last official year of the baby-boom generation, in Marietta, Georgia, a growing suburb of Atlanta. I discovered later, after hearing so many horror stories of the dysfunctional and abusive childhood situations many addicts had experienced, that I had a very typical upbringing. My parents were God-fearing Christians, but not obsessively so. Our family went to church every Sunday. My parents were honest and hard-working. For the first four years of my life we lived on a small street in a small house that my mother would describe to friends needing directions as "the house with toys on the roof."

I was the youngest of three. My sister, Miriam, was three years older than I and I had a brother, Charlie, who was fourteen months older than I was. Because of the closeness of our ages, my brother and I were best friends. Or at least he was to me. To him, I was just the little sister who tagged along everywhere, a bit of a nuisance probably. Whenever he went to his friends', I wanted to go, too. And I learned fast and early how to get what I wanted. I simply begged and cried until my mother was too exasperated to fight me anymore. So I palled around with Charlie. After a while I think I even began to grow on him and he seemed to accept me.

There was no alcoholic father coming home at night, drinking himself into oblivion. No neurotic, abusive mother. Just a regular home on a regular street with regular parents.

When I used to tell my background story in Alcoholics Anonymous, the story of my childhood, I was always aware that there were no obvious outward causes for my later addictive behavior, addictive behavior that began very young and continued unabated for years and years. So I began looking harder at my childhood, trying to remember the emotions behind the external picture, how I felt about myself and my family. I started searching for the sense of belonging, or not belonging, a sense of self-worth. And I found bits and pieces of self-worth.

But as I took this harder look at my life, my history, I also noticed many gaping holes that I hadn't seen before—like a feeling of warmness, a feeling of being valued and being loved simply because I existed. My honest search showed me that those feelings of warmth weren't there. I slowly began to recognize that my childhood, my earliest memories, lacked emotional warmth. In fact, it lacked any real, positive emotion at all. As an adult in recovery, it was only after years of telling everybody how normal my childhood had been that the real reason for my inability to see the truth about my parents and my childhood became clear: I didn't want to accept the fact that my parents may have done a less than stellar job. It was very hard and very painful to admit that although I never lacked for a single material thing, I was starved emotionally.

Even writing this is painful because to this day my mother is one of my very dearest friends and to utter a single word that may hurt her distresses me greatly. For she loved, and still does love, her children very much. But as the mother of three very young children, two of whom needed constant supervision, she was overwhelmed by the simple day-to-day enormity of her responsibilities.

My father had started his own company, selling heavy equipment and big machinery, the same year their first child, my sister, was born, essentially doubling his responsibilities. He was on the road constantly as a salesperson and also had to attend to all of the business of running a company. So he was probably a bit overwhelmed himself.

The whole family attended church every Sunday, the First Methodist Church of Marietta. Although my father seemed very uninterested in religious matters and attended more out of an obligation to his family, I knew that my mother's Christian faith was a very important part of her life. It somehow justified all the suffering she felt she experienced. I grew up witnessing her particular outlook on life, which is that life is suffering. The most we can hope for is but a few rays of sunshine here and there. She always seemed to have her mouth set so firmly, as if she were really squelching a desire to just scream "I can't take it anymore!" My childhood mind knew this wasn't the way life had to be, all suffering and no fun. And I rebelled. I rebelled at her notion that life was suffering and I rebelled at knowing that I was somehow to blame for much of her grimness. My brother and sister seemed relatively easy to care for next to me, or so I had the impression.

As a parent myself now, I fully understand the anxiety that one experiences at the beginning of starting a family. I have a hard time imagining the stress *three* youngsters would cause for both parents, for the one who provides all the financial needs for five people and for the other who makes sure all five people are fed and clothed and that all household responsibilities are taken care of. My mother relied on her religion to help her cope and she probably did a better job than I would have in similar circumstances. But to me, as a child, I needed more than simple material things—having clothes on my back, a nice house, and food on the table. I needed someone to hold me and tell me they loved me. Instead, I always felt as if I were a burden, and unwanted.

Nevertheless, my father's business did well and within a few years we had moved from the small house on Cottonwood Drive where I didn't even have a bedroom to a large two-story house on Church Street, one of the best streets in town. We weren't wealthy but we lived in a typical upper-middle-class fashion, although I wasn't aware of that at the time because many of my impressions about myself and about life had already been formed by the time we made the move to Church Street, when I was four years old.

In fact, my first memory is of being three years old, when we were still on Cottonwood Drive. I had been relegated to sleeping in a crib in the living room because when my mother attempted to put me in my sister's room, I made my feelings on the matter known by pulling all of Miriam's clothes out of the closet and flinging them on the floor. Being old enough to know I didn't want to share a room with my sister, I was also well aware that a three-year-old was much too old to still be in a crib. And in the living room, too!

I don't remember pulling my sister's clothes out of her closet, but what I do remember, my first memory, was one of utter shame and embarrassment. One evening toward bedtime, my parents had company over. I was standing in the middle of the crib when the guests came through the door and my parents introduced me. I felt total humiliation and shame at being *in a crib* and *in the living room*. Here I was, a big girl of three, and I didn't have my own room and I was in a crib! That others might witness this humiliation was horrifying to me. As ridiculously insignificant as this event may sound now, it spoke volumes to my young, impressionable mind that I a) had very good reason to feel ashamed about myself and b) that I didn't even deserve to have my own room as my brother and sister did. To this day it still amazes me that a three-year-old could feel such grown-up emotions. But it's probably the way many of our impressions about ourselves get formed, in seemingly innocent situations that cause a young mind to form attitudes and beliefs that shape a lifetime.

So there in that small house on Cottonwood Drive in an encounter that didn't take even five minutes, my fate was revealed. I have since that time grown up with issues of shame, guilt, and unworthiness that have driven my addiction and fueled my desire to escape. Of course there were a thousand other incidents that all contributed to my feelings of low self-worth, but the fact that my very first memory should be one of shame and unworthiness is very telling to me. It says, on the one hand, that many of my beliefs about myself were already formed by then, and on the other hand, that my childlike sense of the fact that I didn't sleep in a real bed in my own room was somehow my fault, a testament to how undeserving I was.

Much of my later childhood, from the age of four on, reveals similar trivial incidents in which I let something that was happening in my outer world define and shape an inner belief about my myself. One hot summer day when I was about five or so I was out playing with my brother and his friends. His friends kept kidding around, wanting me to show them my body. Because of my overwhelming desire to be accepted by them, I did. As we stood there in a beat-up abandoned warehouse next to the railroad tracks, I pulled my pants down and lifted my shirt up. I feel humiliation even today writing about it. Innocent, curious kids coupled with my desire to fit in, to be accepted, and another nail in the coffin of low self-esteem was hammered in.

Looking back on it, overanalyzing it, I guess I never felt my brother really liked me tagging along. Maybe I was always struggling to fit in somewhere, with my brother, with his friends, struggling just to be accepted for who I was. Maybe I'm thinking too much, but I do know this. I struggled very long and very hard and did many stupid things along the way in my quest to achieve acceptance. And in the end I did win acceptance. But first I had to start with myself. For almost all of my life, I wanted desperately for others to like me. And the secret was revealed when I learned that first I had to like myself. Self-acceptance hasn't guaranteed that others will always, or even most of the time, accept me, but it makes it okay when they don't. My self-image no longer has to be dictated by who I have pleased or who I haven't pleased because that is a losing game since you will never be able to please everyone. Today I follow my heart. And if my heart is joyful because of what I do and who I am, then I am at peace and my life works.

But back then, growing up, and later in my years of addiction, I always felt a little less than adequate. Ever since I was a small child I have always loved to observe others—how they act, who they are. And I always fixated on those who had what I didn't. I had talents, abilities, and interests of my own but it was those who had what I didn't who fascinated me. I loved playing softball and played in a girls' league from the time I was nine until I was fifteen or so. I remember very little of the vast majority of the girls I played softball with through the years. But one particular girl stood out to me back then. She was a pitcher, like me, but she was much better than I was. She was prettier than I was, she was more talented than I was, and she made the All-Stars every single year. This girl had so many of the qualities that I wanted but didn't have. I was devastated each season when I failed to make the All-Stars. I was not good enough, once again, my mind taunted.

In high school, my focus was on the "in" crowd, the popular cheerleader-type girls and the football players. I watched them, was friends with some of them, and envied them all. I was somewhat popular, had a steady boyfriend who was cute and was even two years older than I was, but I couldn't turn my focus away from what I didn't have.

By the time I reached high school, by the time I had my first drink, I was so tired of always being one or two rungs short of the top. All my intellectual gifts, the wonderful friends I had growing up, and my athletic skills weren't enough for me. I could see only what I wanted, what I didn't have, where I wasn't pretty enough, where I wasn't popular enough, where I didn't fit in—lack, lack, lack. All I could see and feel was that I wasn't good enough.

Mind you, I am now thirty-three years old, four years clean and sober, and much of this recognition comes only upon much reflection, trying to understand it all, trying to chip away year after year at that typical upper-middle-class upbringing and get to the truth— some real feelings, real emotions, my real sense of self-worth. The nuts and bolts of it is that I was an addict. From fourteen years of age on I sought to escape. So now let me tell you my story.

My Story

By the time I was twenty-eight years old it seemed as if I had been "addicted" all of my life. In reality, I had only been an addict for half of my life. My life of addiction began when I was fourteen. A harmless nip of gin from a friend's parents' liquor cabinet while spending the night quickly turned into four or five gin and tonics with increasingly more gin and less tonic, accompanied by a raging hangover the next day. Years later, in a treatment center, I heard someone say that "true" alcoholics seem to drink addictively from their very first encounter with the stuff. This was pretty much the case in my own life.

After that first night, I was liberated and would find myself more and more often craving the escape alcohol afforded me. A friend who lived in the neighborhood was usually my accomplice. But I noticed something very different at her house that contrasted with my own home. My friend's mother almost always had a drink in her hand or one sitting on the kitchen counter. It didn't matter what time of day it was. And her mother almost always seemed to be yelling at either her husband or at one of her kids or at anybody within earshot. I noticed that much of her anger fell on my friend's vulnerable fourteen-year-old shoulders. So we drank. My friend drank, I suppose, because her life was too horrible to imagine. But what did I have to drink about? I came from a good home.

So why was *I* drinking? What did *I* have to be miserable about? What did *I* need to escape so badly from that by the time I was sixteen I was drinking two or three pints of liquor a week and smoking nearly half an ounce of marijuana, using money that was supposed to go for guitar lessons for booze and pot instead. Lying about my age at fifteen so I could get a job at Dairy Queen and then quitting on a Friday night because there was a big party and I wanted to go drinking. I should have known better. I was above average in intelligence, I had even been in a gifted class in junior high school. I had been president of my Junior Achievement group. I had a lot going for me. Why was I throwing it all away? Or, more to the point, why were all the good things in my life so very meaningless and empty for me? Why was I addicted?

Of course, this question didn't run through my head at the time. But something deep within me, even then, needed desperately to find some significant reason to participate in life. On the surface, I didn't feel challenged and was bored with life. Deep down, far below the surface, I was tired of always striving to be good enough, tired of always being one step short of where I wanted to be, tired of the feeling of lack that lay deep within me and seemed to be my constant companion.

And that, I believe, was the spark that ignited my addiction. The lack that I had been trying to run away from or deny for all those years had suddenly found an outlet—addiction.

What I didn't know at the time, but came to realize over the years, is that I had started a spiritual journey. I had already sensed a void deep within myself, a longing, a sense of something essential lacking in my life and in me. What I didn't know was that the lack I experienced so painfully in my outer world was really a reflection of an inner lack, a spiritual lack. A lack that I believe would have been there no matter how I had been raised.

There is such a trend nowadays of examining your childhood for the causes of your adult life problems. Did you come from a dysfunctional home? Was your inner child wounded? Were you starved emotionally? What my parents did or didn't do with me as a child has less to do with it than how I *interpreted* those events and let them define my view of myself. My sister grew up in the same emotionally distant family and the way it shaped her is entirely different from the way it shaped me. She became a stronger, more capable person, a smart achiever. I became a bitter rebel, addicted and irresponsible. Same home, different interpretation. But growing up I was so fixated on the outer lack, on what was missing in my external world, that I failed to see that my feelings stemmed from an inner void.

My addictive behavior, which began so dramatically at the age of fourteen, was really just the beginning of a search to find meaning and healing in my life. As Dr. Chopra writes in *Overcoming Addictions,* "The addict is looking in the wrong places, but he is going after something very important and we cannot afford to ignore the meaning of his search."

This void deep within me seemed to have suddenly emerged from its depths and was now demanding satisfaction. Like any good addict, I sensed the void and I responded. I responded with pint bottles of alcohol, nickel bags of marijuana, handfuls of Quaaludes that left me passed out at my desk by the last class of the school day, promiscuous sexual behavior, and in later years food addiction. Not knowing better, I responded to my *inner* spiritual hunger with *external* addictive solutions. It took me years to discover that no external substance could ever fill my spiritual void. And, as I will explain later, religion, with its rigid expectations and requirements for conformity, did not answer my soul's cry either.

It also took me many years to let myself off the hook. Because I had hurt so many people over the years with my addictive behavior, I was a very good candidate for experiencing guilt and shame. Understanding that my addictive behavior was more about my trying to answer my soul's cries for meaning helped me to understand that I was not a bad person, even if I seemed to be acting like one. Everyone searches for meaning in life. To some it is through business success. Others find it by raising a healthy family. Others seek to find meaning through organized religion. Addicts, in my opinion, seem to have a bigger spiritual hole in their lives. To us, the pain of the spiritual black hole within us seems to be felt more acutely and its hunger cries seem to be more insistent.

I believe that people who experience addiction are hearing a call from their souls for healing and for love. Dr. Chopra writes, "In my view, a person who has never felt the pull of addictive behavior is someone who has not taken the first faltering step toward discovering the true meaning of Spirit. Perhaps addiction is nothing to be proud of, but it does represent an aspiration toward a higher level of experience." It is when I tried to answer this spiritual hunger call from within by seeking fulfillment in things outside myself that I became addicted. As much as I tried to consume or pursue externally, this longing wouldn't go away, so I naturally tried to consume and pursue more and more and more. My addictive cycle was now in full throttle and began to rule my life. By the end of my addictive journey, I seemed to experience overwhelming cravings every minute of every day. But there was a solution.

I discovered after years of struggling that it is only by going within and striving to get in touch with myself spiritually, and by responding to the real emotional wounds that I had buried within me, that I could heal myself of my addictions. The miracle is that, as I did this, as I got in touch with my spiritual self and honored my inner life, all of my addictive tendencies faded away from me as easily and as naturally as leaves blowing through the trees on a brisk fall day. I also discovered that I drank for some very real reasons, not simply because I was born with the "disease" of alcoholism. And I needed to do some real work on healing those painful areas of my life before my addiction disappeared completely.

There was a succession of people in my life who wanted to correct my behavior, wanted to fix me, and nearly all of them focused on the external part of my problem and offered me external solutions. At sixteen years of age, my parents took me out of school and put me in a wilderness-type treatment center for teenage girls. There was a corresponding boys-only campus thirty miles away. Our job all day, every day, was construction. We were taught how to build cabins. We hauled wood, mixed cement, poured foundations, dug up trees, sawed, nailed, and painted ten hours a day, six days a week. No school, just hard work. Once a week we met individually with a psychiatrist and every night we had "group," which was actually a particularly meaningless form of group therapy. In later years, the founder of the center was jailed for sexually abusing the young men at the boys' facility as well as for tax evasion and mishandling of funds. The center changed hands and is now run properly and much less harshly.

I was one of the very few at this facility whose attendance was not court-ordered. I learned my second day there what that meant in real terms. It meant that as soon as I became eighteen, I could no longer be kept there against my will. The day I entered, I was fourteen months from my eighteenth birthday. It was a very long, grueling, and lonely fourteen months. Sobriety in the treatment center was a given, because we were not allowed off campus and were closely supervised every minute of the day. I made some good friends and I learned the value of conformity. As long as I did things precisely the way I was expected to, I would progress and gain more privileges. If I attempted to question the rules or do my own thing, I was punished. I felt so angry and repressed at not being given a voice, at being told my needs were unimportant. I was getting my first real taste of how *not* to heal my addictions. I suppose the center was very well-intentioned and I did learn the good feeling that comes from hard work. But the harsh rigidness of the program was slowly and inexorably killing my spirit. One weekend my family came for a visit and my sister took me aside and asked me how I was doing. I burst into tears. I told her I couldn't stand it. Because close friendships were frowned upon and because of the confrontational nature of the program, I was afraid to get close to anyone. I began to stifle my real feelings and instead to pretend that things were okay and that *I* was okay. It was the only way to get ahead in an environment where conformity and an adherence to rules was the norm.

Upon my eighteenth birthday, I had finally earned a "home visit," which wasn't really a visit to home because you had to go somewhere for the weekend that was at least fifty miles from your home, the point being that we'd be sure to get into some type of trouble if we were at our real homes. I told my parents that I would die if I had to go back after the visit, and that I wanted to come home and finish school and go to college. I promised to attend A.A. and Narcotics Anonymous (N.A.) meetings and stay clean, which is exactly what I did. My parents saw the miserable state I was in and agreed to let me come home. Back home at last I began attending classes in the evening in order to prepare for taking the G.E.D. (because I had missed so much of high school, I needed to obtain a General Equivalency Diploma in order to attend college in the fall) and working for my dad during the day. My cousin had several years of sobriety in A.A. and I started attending Narcotics Anonymous meetings with him.

This was part of the deal I had agreed to with my parents in return for their allowing me to come back home. I had agreed to attend weekly twelve-step meetings, and my older cousin graciously agreed to show me the ropes. He had experienced years of drug and alcohol addiction himself and at twenty-one had stopped completely with the help of A.A. and N.A. Seven years older than I was, he was both older and wiser. Having just gotten out of the worst kind of hell I had ever imagined possible, at this point the thought of drinking and drugging again was the farthest thing from my mind. In fact, every night for the next few months, and sporadically for the next five years, I had dark, terrifying nightmares in which I was forced to return to this treatment center, all the while telling my "captors" in the dream that I had been staying clean and at eighteen was too old to go back. The "captors" ignored my pleas and to my horror I was returned night after night to this horrible, lonely, treatment center. If nothing else would, the nightly dreams were sure to keep me sober from the sheer terror of them.

I remember well the first twelve-step meeting I went to. It was held in the cafeteria of a treatment center in Atlanta. As I walked in, I felt instantly intimidated. There were so many people, and although the meeting hadn't started yet, the room was filled with smoke. To my relief, my cousin spotted me and came to my side. He introduced me around and briefly explained the twelve-step approach. In those first few weeks, the steps failed to make any sense to me. With all the references to God, the steps seemed like a sort of religion and I knew instinctively that another religion was not the answer to my addictive tendencies. But I did understand the importance of the people. The people made all the difference to me. They were very welcoming and friendly and helped me a great deal with my feeling of being out of place. Still, no one explained the *significance* of the steps, so I didn't bother with them. I just assumed that the fellowship of other people was what made it all work. I asked a woman to be my sponsor and she said that she couldn't, she had too many sponsorees as it was. So I continued going to meetings, enjoying the people, and focused on taking my college entrance exams as well as the exam for my G.E.D. I was very happy to find out that I had passed the G.E.D. with high marks, and was accepted to my university of choice.

The summer before college many of my friends from the treatment center were released. Some had been there for almost three years. Barely missing a beat, we were suddenly all drinking and using drugs again; it seemed as if we were making up for lost time. I forgot all about my twelve-step program and my nightmares dimmed into obscurity. It amazes me that I was willing to risk everything I had worked so hard for by diving into drinking and drugging again. But part of me had relaxed so much since the treatment center that I was finally ready to enjoy myself again. I had been to hell and back and had survived. I had my college lined up for the fall. Eager to get on with things, I had even begun taking some summer college courses at a local university and planned to transfer the credits to my college in the fall. The pressure I had felt for the past year and a half of my life was finally off. With my renewed drinking I lost all interest in going to twelve-step meetings. But I would occasionally lie to my mother and tell her that I was headed off to a meeting in order to keep her from worrying about me. Of course, at that point A.A. hadn't failed me, I had failed it. I had never really worked at the program and was still uncertain about how it all worked.

College ended up being a blur of parties, booze, drugs, hangovers, and lots of late-night last-minute cramming for exams. My parents remained oblivious to the severity of my addiction because I lived on campus and I was on my best behavior when they did see me. My parents supported me financially during college and I had to pad all my expenses in order to afford my drinking. I always exaggerated the costs of new books and would then buy used ones. I exaggerated the cost of housing, tuition, and meals. They were paying my housing and tuition directly to the university, so I would exaggerate the cost of everything and then get the university to refund the extra amount directly to me. It is very shameful behavior to look at now, but I didn't question it at the time. My addictions had to be fed, and integrity was not a well-known concept to me then.

After college, my finance degree got me a good job as a commodities analyst with E. F. Hutton. At twenty-two, it was not until I was in the real world of eight-hour workdays, alarms set at 6:30

A.M., bills, and adult responsibilities that I realized anew that I had a problem with drugs and alcohol. In some amazing fashion that only youth can explain, I was able to drink at a local bar almost every night to the point that many nights I didn't remember driving home and yet got up and made it in to work every morning. I swallowed a lot of headache powders, but I did make it in.

It wasn't long before I found a partner in my addiction. I hooked up with a boyfriend who partied just as hard as I did and also enjoyed cocaine as much as I did. Unfortunately, he also had the financial resources to provide an unending supply of "party favors" such as cocaine. Before long, I had moved in with him and we were spending thousands of dollars on drugs, late-night bars, fast cars, and exotic trips. My work suffered greatly until I realized that, because of my boyfriend's generous cash gifts, I was spending more in a month than I earned in a year. So I ditched the job and lived it up. With nothing but time on my hands, I increased my drug use to the point that the moment I stepped out of bed in the morning, I cut a few lines of coke on the dresser before even getting into the shower. I then continued to use coke all day before going out all night and boozing it up.

And if all this wasn't enough, I innocently added another addiction to my arsenal—bulimia. Although I wasn't overweight at the time, I was obsessive about my weight and was forever trying to lose ten pounds. At five feet seven inches and one hundred twenty-five pounds, I thought I would be much more attractive at one hundred fifteen pounds. My boyfriend was a closet bulimic, and in the beginning of the relationship, I was oblivious to what his trips to the bathroom after meals were really about. But the mornings were filled with evidence that something was going on. The kitchen would be a wreck; dirty pots and pans were everywhere—on the stove, in the sink, cabinets wide open—with half-eaten meals in each. And he hadn't come to bed the night before. It finally dawned on me that he was staying up all night, making food, eating it, and then throwing up.

One night we had friends over for dinner and my boyfriend made us a particularly delicious meal. It was so good, in fact, that I ate two servings and was stuffed afterward. Too full, in fact. I immediately started obsessing about my weight and how I was going to burn off the calories I had just consumed. And then, as if it were the most natural thing in the world, I simply went upstairs to our bathroom and made myself throw up. I instantly felt better, with no more obsessing about how much I had eaten. Just like when I had my first drink at fourteen, I suddenly felt liberated all over again. I had just enjoyed a wonderful meal and didn't have to experience any remorse. I brushed my teeth, fixed my hair, and went back downstairs to join my friends. No one had any idea what I'd just done.

I had no idea at the time how much what I had just done would very soon come to rule my life. Between my cocaine abuse and my fastly developing bulimia, I finally lost that ten pounds. In fact, I lost twenty-two pounds. At twenty-three years of age, I weighed one hundred and three pounds and thought I looked great. Everybody else just thought I looked malnourished.

The bulimia played perfectly into the shame from my childhood that I had repressed and run from so long ago. It quickly became a new escape hatch for me, and I noticed that the greater my hatred of myself and my lifestyle became, the more I was compelled to eat and make myself throw up afterward. But in less than six months time, I had become fed up with this life of boozing, clubs, cocaine, and my secret shame of bulimia.

By the end of the year I ended the relationship with the boyfriend, and prayed to God to help me. I found a job in sales to support myself, yet I was actively very addicted, specifically to tequila, cocaine, and now food. I couldn't get through a single day with feeding one, two, or all three of these addictions. I was thankful that my new roommate didn't notice the bulimia because it was so humiliating and shaming to me. My only friends were people I knew who partied to the same extreme degree that I did. I was more and more estranged from my family, ashamed of myself, and rarely spoke to either my brother or my sister.

In fact, I was ashamed of my whole life. I had just turned twenty-four and my life was still a chaotic mess. I began and ended a series of relationships. I tried, without success, to get business projects off the ground. I even contemplated moving to Los Angeles at one point, and went as far as finding a place to live on one of my several business trips out there. But before long, I was back in my miserable little life. I had so much desire to do things, to accomplish things, but I could never get anything to work out. And I was sure it was because of my addictions.

And as my addictions worsened it was also becoming harder and harder to support myself. When I left the boyfriend, I found a job that paid most of my bills. During the months when I was short, my parents helped out, wondering why, at twenty-four, I couldn't support myself completely but lovingly wanting to help me. They were still oblivious to the degree to which my addictions ruled my life. But before the year was out, I had lost the little bit of money I did have in a short-term business venture that failed. My roommate and I had spent all we had to rent a kiosk in a local shopping mall for the Christmas season to sell personalized Christmas stockings. We predicted we could net between four and five thousand dollars for the six-week period.

The planning stages for our venture went well, and the kiosk was very busy the whole season. But my addictions held me prisoner. Instead of helping her oversee the kiosk, I repeatedly abandoned my roommate because I was either hungover or bingeing and purging on food all day. It was so humiliating to see our little venture that we were so excited about go down the tubes just because I couldn't get my act together. Instead of making four or five thousand dollars, we lost fifteen hundred dollars. As humiliating as it all was, I hadn't hit bottom yet. Feeling utter shame, I moved back home with my parents the month before my twenty-fifth birthday.

At this point, I settled into a sort of routine. I had a favorite bar I'd been going to for four or five years, since college. I ended up spending nearly seven years of my life at this one bar. The bar had a *Cheers*-type atmosphere in the sense that there were a dozen or more regulars, we all knew each other, and we were all friends. It seemed perfectly normal to me that my only real friends were the regulars in this bar. We were a diverse group, from a self-employed millionaire, to a stockbroker, to various salespeople and other professionals, to a general contractor. In fact, it was through one of these regulars that I got my first job out of college, the job with E. F. Hutton. This, again, was perfectly normal to me—that I found my first real job through someone I knew from a bar.

Most any night of the week, you could find my car parked outside this bar. It was the central meeting place for our nightly activities. The usual routine was to go to the bar, meet a few friends, score some cocaine, hit a few of the more exciting nightclubs in town, and wind up at six in the morning wired on cocaine and dreading the day ahead. Things always stayed interesting because you were never sure exactly what mix of regulars would be at the bar and therefore who you would be running all over town with snorting cocaine and partying all night. If there was no one I knew at the bar, I would spend the evening by myself, barhopping and hanging out.

Someone asked me once how I afforded all of this boozing, clubs, and cocaine. As any good female alcoholic will tell you, it's not hard to drink all night long in bars and not spend a dime. Men offer to buy you drinks. Bartenders offer you drinks. People offer you cocaine. For any young, attractive female doing the club scene, everything is free and at the end of the night you dump whoever financed the evening's follies before anything is expected of you. I had several girlfriends who hung out with me and it was actually easier to get men to buy us drinks and cocaine all night when we were together. Our behavior was shameless, and in retrospect inexcusable, but at the time we were innocently trying to have some fun. When all else failed, I even used to bug one local dealer who hung out in the bar to give me drugs. He usually gave in just to get me to stop harassing him.

I made a little money with the off-and-on jobs I held as a stockbroker, but I could never get a job with a good brokerage firm so I never stayed anywhere very long. (I had previously gotten my stockbroker's license shortly after leaving E. F. Hutton.) Oblivious to my addictions, my parents supplemented my income. This final point, my parents still helping to support me, was a *huge* source of guilt and embarrassment for me. Everyone else I went to college with was able to support themselves, work at a steady job, have their own apartment. Me, I couldn't hold a job longer than six weeks. I was so certain that something was wrong with me, that I had just been born faulty. "Why was simple existence so hard for me?" I asked myself so many times. Alcoholics Anonymous would later underscore the whole belief in this unworthiness I kept feeling by having me focus even more attention on my faults. But back to the story.

The mornings after a binge were always the worst. To me, the most miserable feeling in the world was seeing the sun rise after staying out all night snorting cocaine and going to clubs. Every time I saw the sun, the feeling of loathing toward myself and my life was at its greatest. The sunrise to me signaled two things: the onset of a huge guilt trip for having stayed out all night, and the fact that the day ahead would be wasted. Because I would have to go home, try to sleep off the previous night's effects, and wind up getting up sometime in the afternoon with the day half gone. During the years I was living at home with my parents I felt especially guilty for staying out all night and worrying them sick. By now they knew all about my addictions, and when they woke up in the morning and my car was still not in the driveway, my mother's whole day would be filled with worry and despair. My parents didn't know if I was dead, lying in a ditch somewhere. To avoid the confrontation and the inevitable guilt, I would have to wait until they left for work in the morning before I went home. I then made sure I left the house before they got home.

They tried confronting me about my behavior and I assumed then that I was going to try to do better. But nothing ever changed and, loving me, they didn't want to throw me out. They didn't know quite what to do with me. They endured a living hell, I'm sure, because of my inexcusable and selfish behavior.

I was very aware of how screwed up my life was. My guilt and shame were overwhelming. I was hurting those who cared about me the most. I was throwing my life away. And I wanted to stop this insane behavior more than anything else. But it seemed as if my addictions were self-perpetuating. I would feel guilty for my behavior and so would be compelled to use again and again in order to avoid facing up to my feelings. I truly did want to move forward with my life. I had a stack of self-help and personal improvement books beside my bed and was always setting goals and making lists of what I wanted to achieve. But my addictions seemed to drain all the strength and hope out of me every time I resolved to change and do better.

So night after night, I sat in my bar, with my "friends," and repeated over and over again the behavior that was destroying me. I looked around at my friends and was perplexed by what I saw. No one but me seemed to have any remorse over what they were doing. We were all sitting there night after night throwing our lives away. My perceptions told me that these people were living in some sort of fantasy world where alcohol had created the delusion that they were doing something productive with their lives. But I watched one day at the stockbroker's house as he snorted cocaine, with his five-year-old daughter in the next room. And I watched as the millionaire had yet another business deal go down the tubes. And I saw the salesman lose another job. And I wondered, Don't they know? Don't they realize? Doesn't anyone here want more out of life than this? Are our expectations so low that this life of drugs and alcohol is acceptable? And am I the only one who wants off this senseless merry-go-round? The pain in my life was acute.

And then one night I was sitting there, in the bar, talking to a friend and bemoaning my life and how disgusted I was with myself. I said I was thinking about going to an Alcoholics Anonymous meeting. "I'll go with you," my friend said suddenly. I was shocked and elated that someone shared my feelings of being fed up with this lifestyle. So off we went. We found a meeting nearby and at the beginning of the meeting, the speaker asked if there were any newcomers. We both raised our hands. After the meeting everyone was very nice and friendly to us, just like I remembered twelve-step meetings as being. They gave us each a Big Book and told us to read it.

I read the entire book during the next two days. I read and reread the twelve steps listed in the book. They are as follows:

1. We admitted we were powerless over alcohol—that our lives had become unmanageable.
2. Came to believe that a Power greater than ourselves could restore us to sanity.
3. Made a decision to turn our will and our lives over to the care of God *as we understood Him.*
4. Made a searching and fearless moral inventory of ourselves.
5. Admitted to God, to ourselves, and to another human being the exact nature of our wrongs.
6. Were entirely ready to have God remove all these defects of character.
7. Humbly asked Him to remove our shortcomings.
8. Made a list of all persons we had harmed, and became willing to make amends to them all.
9. Made direct amends to such people wherever possible, except when to do so would injure them or others.
10. Continued to take personal inventory and when we were wrong promptly admitted it.
11. Sought through prayer and meditation to improve our conscious contact with God *as we understood Him,* praying only for knowledge of His will for us and the power to carry that out.
12. Having had a spiritual awakening as the result of these steps, we tried to carry this message to alcoholics, and to practice these principles in all our affairs.

At the end of reading the Big Book, I went, "Huh?" But I knew meetings were the answer. They had worked for my cousin. It was also the only real solution to alcoholism anyone ever talked about. I didn't do any research into other treatment options. I assumed that because of its high profile, A.A. was the answer. So I went back. And went back.

And suddenly one bright, beautiful, fall morning, I found myself at a pay phone on a street corner in downtown Atlanta dialing my mother. "Please help me," I cried out to her when she answered. The night before, I had dutifully gone to a meeting, but in the middle of the meeting I had been seized by overwhelming feelings along with an overpowering craving to use. Fifteen minutes later, I was sitting at my bar, drinking a few shots of tequila and arranging to purchase some cocaine. The next ten hours were a blur of sleazy, late-night bars, too much booze, and the company of similarly addicted "friends," all of this accompanied by the horrible wired feeling you get from too much cocaine. And then the phone call to my mom. I felt again as if I were in the depths of despair. I hoped A.A. would be the answer, but I still couldn't quite make out what A.A. was about. I had read the steps, admitted I was powerless, had prayed to my Higher Power, had turned my will over, had begun a fourth step, yet still I drank. Where was all this relief I had been expecting? The steps themselves had little or no effect at all on my desire to drink, use, or binge and purge. In fact, the steps seemed to say that my addictive behavior was somehow a result of my moral wrongs, character defects, and shortcomings and not about my spiritual and emotional pain and my empty, painful life.

Desperate for relief, I checked into Willingway, a nearby treatment center in south Georgia, for six weeks. The center used the twelve steps as its foundation. With the fog finally starting to lift, I began to understand more about the program and how it worked: "It works if you work it." I got indoctrinated in all the slogans. I did a lengthy fourth step, read it to a counselor and God, and then burned it as a final release from all my horrible wrongs. I prayed every day. I was sober!

But I still hadn't given up my bulimic behavior. I assumed that it was the alcohol and drugs that were causing me the real problems, that they were hampering me in my ability to get on with life. I wasn't yet ready to give up all my addictions. Giving up the alcohol and drugs did an immeasurable amount of good toward helping me feel better because at least I was no longer hurting my parents. With the food, I was only hurting myself, so it was acceptable. I even binged and purged my way through Willingway, an easy thing to do because all the meals were served buffet-style, and we each had our own room with a private bathroom attached.

I knew that it was hypocritical to give up only two of my addictions while hanging on to the third. But I was at least making progress. In my mind, although I did still have an active addiction, I didn't think it was all that different from those sober people who plied themselves with cigarettes and caffeine. They, therefore, still maintained an addiction or two, albeit less destructive ones.

After treatment I returned to my parents' house. They had been extremely concerned about me and had supported me through Willingway, both financially and emotionally. My mother, an endless well of compassion, love, and understanding, was becoming the bedrock of my support system. I was connecting with her on a much deeper level than ever before and was eternally grateful to her for her constant, unconditional love. I wrote to her constantly while in treatment and both my mother and father drove down for family counseling sessions. I was beginning to feel as if they were the only two people who had always been there for me and had never wavered in their love and concern for my well-being. I was starting to feel hopeful for the first time in a long time.

For the next twelve months, I attended A.A. meetings regularly and did everything I was told to do, in triplicate. At twenty-six I started graduate school, and life was good. I led A.A. meetings, I took my inventory, I carried the message. I still binged and purged secretly at my parents' house and occasionally at school. But in my mind that had little to do with my sobriety in A.A. I felt a bit guilty and false for not coming clean about my bulimia to the people of A.A., but I felt so raw and vulnerable just trying to deal with giving up alcohol, my friend and enemy of twelve years. I was doing all I could and I had to let that be okay. I did drive all the way back to Willingway in order to modify my fourth step to my counselor. I confessed my bulimia to her and told her I had binged and purged while there and was still doing it. But because the bulimia was still steeped in so much shame for me, I was unable to tell anybody else about it.

Perhaps because I still had an active addiction it was just a matter of time before it all came crashing back down on me. A month shy of my one-year chip in A.A., I was drunk and had used cocaine again. When I found myself in Philadelphia for the weekend with two of my best girlfriends from my partying days, the thought of watching them party all weekend without me was unbearable. I agonized over it for a few hours and then took my first drink in over eleven months; we also scored some cocaine at a local nightclub. The rest of the weekend was a blur. I returned home, ashamed, but with the secret of my relapse intact. Unfortunately, the alcohol cravings that had been quiet for so long now returned anew. It was a miracle I made it through graduate school at all. I binged and purged three or four or sometimes more times a day. I drank more and more. I had become one of the unfortunate 70 percent who relapse in A.A. I was miserable.

I was racked with confusion and despair. When would this merry-go-round end? What was I doing wrong? Why was I unable to stop destroying myself? Why couldn't I give up *all* my addictions? I wanted so much more out of life than this. When would this pain that consumed my life end?

I had no idea at the time what sort of pain I was trying to run from. All I knew was that I couldn't bear my life while "using" and I couldn't bear the thought of not having an addictive escape in which to flee from life. I used addictive substances because I felt pain, and then having used, I felt more pain and so was driven to use again. I believed I had done everything A.A. had taught me yet here I was, once again caught full throttle in the addictive cycle. If A.A. wasn't the way, what was?

Not knowing anything different and convinced that A.A. could help me, I redoubled my efforts. I started attending Overeaters Anonymous for my bulimia. I got sponsors. I did another fourth step. I led more meetings. I opened up more. And I worked on trying to better understand myself and all my emotional pain. I started trying to see why my father was such a shadow figure in my life even though I had always tried so hard to please him. One of the things I was beginning to learn about bulimia was the fact that the majority of girls who suffer from it were reportedly sexually abused. Bulimia was a shameful "disease" for me, and I could see how sexual abuse could cause bulimia because all the people I knew who had been sexually abused talked about how *ashamed* they felt and how they felt they were somehow to blame for it. Bulimia was just another arena in which many of us continued to relive our shame over and over again.

Although I wasn't sexually abused, I sensed that somehow my food issues seemed to center around my searching for love and comfort, perhaps the love and comfort I had been longing for from my father my whole life and had never received. I was growing closer and closer to my mother, but my father still remained an unreachable enigma to me. He had always been there physically and materially for the family, but emotionally I felt as if I had never gotten his approval or respect. And as a little girl, I had longed for it. Part of the reason for my promiscuous behavior in high school had been my search for love and affection and now, as an adult, this empty hole in my heart still plagued me. I was trying to fill this hole with food, but it never seemed to get filled.

By reading self-help books and seeing a good therapist, I slowly learned to accept my father just the way he was. As the sole financial provider for five people, he did everything he felt was demanded of him. He did not himself grow up with examples of lavish love and affection. In fact, his own father had died when he was nine years old and he was sent to live a hard life in the country at the rural home of an older childless aunt and uncle. After two years, when he'd finally learned to fit in, he was called back home to Marietta; because of the poor quality of the rural schools he'd attended, he was a year behind in school.

I could either spend my life trying to chase after this lost love and affection from my father or learn to love myself and accept my father just as he was by recognizing that he hadn't received love and affection himself. I chose the latter, and as I did so my gratitude for all he had done for me overwhelmed me. He had shown me in countless ways over the years how very deeply and dearly he truly loved me, but because it was never in the form *I* wanted (physical hugs and kisses, the words "I love you, I'm proud of you"), I overlooked all the many sacrifices he had made in my name. I was beginning to see clearly now.

I achieved sobriety again, and at long last, I achieved freedom from my bulimia. The sobriety felt very precarious. Even though I was doing everything I had been told to do, and even though I was sober and abstinent, I still felt as if I was skating on thin ice and that if I wasn't hypervigilant, I would relapse. Sobriety felt like such hard work. I hadn't imagined it to be so hard or to be something I had to be so attentive to. I had always felt deep within that I could heal this addictive part of myself, and be done with it, not feel as if it all hinged on how many meetings I was going to, or whether I was sharing enough or calling my sponsor often enough. There seemed to be no end to all the things required of me by the program. And there seemed to be no encouragement to do what felt right inwardly, such as ex-amining my negative beliefs and my low self-esteem. Instead, A.A. and O.A. started feeling very dictatorial and forced. Something about the programs seemed to me to be false. I was doing everything I was told to do but I could still feel that inner void looming deep within me. The void spelled dissatisfaction and symbolized a lack of real fulfillment. Although sobriety and food abstinence in itself was ful-filling, it had a superficial quality to it, sort of like eating ice cream when your body is hungry for a real meal. It would quell the hunger pangs but it wouldn't give your body the nourishment it was truly needing. A.A. and O.A., although helping me in some ways, did little to truly satisfy me except to give me a rigid doctrine with which I was expected to live my life. And I didn't like that.

Then I started having cravings again. At first, they were vague stirrings, but they soon became insistent cries for satisfaction. My sponsor said I needed to go to more meetings. I did, and it seemed to make the cravings intensify. By my ignoring the real reason for the cravings, and putting the Band-Aid of a meeting over them, the cravings became more vociferous and demanding. Had I only known what I know now about cravings, I could have worked on responding to my unmet needs and the conflict that the cravings were signifying. My sponsor didn't lead me in the right direction because she herself didn't know. She was never taught the meaning of cravings either.

It was the beginning of A.A.'s abject failure to heal the real wounds and the real reasons that lay at the core of my addictive behavior. And it was also the beginning of my journey of self-healing.

I did some research into A.A. and its origins and discovered that back in the 1930s, when A.A. began, because of the societal views of the day and partly because of the views of the Oxford Group (the Oxford Group was a religious group Bill Wilson attended prior to founding A.A. and its steps had a profound effect on the formation of the twelve steps of A.A.), alcoholism was thought to be the result of moral weakness and sin. This view would explain the A.A. emphasis on doing a moral inventory that only focused on our perceived moral wrongs, making a list of our shortcomings, and praying to have our character defects removed. If I was truly an alcoholic because of moral weakness and sin, then I would certainly think that listing my moral wrongs and turning my life over to God would relieve me of my disease.

However, I was a woman living in the latter part of the twentieth century and the notion that my addictive behavior was the result of moral weakness and sin was ridiculous. I drank for many reasons, probably many complicated reasons. And until I resolved those reasons, I believed I would remain addicted. All the "fourth steps" in the world would never get at the real heart of my addiction.

I continued my research into A.A.'s origins. I was truly baffled as to why, if A.A. had worked so well for so many, it didn't help me. Was there something wrong with me? I was still convinced that the problem must be with me.

I was reading *A.A.: The Story* by Ernest Kurtz, a book about the background and history of A.A. I was suddenly very intrigued by its explanation for A.A.'s success. "It was the claim to *specialness* that was the root of (the alcoholic's) troubles [emphasis mine]. The program of A.A. worked because it deflated the alcoholic's claim to specialness."

If this is indeed true, it might explain why A.A. works so well for some, but for others fails miserably. A.A. was founded on the experiences of one hundred men and one token woman. All these men were white, privileged, and, in Bill Wilson's own words, suffered from "self-will run riot." Bill Wilson perceived the main problem with these alcoholics, as seen through his own experiences, to be ego related. Therefore, the original intent of A.A. was to completely deflate the ego by surrender and the A.A. form of confession, the fourth and fifth steps, admitting our wrongs. It further focused on defects and shortcomings to ensure that the ego remained humble and subservient.

But this is no longer the 1930s. The world of today's addict is much more complex, and the reasons for being addicted go far beyond a "self-will run riot." In fact, for many addicts, myself included, it was the very fact that I had felt so inferior and so *un-special* all my life that contributed to my addictive behavior. I longed to actually feel special. If I could but feel special, perhaps it would help me. People with low self-esteem need to develop a healthy, strong ego. It is very harmful to someone with problems of inferiority and low self-esteem to tell them they need to completely deflate their already nonexistent egos.

This would explain why A.A. works so well for those who need to be humbled and get their egos in the right perspective. But for me, I needed to be built up, not knocked down. I needed to learn that I was a divine creature of the Universe. My addiction was about my self-hatred and my negative beliefs about myself. Doing moral inventories, listing my defects and shortcomings, all this did was sink me lower than I already was. It is a testament to my will that I found sobriety in A.A. at all. A.A. does stress the need for a belief in a Higher

Power and I do believe that the spiritual aspect is very important. But it is also vital to people who are in my position and suffer from low self-worth and low self-esteem to honor the things that are right and beautiful about themselves; we need a model that will teach us about our own inner power and how to connect with it.

While all the people in A.A. were fun, friendly, and engaging, I needed to chart my own course if I were truly to heal my addictions. Which is exactly what I began doing. It took me four long years, and much soul-searching and inner work, but I did it. I found my way out of active addiction. Long after I had achieved sobriety on my own terms, I discovered that many other people had charted their own course toward sobriety and, interestingly, they had all found similar shortcomings with A.A. Charlotte Kasl, author of *Many Roads, One Journey: Moving Beyond the 12 Steps*, Jeane Kirkpatrick, founder of Women for Sobriety, Dr. Albert Ellis, founder of Rational Emotive Therapy (a cognitive approach to sobriety), Jack Trimpey, founder of Rational Recovery and author of *The Small Book*, all these people discovered that it is possible to fully recover from the "disease" of alcoholism. As Jack Trimpey says, it is an "irrational belief that alcoholic people cannot choose to become non-addicted. The truth is many do it and do it every day." It is a limited belief that you need A.A. for life and one which you can discard if you choose to. I had always imagined that deep within myself I could one day be "recovered"—instead of "in recovery" for the rest of my life.

Shortly after I stopped attending meetings, a friend from A.A. said sarcastically, "What—are you cured now?" "Why not?" I replied in all seriousness. Why should I have to be addicted for life? The truth is that I don't have to be addicted for life unless I choose to be.

I'm married now, very happily. I met my husband at an A.A. meeting when I was twenty-five. He's seen me drunk, sober, binge-ing, and abstinent, and has loved me through it all. Conversely, I've seen him go through his share of hard times as well. Today I am happy and fulfilled by life. We have a two-year-old son and a five-month-old. My life is light years from the bars, the binges, the drugs, and the remorse that consumed me every single day just a few endless years ago.

I have rediscovered that the world is a magical, wondrous, beautiful place, even amid hardship and despair. This book is about my journey, in the hope that through my own struggles you can learn to become empowered in your own life.

2

Meetings Quit Working

WHEN, AT THE AGE of twenty-five, it became really important to me to quit drinking, I discovered that I couldn't do it alone. I found myself "hopelessly" addicted to alcohol. No matter how hard I tried, I seemed unable to stop drinking. After spending six weeks in treatment, enlisting the emotional support of family and friends, and relying heavily on A.A., I finally became clean and sober. However, after about a year of sobriety, aside from the fact that I didn't need to drink to get through the day, I still felt no better inside about my life. My days seemed increasingly filled with drudgery and routine. Attending meetings in the evenings would give me a bit of a lift, but more and more it seemed like a very superficial sort of lift. It had no substance or energy behind it. I would enjoy being with the people and interacting with them, but after the glow of the meeting wore off my life still felt drab and unexciting. What was wrong with me?, I asked my sponsor. She felt I obviously needed either to do another inventory, or work on my character defects, or go to another meeting. In other words, it was obviously because I wasn't doing enough work on myself that I felt this way. After a while I couldn't stand it anymore. I was so tired of always working on myself, always trying to improve, and the gains I did achieve were so short-lived and superficial. Long-term happiness just did not seem to be in my future. And I became very tired of hearing all the rhetoric and clichés in A.A. "Well, just go to a meeting," or "Have you done a fourth step on this?," or the inevitable "Just let go and let God." Well, I had let go and let God and I was tired of waiting for him to give me my happiness, was tired of feeling like a continual failure in my inability to find fulfillment. I was on the verge of using again and I was desperate for answers that nobody seemed to be able to give me. If I heard one more person tell me I just needed to go to a meeting, I was going to scream.

Deep within myself I was aware of a still, small voice that said meetings weren't the answer for me. "But how could that be?" I asked myself. The program works if you work it, everyone knew that. My feelings made me feel like a traitor. How could meetings not be the answer? I must be in some sort of denial. My mind is trying to trick me into pulling away from the meetings so I will use again. "No, that's not true," said another part of me. "Just trust me." I was very scared to stop going to meetings. I felt certain that I must be in denial about something and was being tricked by my subconscious. But another part of me seemed to be begging me to honor it. I slowly became aware that a part of me was trying to tell me something and that I would do well to listen. So after much inner anguish and thought, I decided to quit going to meetings. They were not working for me and it was fine if they worked for others, but I had to honor the part of myself crying to be heard.

Meetings had become more about doing what I *should* do rather than what I felt my inner urgings were leading me to do. The program, for me, had become too rigid and authoritarian and always kept me questioning my every motive. I noticed that I was always labeling my thoughts, feelings, and reactions to the circumstances in my life, e.g., "Was that reaction co-dependent?," "Did I eat that dessert in order to avoid feeling something?," "Is this really a healthy relationship for me?," "I should really confront this person and draw boundaries."

Instead of leading me toward inner harmony, meetings had become a dreaded chore. I was no closer to being fulfilled inside myself.

At the time, I was reading one self-help book after another and slowly becoming aware that I was attending meetings more from fear than anything else.

I was fearful that if I quit going to meetings I would drink or use again and would die. I was also afraid that if I didn't have some external checks on my behavior (from sponsors and others in the program), I couldn't be trusted. So I was fearful of my own nature. It was this fear that was beginning to cause me pain. The program that had initially relieved suffering was now causing suffering. Even though I was afraid to listen to my own inner authority, I knew I needed to. I could no longer live my life from a position of fear. I had found sobriety in A.A. Now I needed to find the rest of my life.

At the time I stopped attending meetings, I wasn't exactly sure what I was doing. I didn't know why meetings seemed to work so well for everybody else but left me feeling empty. I wasn't aware of how the rigid expectations of A.A. were causing me to feel uncomfortable. At the time, I just felt a strong dissatisfaction with the program and I had an inkling that there was another path for me, a better path. So I responded to my inner urgings and left A.A.

I was now twenty-eight years old and was living with the man who would become my husband. Having finished graduate school and obtained a master's degree in international business, I secured a contract with a publisher in Great Britain to write a book to be titled *Selling to America*, targeted for foreign companies who wanted to export their goods to the United States. It was the culmination of a long-time dream and I felt that being a published author would surely quell my inner emptiness. I was wrong. It was a wholly empty victory. After writing the book, I worked briefly at a market research firm in Atlanta, and when my book came out, I used my newfound skills to start my own consulting business, assisting foreign companies with their research needs in the American market. Having always wanted to work for myself, I again felt that this would fulfill me. Instead, it was another empty victory even though I was getting more work than I could handle.

Where on earth, I wondered, could I find fulfillment? I didn't find it in A.A. or in sobriety. I didn't find it in the outer world, with my book or in business. Perhaps the inner urgings that were prompting me to leave A.A. and pursue my own path held some clues that might help me in my quest for contentment and satisfaction.

The inner search for meaning and fulfillment suddenly assumed primary importance in my life. I had to start charting my life based on my terms and pursue things that were meaningful to me. I had been pursuing what was meaningful to everybody else all of my life. I allowed my father's influence to dictate my college career. It was his desire, made known to me at the age of twelve, that I go to Harvard and study business. Having scored in the top 1 percent of the class in IQ tests at school, he suddenly decided that I was to be the one everyone's collegiate expectations were focused on, although my sister was sitting at the table as a junior in high school with college admission applications spread before her. But I didn't question his expectations. Instead, my overwhelming desire to please him had me listening earnestly to what he said and vowing to make him proud. Similarly, I had allowed my mother's influence to chart my religious life. I had become a born-again Christian at twelve partly because I wanted to, but deep down I knew that it was the "right" thing to do and that my mom would be greatly pleased. I had no inner integrity that guided me to follow what was important to me personally. I had been living for everybody else for so long that I had no idea what was even important to me personally. Even my international business degree, my book, and my consulting was done first, as a way to please my father and second, as a way to please my live-in boyfriend. But now, at twenty-eight, I could no longer ignore my inner promptings, promptings I had been feeling for a long time but was too afraid to listen to. Now was the time to begin listening. One of the first things I felt was an overwhelming desire to know God better. I sensed that at the heart of my understanding of God I would find myself and I would find healing. But the more I searched for God, the more I kept hearing the voices of everybody else's definition of Him, if God even was a Him.

For reasons unknown to me, perhaps guided by this newly emerging inner wisdom, I started making lists. I wasn't sure where I was headed, but I knew that I could no longer continue living my life from the standpoint of fear. I was being intuitively guided to pursue a path of love, and the way to do so was unfolding before me. I wanted to better understand exactly what fear did for me and what love does for me. So I made two separate lists. The first was a list of the things fear had done for me. The second was a list of what love does for me.

3

Healing Our Addictions

LIST NUMBER 1—a list of the things fear has done for me. Fear keeps me

- questioning myself and my motives
- dependent (on an external authority to tell me how to live)
- weak and powerless
- guilty
- indecisive
- unworthy
- insecure
- a victim

List number 2—a list of the things love does for me. Love

- energizes me
- accepts me
- forgives me
- uplifts me
- inspires me
- empowers me
- expands me
- heals me

Now that I was finally stopping long enough to listen, there seemed to be a wellspring of wisdom and guidance bursting forth from within me. Insight and realizations that had been there all along were suddenly coming into focus and everything about my previous actions made sense.

As I meditated on these things and asked for further guidance, I was led to one book after another that clarified my confusion and answered my many probing questions. Some of the writers are very well known: Dr. Wayne Dyer, Dr. Deepak Chopra, Dr. Bernie Siegel, Lee Jampolsky, Gerald Jampolsky, Louise Hay, Shakti Gawain. I integrated their teachings with what I knew to be true in my own life and applied their insights to what I knew about my own addiction and recovery. Many of their insights helped me to see where I was hampering my own success and sobriety by letting others provide the answers for my life.

As I began living these new insights I saw, crystal-clear, how I could begin to heal my addictions. It had to do with doing what felt right to me based on love, rather than letting others tell me what to do and how to recover based on fear.

I realized that there are two basic ways to heal ourselves of addictive behavior. We can heal either through fear or through love. Twelve-step programs today have fear as their basis of healing. Slogans such as "Our only options were jails, institutions, or death" served only to plant and keep the fear (of these things) as the motivating factor for my recovery. The program further requires us to give up our power (admit we are powerless) and conform precisely to the A.A. code of conduct. "Rarely have we seen a person fail who has *thoroughly* followed *our* path. . . ." And the program uses shame to keep us in check: "Those who do not recover are people who *cannot* or *will not* give themselves to this simple program." (Emphasis mine.) The message here is obviously intended to be helpful and, fortunately, the twelve-step model has helped thousands to recover; but it is nevertheless a model grounded in fear and is dependent upon conformity and adherence for its success. I was learning that spiritual growth occurs most often when we are willing to embrace our inner guidance and not the rules and regulations handed to us by an external, rigid model of behavior.

I was also learning about the real differences between fear and love. Love as a basis of healing asks us to find our own inner authority, to connect with the inner wellspring of our spirit, which gives us a sense of powerfulness and empowerment instead of powerlessness and dependency. Healing through love means going directly to the core of the spiritual hunger pangs that are the cause of our cravings. The twelve-step model views alcoholism as the enemy, to be conquered and overcome. This message tells our bodies to be on the lookout for signs of "stinking thinking" (defined as continued defeatist, negative thinking) and keeps us waging a constant battle within ourselves. I found myself categorizing my thoughts and labeling them as acceptable or unacceptable.

This is especially draining for those people who have never learned to validate their own thoughts and feelings. Telling them that their thinking stinks is shaming and demeaning. Love does not want us to view a part of us as separate and diseased. Instead, love wants to lead us to wholeness. Love asks us why we are having cravings. By examining *why* we are having cravings we can better get at the solution. We may be having cravings because we feel very worthless and defeated, or we may have cravings because there is some aspect of our life that we do not want to deal with. Dr. Deepak Chopra, in *Overcoming Addictions*, in a section regarding eating and addictive behaviors writes that "If you are unhappy with your work, you should have a talk with your supervisor. If you're not satisfied with a relationship, you should express your feelings. And if you're really hungry, regardless of whether you're overweight, by all means eat. But if you're not hungry, don't eat." He is referring to the fact that we should deal with whatever is going on with us emotionally, rather than hiding behind addictive behavior, whether it is eating or any other addiction.

There are a number of reasons for experiencing cravings. To view cravings as simply a sign that I should go to more meetings did nothing to relieve the cravings In fact, it tended to make the cravings intensify because I still had not gone inward to listen to what the cravings were all about. More meetings *were not* the answer. Identifying the under-lying message of what my body was trying to tell me and honoring it was the answer.

Love wanted to draw me away from the battlefield. It wanted to connect all the fragmented and splintered aspects of myself and fill in all of the holes. Love wants to lift us up and inspire us. Love helps us to accept ourselves and forgive ourselves (drunk or not, we are worthy of love's blessings). Love wants us to find the Higher Power WITHIN OURSELVES, to heal us and make us whole.

Love lightens the load in every area of my life. It allows me to accept full responsibility for every circumstance that I find in my life and further allows me to see the positive aspect of each situation. It gently encourages me to learn and grow. Love allows me to see past the labels of good and bad.

Fear, on the other hand, wants to keep the answer outside our-selves in an external God (who may or may not decide to relieve our cravings). Dr. Bob (one of the founding fathers of A.A.) admitted that after achieving sobriety he had cravings for the rest of his life. Did God decide that Dr. Bob didn't need to be relieved of his cravings, or were there other forces at work?

I saw how fear and dependency go hand in hand. I had a strong sense at this point that I had unknowingly embarked on a journey. A journey of understanding and knowing, a journey that was clarifying all the questions I had ever had about addiction and about fear. My innately curious mind wanted to know more. I especially wanted to know the origins of the fear-based thinking that underpinned A.A. and to more completely understand its effects.

4

Fear and Dependency

I BEGAN RESEARCHING the origins of fear-based thinking, and because of my own early experiences with Christianity, I started there. I had been raised in a Methodist church. The Methodist view is one of traditional Christianity.

Traditional Christianity sees mankind as sinful and in need of redemption. We are taught to view ourselves as sinners who cannot trust our own urges and instead must rely upon the church and an external, judgmental God for guidance in all matters. We are taught to view circumstances and urges in terms of right and wrong, good and bad. And we are given the message that we must be vigilant at all times because Satan is always tempting us and is just waiting for us to be "weak." The golden rule is the basis for how to conduct ourselves, and we are allowed to feel worthy and useful if we are always seeking to help others. The inherent message is that God likes us better when we are being good.

This view of Christianity deepens our fear and dependency by keeping the authority and voice for our lives outside ourselves and in an external God who judges us. Furthermore, the teaching that our own sinful natures are not to be trusted and must be controlled at all times leaves us feeling powerless and weak. In always looking to the church for how to live our lives, we give away the power to make our own choices and to find what truly works for us. We are forever trying to pigeonhole what feels right for us into one or more of the beliefs of our religion. If what feels right for us doesn't fit into any of the views of the church, we simply accept that we must trust the church and give up on trying to find our own way.

No one is encouraged to question the teachings of the Bible or of Jesus. In fact, blasphemy is a frowned-upon offense. However, the church leaders do not tell you (probably because they don't know themselves) that the Bible has throughout history been modified (starting in the fourth century with Emperor Constantine) to suit the designs of the church leaders, which were to keep the flock dependent, fearful, and powerless. So the teachings that were meant to empower us have over the years become a tool to manipulate followers into fearful submission by declaring one could or couldn't get into Heaven without meeting precise requirements.

We even expect our church leaders to be immune to those things we experience in everyday life. In our city, an extremely popular minister was being asked to step down by his congregation simply because his wife had filed for divorce. I wonder how many of those crying the loudest for his removal had been divorced themselves or had a family member who was divorced.

Many of the beliefs and practices of Christianity are grounded in fear. Fear of sinning, fear of being "bad," fear of ourselves, fear of being "selfish," etc., etc. Our behavior is only acceptable if the church deems it to be acceptable. We are never taught how to trust ourselves or listen to our own inner authority. We are given rules and regulations to live by and are expected to play by them. We are not taught the limitlessness of our potential, and we are not given the tools to find our own spiritual paths. There are a number of churches today, such as the Unity denomination, that are deviating from the traditional model of Christianity in that they allow diversity of experience and even encourage members to find their own version of God rather than force-feeding them one based on a limited interpretation. Not surprisingly, Unity church memberships are increasing every day.

The similarities of traditional Christianity to A.A. are numerous;

many are obvious. We are told that the first thing we must do is admit powerlessness and turn our will and our lives over to the care of God, as we understand Him. We are told the program of recovery rarely fails if a person "thoroughly follows our path." We are taught continued dependence on the model by such phrases as "If you ever use again you'll die," and we all hear numerous stories about those poor unfortunate souls who quit going to meetings and wind up drunk again and worse off than before. We are told to make lists of our shortcomings and are expected to continue to work on our character defects for the remainder of our time in the program. We are expected to blindly accept that the steps are the only way out of addiction. If we question them, we can anticipate the wrath of the group upon us. I questioned the steps once and the whole group came down on me; I felt that I had been shamed for even bringing it up. The program had worked, and still does work, for thousands, was the response. But I don't think the original founders, given the variety and complexity of addictions today, would have wanted the steps to become so rigid and fixed.

A.A. correctly anticipated the problems they would encounter in placing reliance upon a Higher Power and so decreed that a Higher Power could be anything we interpret it to be, even a tree. However, the focus was still on something outside ourselves.

But I was starting to discover that in order to find our own inner power we needed to find that personal aspect of God WITHIN us. "We need to know God and have a sense of his/her presence," writes Joan Gattuso in her book *A Course in Love*. We can find our God consciousness in our minds and our souls. When we keep viewing God as external, it then keeps our power in something outside ourselves. It was God *acting through* Jesus who allowed him to perform the miracles; he said, "This and more will you do also." We *can* perform miracles when we find the God within us. God acting through Jesus means that Jesus had God's energy manifesting in his body. I believe we have God's energy manifesting in us every day of our lives.

Gerald Jampolsky, in his remarkably insightful book *Love Is the*

Answer, describes how our addictions keep us unhappy: "Our addictions keep us from recognizing our spiritual essence and discovering that true happiness is found only by going inward."

We need to go inward, not upward. Going upward (to an external God) kept me feeling separate and as if I had to "earn" love or do right for good things to happen to me. Similarly, looking to a Higher Power (upward) causes us to feel that our sobriety, happiness, and peace of mind depend on forces outside ourselves.

As we go within and connect with our inner self, we discover that we have a Higher Power within us, our Higher Self.* This Higher Self is our spiritual, invisible, formless self and is not limited by physicality. Our Higher Self wants to heal all of our missing parts and lead us to create meaningful lives filled with purpose, happiness, aliveness, and vitality.

One of the drawbacks of relying upon fear and dependency for guidance is the limitations they impose. Some of the limiting beliefs in A.A. include the idea that we are addicts for life and must be in recovery for the rest of our lives to ensure that we don't use again; if we drink again, we will die. We are encouraged to be overly dependent on meetings and on sponsors. Oprah Winfrey has admitted that for a long time she did not believe herself to be worthy of both fame *and* fortune *and* beauty. Therefore, she continued to battle her weight, and in many of her early shows she is very heavy. She finally discarded these limiting beliefs as simply not having to be true for her any longer and she is now radiantly beautiful (and still rich and famous).

Why do we argue and fight so strongly for our limitations? There are no outer limits to what we can achieve. People who do not believe in limits prove this every day. Space travel is a good example of what can be accomplished when we discard limiting beliefs.

The thing about beliefs is simple: What we believe to be true will

---

*By our Higher Self I am referring to the higher power of the Universe, or as Shakti Gawain describes it: "a higher intelligence, a fundamental creative power, or energy, in the universe which is the source and substance of all existence." Higher Self is that force which created us and lives and dwells within each of us.

be true for us. If we believe that we will always be addicts, then that is what we will experience. If we discard this belief as simply not true, we can believe that we can heal our addictions so thoroughly as to transcend them. We no longer have to live as addicts fearful of using again.

Bookstores today are filled with books that talk about the mind/body connection. Renowned authors such as Bernie Siegel and Deepak Chopra speak of how our minds affect our bodies. Stories of spontaneous remissions, miracle cures, cancerous tumors that had disappeared by the time surgery was scheduled—these are no longer uncommon. What each of these stories has in common is that upon receiving a diagnosis of disease, each patient became proactive in regaining his or her health, often ignoring traditional medical advice with its predictions of doom and gloom. At the root of each of these success stories is a belief in their own power to heal themselves through whatever methods they choose, be it the power of prayer, focused relaxation, visualization, or alternative therapies. Each patient with a remarkable story of healing changed his belief system from one of sickness to one of wellness. Likewise, we can do the same with our negative beliefs that our addiction is stronger than we are or that we will be addicted for the rest of our lives.

As I walked through the doors of my first Overeaters Anonymous meeting, I was filled with purpose and looked forward to finally being able to put my years of food addiction behind me. But after months of O.A. meetings, late-night calls to sponsors, endless inventories and lists of character defects, I still felt no real relief. I still experienced cravings on an almost daily basis. In many ways it seemed as if the harder I struggled, the more entrenched my addiction became. It slowly began to dawn on me that all anyone talked about during the entire meeting was *food*. "Abstinent eating" was defined as three meals a day with nothing in between. People were constantly beating themselves up for eating between meals, having seconds, having dessert. And those who had achieved long-term abstinence were viewed with a mixture of awe and envy. I felt like a failure the whole time. The model of behavior was far too rigid for me. And I especially did not like to focus so much on the food. The food had nothing to do with it. My binge-purge behavior was a result of the *pain* in my life along with my feelings of unworthiness and despair. Forcing myself to adopt a rigid set of rules was not the solution. Identifying and releasing my pain was the only true way to heal. And this could be done with love.

I stopped going to meetings and focused on getting my life in order. My first priority was to start pursuing things that made me feel good about myself, which meant doing things that I felt like doing instead of forcing myself to do things that didn't feel right. O.A. meetings did not make me feel good about myself unless I had been "abstinent." Otherwise, I felt "bad" or "guilty," two messages that are neither healing nor empowering and actually echo Christianity's message of sin and redemption. I hated the duality of good/bad and abstinent/relapsed. It kept me fearful and dependent. I was fearful of failing and dependent upon abstinence to feel good about myself. This type of thinking is a trap and will rarely lead to long-term recovery.

When I finally "dropped out" of O.A., it was not a conscious decision on my part. The program itself just did not satisfy me. After attending O.A. meetings for a little over six months, I did achieve abstinence. But, sadly enough, even when I achieved a full year of abstinent eating I still felt no inner fulfillment. Instead, working their program felt as if I were imposing a harsh set of behavioral expectations on a poor body and soul that was already weakened: "Don't eat that. That's a trigger food for you"; "Remember, don't let yourself get too hungry, angry, lonely, or tired"; "You'll go to a meeting tonight, whether you like it or not"; "You had better be willing to call your sponsor. Your abstinence depends on your willingness to do so."

These were all things I told myself in my zeal to do exactly what I was told.

Tired of the constant battle within between my will and that of the program, I slowly stopped attending as many meetings. If I really didn't feel like going to a meeting one night, I let it be okay. I would still feel guilty for not being willing to go, though. On the one hand, my twelve-step groups were very clear on what I needed to be willing to do. And on the other hand, my heart was aching to be heard and responded to. And my heart was very clear as to what its message was: "It doesn't have to be this hard. Lighten up, Marianne, and go a little easier on yourself."

My heart was begging me to be gentle with myself. So despite my guilty feelings, I made fewer and fewer calls to my O.A. sponsor, I attended fewer and fewer meetings, and I slowly tried to stop obsessing about how much, what kind, and what time of day each morsel of food went into my mouth. I started trying to relax around the whole issue of food. And I learned a lot. As I relaxed, things began to get much easier. I began to see that food really wasn't the issue, and that if I focused instead on the *feelings* that made me want to escape into an addictive episode with food, I could heal a whole lot faster.

I also began to recognize that my own self-hatred was a primary component in fueling an addictive encounter, the theme that had been played out over and over by myself. I failed to live up to my expectations about my weight, my career goals, my personal goals, my relationships, and so my self-esteem would plummet. Not wanting to feel these painful feelings, thoughts of Domino's Pizza, ice cream, and Coca-Cola would loom large in my mind and off I'd go to the grocery store to buy all my favorite binge foods. Afterward, feelings of remorse would quickly surface as my self-esteem took another hit. By not actually dealing with my demons, and instead running from them all the time, I never developed any healthy strategies with which I could deal with life on life's terms.

As I began to see the root cause of my addictions, I began to see how my insistence on living in a fear-based manner made it inevitable that I would be continually overwhelmed by life and its problems. Today I live in more of a love-based manner that allows me to take healthy responsibility for all of my life's circumstances and trust that the Universe will support my actions. It also allows my heart and my body to work in harmony. Today I no longer have any need to force myself to continually do things that feel wrong to me. And that is perhaps the most healing thing I could ever have learned.

As it turns out, as I turned my focus from food and instead on to myself, my cravings began to go away. It was as if my body had simply been trying to get my attention all along and now that I was really responding to its needs, I was getting better. I was learning that the feelings of guilt and remorse only tended to set me up for another addictive episode. And if I could let a binge be okay, I was moving much closer to self-acceptance and farther from self-hatred, the fuel of my addiction. I slowly kept moving forward in this fashion, listening to my heart, responding to my body's needs, until one day all feelings of wanting to binge and purge had left me completely.

I relate my Overeaters Anonymous experiences because O.A. had more fear-based messages for me than any other twelve-step group. I found myself continually feeling shamed, and I continually questioned every morsel of food I ate. Instead of being able to relax and enjoy food, I was constantly trying to be vigilant about not eating between meals, not eating for emotional reasons, not eating too much, etc., etc. It was exhausting! The more I focused on my eating, the guiltier I felt for not being able to live up to the "ideal" and so the more I ate. There is nothing empowering about this sort of thinking.

Alcoholics Anonymous and other twelve-step groups use their steps as the model for recovery. But those of us in the programs are not given the encouragement to follow the beliefs and practices that feel right for us if they do not resound with the twelve steps. Every meeting started sounding like so much rhetoric and so many pat answers. Having achieved sobriety, I was never given any real solutions to my problems and the pain in my life. I was not encouraged to continue developing personally other than to keep working on my character defects and shortcomings.

I wondered if other people in A.A. were really satisfied with their lives. The O.A. members didn't seem particularly satisfied with life whether they had achieved food abstinence or not. They seemed a bit rigid and obsessive to me. I looked around at the A.A. members and saw that many of them truly did seem happy. They had no trouble remembering how bad things had been and how wonderful things were now. And many of them were trying to develop more spiritually meaningful lives by pursuing different spiritual and religious outlets. But the fact that I was told I would have to attend these meetings *for the rest of my life* strongly implied that I could not or would not live the right kind of life without A.A.'s omnipotent guidance to ensure my continued sobriety. I resented the implication that I didn't know what was best for me without A.A. overseeing me and keeping me on track.

Where was the affirmation of the positive traits I had? The steps never told me to include anything positive or healthy or beautiful about myself when taking a personal inventory. Instead, the whole focus was on my wrongs—categorizing them, telling them to others, and promptly admitting them. And where was the support to pursue my own guidance and answers? I was stunted in my development until I began to honor that voice. I thought it ironic that as soon as I began to honor my *own* voice, my pain, along with all of my cravings, began to disappear.

5

Questioning Not Allowed

No one in my church would ever have questioned something that was written in the Bible. The Bible is sacred. If something is in the Bible, then it is written in stone. However, you do not have to be very creative to be able to twist any quote in the Bible to serve your aims. The church I grew up in, the First United Methodist Church of Marietta, always depicted God as vengeful and judgmental, which kept me fearful and dependent upon it for guidance.

In the model of traditional Christianity, questioning is not at all encouraged. The teachings of Jesus, and the teachings of the Bible, are sacred. Furthermore, the church deems itself the absolute authority to decide what is and what is not acceptable behavior for its members.

Alcoholics Anonymous is very similar. The Big Book of Alcoholics Anonymous has become sacred among twelve-step devotees. I can remember a number of times that I brought a very troublesome problem to the group only to be quoted something pat and superficial from the Big Book. The devotion given to this book is almost cultlike.

I have nothing against using whatever works for you, but you can become so rigid and dogmatic in your application of a written text that it is no longer able to serve the purpose for which it was written. When you take the flexibility and objectivity out of the Bible or out of the Big Book, then it is no longer able to support your continuing personal development. You become stuck in a rut, having to check everything you do with the Higher Authority of another person's point of view.

The underlying danger in any program that discourages questioning is that you will never be able to fully develop until you find your own voice and your own inner authority. If the inner authority for your life tells you that the A.A. or the Christian model is right, then by all means follow it. But more often than not, it is the voices of guilt and fear that are really encouraging you to give the authority for your lives away.

For many people, especially those who have never let themselves be heard, the need to question is acute. Without questioning the beliefs that are handed to us by well-meaning parents, churches, support groups, therapists, and so on, we are not able to truly know what is best for us. We need to ask ourselves: Does it feel right? Does it resonate with me internally?

I used to feel that Christianity resonated with me internally until I realized that I was constantly trying to pigeonhole what felt right for me into one or more of the beliefs of the religion. I was not living by my own authority. If what felt right for me could not find a home in one or more of the religious beliefs, instead of the belief, it was my inner longing that was the first to go.

For instance, at the very beginning of my struggle to achieve food abstinence, I read a great many religious books, especially books by Dr. Norman Vincent Peale, author of *The Power of Positive Thinking*. Having achieved sobriety from alcohol and drugs, I was searching for the strength to help me overcome my food addiction. In his books, Dr. Peale reiterated over and over again how we could overcome absolutely any obstacle, no matter how stubborn it might be, by faith in the power of Jesus Christ. Jesus gives us the power and the strength to believe that we can achieve anything, was Dr. Peale's message. As a very well-known minister and lecturer, Dr. Peale believed fervently in his message. And it was the message of Christianity in general: "It is through Jesus that we are saved and through Jesus that all good things come to us."

I have to admit honestly that I had a hard time with this message. Having grown up in the church, I had accepted Christianity pretty much without question. The church taught us about God and about Jesus, and how Jesus came to earth in order that we sinners might have salvation. If we turned our will and our lives over to him, we could gain salvation and entrance into heaven. But even as a young child I had questions about all of this. I was curious as to the fate of babies and small children who were taken from this world before they had a chance to ask Jesus to save them. Did they get to go to heaven? Or were they forever banished to some sort of otherworldly holding pattern? Having been taught only of the existence of heaven and hell, with no in-between places, the conclusion must be that those who didn't go to heaven went to hell. But surely little babies didn't go to hell.

And what about all the poor, starving children of Africa who have never even heard of Jesus?, my young mind queried. Since they had never heard of Jesus, did they not get salvation either? I asked these questions of the church and was told that God looks after all of His children. Well, if he looks after all of His children, then that must mean that the innocent people who die never having heard of Jesus got into heaven anyway because they were innocent. But if you get into heaven based on guilt or innocence, why do we need salvation? The Bible is very clear on that point—because we are all sinners. But if we are all sinners and only through salvation can we bypass our sinfulness and get into heaven, then we're back where we started. What happens to those innocent ones who die without ever having heard of Jesus?

The church couldn't satisfy my youthful curiosity so I quit asking and just started believing what I was taught, ignoring my reservations and the flaws I had found.

But perhaps the biggest reservation I was having about Christianity and the problem I continually encountered in my reading would not just go away this time the way it had when I was a child. My biggest resistance to all the words I was reading in my religious books related to the omnipotent power given to Jesus. All good comes through Jesus. From God ultimately, but *through* Jesus. Jesus is our salvation, the way, the truth, and the light, I was told. Something inside me welled up every time I read this. At first I thought it was simply my ego resisting turning over its will to a Higher Power. So I continued to read the Christian word and whenever I felt resistance to a particular message, I suppressed my feelings, overrode my resistance, and forced myself to stay faithful to the message, no matter how I felt internally. The struggle was still there, inside me, but I buried it down deep.

Because I had been reading all these Christian books in order to gain strength to overcome my food addiction, I expected to feel more powerful as I forced myself to adopt their message. *The Power of Positive Thinking*, in fact, assured me that this would be the case. But I wasn't feeling more powerful. In fact, I was feeling less powerful, given the message that I was a hopeless sinner and was powerless without Jesus. To make matters worse, my food cravings were not lessening. I was attending O.A. meetings, but there I just received more messages of how powerless over my disease I was, and that I was in full-blown denial if I believed I could overcome my bulimia by myself.

And then one day I was reading a book by Shakti Gawain, *Living in the Light*. In it she had written a chapter on intuition that talked about how at the "core of our being lies a loving, powerful, and creative nature" but that from childhood on we are taught not to trust our feelings, that the rational, logical side of ourselves is superior. She really grabbed me by her next statement. She said that addiction is what happens when we deny and suppress our intuition. I had an instant reaction within myself. Maybe all the resistance I was feeling toward Christianity was valid and was actually my intuition trying to speak to me. I knew within that this was so. I read on, and the following passage felt as if it had been written directly and personally for me to read:

Our established religious institutions support this fear of the intuitive, nonrational self. Once based on a deep awareness of the universal creative principle in every being, many religions only pay lip service to that idea now. Instead, they seek to control the behavior of their devotees, using elaborate rule structures purported to save people from their deep, irrational, and basically "sinful" natures . . . We've grown increasingly fearful of this intuitive aspect of our natures. We've attempted to control this "dark force" by creating authoritative rule structures that define right and wrong, good and bad, and appropriate and inappropriate behavior in a very heavy-handed way . . . Both personal and social problems are the result of fear and suppression of our intuition.

Suddenly, it was all so clear to me. My intuition had known all along. It had been trying to get through to me, by my feelings of resistance, to tell me that if traditional Christianity didn't feel right for me, then to honor that. My intuition was trying to guide me down a different path, my path, and my fear and suppression of this new side of myself was only making my addiction more entrenched. I felt I had been given a spiritual awakening similar to the one Bill Wilson had in his hospital bed at the beginning of his sobriety when a bright light filled him with peace and forever set him on the path to sobriety. From that day forward, my spiritual journey took a vastly different course. I instantly became empowered as I recognized that I had a wisdom inside me that knew precisely what was and wasn't right for me personally. I felt validated for perhaps the first time in my life. It had simply never occurred to me that the religion itself might be flawed, and not me. I had been thinking it was all me, that it I was unwilling to go against my own will, I just wasn't spiritual enough or pleasing in the eyes of God. Now I was seeing that perhaps it was the religion itself, with its rigid expectations and dogma, that wasn't right for me, not that *I* wasn't right.

I was careful to not throw out the baby with the bathwater. Christianity has many helpful components, and just like twelve-step programs, has helped and continues to help thousands every day. Christianity in its simplest form means, to me, trying to live our lives based on Jesus' example of love, tolerance, and patience. But traditional Christianity had been interpreted and reinterpreted for two thousand years by humans, humans who are subject to power struggles, mistakes, fears, greed, and prejudices that color their views. I believe that if Jesus were here in physical form today, he would encourage us all to learn to look past our limited views and see our true unlimited potential, not to get caught up in endless dogma and empty rituals. I believe he would want us all to try to harness the same spiritual energies that he did. The Christian belief that I was a hopeless sinner and powerless sent warning bells off inside me.

What I had been doing, again in my zeal to stay loyal to the Christian religion, was throwing out any belief of mine that I couldn't somehow fit into one or more of the tenets of Christianity, even though many of the beliefs that I threw out had felt right to me, had clicked with me internally. Understanding intuition as I now did, I saw how these beliefs that clicked with me internally were little indicators from my intuition that there was a belief that was right for me.

So I had to go back and look at each and every one of my beliefs. Did they feel right for me? Did they serve me or hinder me? Did they strengthen me or weaken me? Did they shackle me or free me? I began honoring the beliefs that felt right to me and letting go of those that didn't.

The first belief I questioned was the belief that we must turn to Jesus for all of our power. What about his own words, "These things and greater shall you do also," or "The kingdom of heaven is within you." I believe that Jesus is the greatest example of how we can live our lives, but I honestly believe that he would be appalled by how the Christian religion has turned him into such an idol, the very thing he said he didn't want. I believe that power exists within each and every one of us, and was what Jesus was referring to when he said "These things and greater shall you do also," and that calling ourselves "sinful" and "hopeless" and "powerless" is simply our fearful way of running away from our own power and our own vast potential. By putting the power outside ourselves, in a church or a twelve-step program or something else, we are relieved of the responsibility for harnessing it ourselves.

I began questioning other beliefs, questioning everything in my life for the first time, placing it before the inner authority that was beginning to emerge from within me. I realized that we all have a unique, individual, highly personal set of beliefs that we live by. I also recognized that many of the beliefs that we live by are outdated. Many others may work for some people but not for others. The tendency is for groups to make what works best for them become a rigid belief that everyone else would do well to live by, when the truth is that a variety of beliefs is best. That way we can pick and choose. As my mother always says, the reason we have chocolate, vanilla, and strawberry ice cream is so that everyone will get what they want. In other words, what works for me may not necessarily be what works best for you.

A.A., however, wants to force-feed you a set of beliefs that you are not expected to question or change. If the set of beliefs they hand you does not resonate with you internally, there is no encouragement to honor what feels right for you.

One belief that we are especially discouraged from questioning is that of being an addict/alcoholic *for life*. If we have found sobriety in A.A., we are expected to continue A.A. meetings for as long as we wish to remain sober. Every A.A. meeting hall I was ever in resounded with stories of those poor unfortunate souls who had succumbed again to their disease after years and years of sober living. The statement, "You know, he stopped going to meetings," is always the final refrain in the story. The message is clear. If we stop going to meetings, we'll drink again. Maybe not tomorrow or next week, but eventually. And then the dreaded disease, the "monster," will have us again.

There is even a medical model that explains the progressive nature of alcoholism. Treatment centers give us the whole unpleasant picture in these medical terms. We are shown charts of how the "disease" of alcoholism will progress even in sobriety, meaning that if we are unfortunate enough to ever drink again, our disease (and our subsequent behavior) will be far worse than ever before. Not to knock seemingly sound medical models, but why do we have to focus so much attention on the disease, placing limitations, labels, and expectations on it? And why do we unequivocally accept that we will have to continue meetings in perpetuity if we expect to remain sober?

I have yet to meet an ex-smoker who continues to lament how bad his life was before he quit and how grateful he is to not smoke today. Neither do you see ex-smokers who feel compelled to focus on their previous addiction for the rest of their lives. You never hear an ex-smoker say, "I'm a recovering smoker." Why? Because it would be ridiculous. And yet numerous reports cite smoking as *the* hardest habit to quit and liken it to a heroin addiction, but more intense in terms of the compulsion to use. And yet the vast majority (reportedly over 90 percent) of smokers who successfully quit do so without the assistance of stop-smoking programs, patches, gum, hypnosis, or any other external agent.

So why do we feel compelled to spend an inordinate amount of time and energy focusing on our alcoholic (or overspending/promiscuous/eating/drug-taking) addictions? Why do we have these diseases *for life*, yet not the smoking addiction? I question the whole "diseased for life" concept. I do not personally feel that labeling myself as "in recovery," attending a lifetime of twelve-step meetings, taking and making phone calls to and from sponsors, making lists of shortcomings, and praying to have my character defects removed is my answer. I questioned this belief at its very core when I stopped attending meetings. But this decision was based upon the guidance of my own inner authority.

To reiterate, if you do not question the beliefs that you have about life, relationships, work, and family, and instead choose to blindly accept the beliefs handed you by family, church, school, and well-meaning friends, you will never develop fully. You must find your own voice, your own authority, and do what feels right internally.

It is very important in doing this to realize that your own inner authority will never lead you to do anything that would harm another. I have learned that the highest good for ourselves is that which is the highest good for others as well. It is one of the universal principles of love. If you feel that your inner voice is guiding you to do something that harms another, you are simply being deceived by what your own secret wishes and desires are. And I had to learn to differentiate between what actually harming another meant as opposed to taking care of people when they should be taking care of themselves. I was afraid that if I didn't take care of my significant other in certain areas of his life I would be harming him, when in actuality I was only harming myself by doing for him what he needed to do for himself. Your inner authority may guide you to take more responsibility for your *own* actions and *less* responsibility for your spouse's or family's. Forcing them to grow up by no longer taking on their responsibilities doesn't harm them. However, they may not like it.

6

Food and Cigarettes

I RAN ACROSS an article in a local Atlanta newspaper recently that discussed bulimia. The caption read, "Love-Hate Relationship with Food." The article was an interview with several bulimic women, and one—a young girl in her mid-twenties—described how she hated the feeling of food in her stomach. With a jolt I remembered all the painful and fearful feelings about food that I myself had experienced during my years of bulimia.

While I was actively bingeing and purging, my main concern was to gorge myself as much as possible and then quickly expel all the food from my body through vomiting. The whole binge cycle usually lasted as little as thirty minutes or as long as two hours. And the main objective was to *stop feeling all feelings.* I thought for a long time that it was the food itself that was so alluring. Prior to a binge, thoughts of eating gooey brownies, thick, cheesy slices of pizza, cookies, and ice cream would invade my mind. But it wasn't the food so much as it was the *escape* that the food offered me, much in the same way that drinking and drugs offered me an escape. But with food, I could be utterly alone. Just me and my feelings of inadequacy, my loneliness, my disappointments. I didn't have to sit in a bar with my friends and be engaging. I didn't have to obsessively scour the bars for drugs to keep the night going. After I tired of that whole lifestyle, food was there. Food accepted me just the way I was. I could sit at home and binge. I could wear what I wanted. I didn't have to answer the phone. I could look and act as disgusting as the binge-purge behavior is and food didn't mind. Food became the arena in which I dumped all my pain, all my striving to become worthwhile and the letdowns and failures I felt along the way. All the feelings of shame, all the stresses of life—everything was given a voice when I was bingeing. And later I would fall into bed, numb, my eyes expressionless, all pain gone, only emptiness remaining.

In later years, when I was trying to overcome my bulimia, I had to relearn how to eat. I had to eat moderately. Of course, I knew *how* to eat moderately. Most of my daytime meals were moderate meals. But now I had to learn how to eat moderately all the time. This is when I suddenly became aware of how uncomfortable food can feel in your stomach, especially if you've eaten too much. Even one bite too many would send me off on a purge, I was so unable to bear the thought of a whole meal being in my stomach. Fear would invade my mind: "You're going to get fat with all that food you just ate. Better get rid of it," or "You had way too many calories" even if I had had only a reasonable amount.

I was so terrified of gaining weight, so afraid that I would be mediocre again. Having battled a self-image problem for so long growing up, and having finally developed really good feelings about my looks in my twenties, I was determined to never again become pudgy, to never again experience that self-consciousness. I had so much riding on it, in fact, that I would rather make myself throw up than let myself gain weight.

So the first few months of food abstinence and moderate eating were *very* uncomfortable for me. At some point, I knew I would have to just trust that I could eat, and digest, three meals a day without my whole world falling apart. But in the beginning that's exactly what I felt would happen. I felt that everything would fall apart if I wasn't thin. It was an issue of control with me, and I was fanatical. I finally had control over my weight, as warped as that control was, and I was clinging to it for all it was worth.

I read somewhere that bulimia and anorexia often develop as the only way people can exert any control over their lives. They may live in a very strict home or may be very strict with their own high expectations, and they see food as the one area in which they can have absolute control. This was true for me, but it was also about fear. I was fearful of life, afraid and unable to feel any more pain than I had already experienced to this point. I was also afraid that I would not be as lovable or worthwhile if I was chubby.

But, like the many ironies of addiction, the more control I exerted or mistakenly thought I had exerted, the more out of control my eating became. There were times in my life, especially during graduate school, when I was completely at the mercy of my food cravings. I would leave class early to go binge. Some days I never made it to class at all. Or I might spend the whole morning bingeing and make it to my afternoon classes, struggling to stay awake because I was exhausted from the morning's purging. When I was learning how to achieve food abstinence, I realized that I had to reevaluate the area of control. Although I might be controlling my weight, did I really have any control over my eating habits? The answer was no.

So, the burning question then became, Can I learn to trust that if I let myself digest my meals, even when I think I've eaten too much, that my world will not fall apart? The hardest part of food abstinence was knowing that if I stopped purging, I would gain weight. And to my sick bulimic mind, I had to think really hard about whether it was worth it or not. Any normal, sane person would not have a moment's hesitation, but because I had so many self-esteem feelings tied to my weight, I had to really become comfortable with the idea that giving up purging would mean gaining weight. As it turned out, when I stopped bingeing, I actually lost a few pounds because I was no longer consuming sugary items.

Next, I had to make peace with all the other painful feelings about myself I had been trying to run from. Again, it was very similar. While I imagined that the very *worst* would occur if I faced my negative feelings about myself, the opposite was true. I had been fearful that if I ever turned inward and looked squarely at my beliefs that I was less than enough, faulty, or simply inadequate, I would have to accept these "truths" once and for all. But when I finally did turn inward, I kept getting the same message over and over: that I really was worthwhile, and lovable, and that the programs or belief systems that wanted me to believe otherwise were wrong, not me! What a relief! I had been running from shadows all my life. But I suppose fear will have it no other way. My fear didn't know what the unknown held, and so told me to suspect the worse. "After all, you've been let down before. Why should this be any different?" seemed to be fear's rationale.

ARE WE TRULY HEALED IF every time we get in our car or every time we finish a meal or anytime we feel a moment of either stress or happiness, we reach for a cigarette? While waiting in the doctor's office one day, I read an article about smoking. The writer of the article suggested that smoking is really nothing more than a *smoke screen*, a smoke screen between ourselves and our feelings, and between ourselves and others. It is a way to dull our senses to stress, or a way to heighten our sensation of pleasure. It is an addiction. And like any other addiction, it keeps us from fully experiencing life.

Several years ago I attended an A.A. conference that was being conducted by a very popular twelve-step speaker. The large auditorium reserved for the conference was filled to capacity. We had all dutifully brought our Big Books and were following along as the leader spoke. Everyone attending the conference was looking to further his understanding of A.A., and I assumed that they were also, like me, seeking guidance as to how to lead a better life. So it seemed a bit ironic to me that at every break, as hundreds of people streamed into the lobby, the smoke detectors would start wailing. There were so many people smoking during the breaks that the lobby was filled with smoke so thick it looked like a foggy morning in England. I am not saying people shouldn't smoke. But I do think it is just an addiction, like any other, and that one should look at the motivation in choosing to smoke. Smoking is, of course, less destructive than alcoholism in terms of resulting in fatal accidents, broken homes, etc.

However, it claims more lives in the forms of lung cancer and emphysema and overall poor health than does alcoholism.

I personally didn't feel like I was completely healed from addiction as long as I still smoked. It had, for me, indeed become a smoke screen. So when I decided to quit, I chose the way I had heard was the most successful, cold turkey. I was very fortunate in that a year or so prior to this, a very wise friend had given me her "stop smoking" pep talk. My friend told me in her enthusiastic and infectious way that what you believe to be true about quitting smoking is what you will experience. If you think that it is going to be awful, that your cravings will be unbearable and last all day long, that you'll be irritable, and that it will basically be the worst ordeal you've ever encountered, then this is very likely what will happen. However, if you think that it will be bad for just a few days, that your cravings will be short-lived and tolerable, and that overall it won't be too horrible an experience, then that is what you'll likely experience. My friend also gave me the speech about how I needed to stop being a smoker in my thoughts by always thinking of myself as a nonsmoker from now on. This, I found out, was very important, for it saw me through the times, months later, when I wanted to smoke but decided not to. Perhaps the zeal with which she delivered her speech was what affected me the most, or perhaps it was just the truth of her words. Nevertheless, the long and short of it is that my friend was exactly right. Once I made the firm decision to quit, instead of simply waiting around for that perfect moment to quit that never actually occurs, I resigned myself to simply being uncomfortable for a few days, a week at most. The first three days were bad. Not unbearable, but uncomfortable. And after those three days, the worst was over. I would occasionally crave a cigarette, but would not have one. As time went on, when I would crave a cigarette, the thought of actually smoking one was enough to keep me from lighting up. Because by then I had become a nonsmoker and the smoking habit was smelly and repulsive to me; it still is to this day.

Since I've stopped all my former addictions, I've found that other ways to *stop feeling* will try to entice me. The television might beckon me every night, or I might become immersed in some activity, such as reading or writing, that I will do compulsively. Or if I am feeling particularly depressed, I might crave movies or want to lie curled up on the couch all day. Addiction can be a sneaky thing in that it wants to draw us away from what is really going on with us and divert us on to its track. And it does that by the use of cravings. But I discovered that when I can respond to what the addiction or the craving is really about, the healthier and happier I become.

7

The Meaning of Cravings

THE PRIMARY ASPECT of addiction we suffer from the most when we are in active addiction (or even in sobriety) is cravings. A.A. members tremble at the thought of going through a series of cravings, and usually the twelve-step answer when experiencing cravings is to go to meetings, meetings, and more meetings. It is not at all rare to be attending an eight P.M. meeting and hear someone share about how that meeting is their third or fourth or fifth that day.

However, we do not need to be afraid of cravings any more than we need to be afraid of our stomach sending us hunger pangs. Cravings are simply nature's way of telling you that something within you is out of balance. Just as hunger is nature's way of telling you to eat, cravings are a message from your Higher Self that there is something you are avoiding that needs to be tended to.

Seen in this light, cravings have *less* to do with the disease of addiction and *more* to do with personal responsibility. I can be a so-called alcoholic or suffer from any addictive "disease" and be completely free of cravings, so they are not so much related to the addiction itself. Cravings, therefore, are a sort of inner barometer. If you are taking care of yourself, are giving voice to your inner guide, and are accepting responsibility for your actions, you will probably experience very few cravings. Cravings will, however, creep into your life when you are under stress or are not taking responsibility for some part of your life. There's an old A.A. saying about never getting too hungry, angry, lonely, or tired, which is one slogan I happen to agree with.

When I experienced cravings, I took it as a warning bell from within. My inner guidance was gently trying to send me a message to shape up in some area of my life. I had to ask myself what I was trying to avoid or escape and then be really honest. If instead of going within and listening to my inner wisdom, I shrugged it off or ignored it, my cravings would intensify.

Cravings can also signify pain. If I was experiencing a particularly painful episode in my life, I would very likely feel like escaping into one of the many tempting black holes of addiction.

There are basically two ways to view cravings. The fear-based way of thinking sees cravings as problems, and as obstacles to be overcome. Cravings are seen in a negative light. The most common form of treatment is to attend more twelve-step meetings. Rarely did attendance at a twelve-step meeting relieve my cravings. They may have temporarily delayed the inevitability of my using but they did very little to relieve the desire to use. The negative way of seeing cravings as obstacles to be overcome causes an inner war to be waged within you. One part of you craves the addictive substance, another part craves sobriety and abstinence. Since there is no internal resolution, a battle wells up within you and the cravings intensify. The more you try to respond to your cravings with external solutions, the stronger the cravings seem to become. In these instances, even prayer can be viewed as an external solution. When we pray pleadingly to an external, judgmental God to relieve our cravings, we are still leaving the solution to our problems outside ourselves. What, then, is the answer? The very best way to respond to a craving is to let go of the struggle, and it is love that helps us to do this.

The second way to handle cravings is with love instead of fear. Love-based thinking views cravings as a message that something in our lives is out of balance. We may be experiencing a great deal of stress, or pain, or we may be avoiding taking action or assuming responsibility in some part of our lives. I experienced cravings for many, many years simply because of an accumulation of pain in my life. I had never felt worthy on a number of counts and all the painstaking efforts I put forth to try and measure up went largely unnoticed by the people to whom I had given over my self-esteem.

For instance, I could never quite be the business person my father wanted me to be. All I heard from him my last two years of college was that I should get a job with a Fortune 500 company. That's the only way to go, he repeated over and over. I did get a job with a Fortune 500 company and before the year was out, the company had been bought and all my coworkers were laid off. I had already quit, disillusioned and unhappy with corporate life but also too addicted to show up for work every day. So I let my father down. I felt like a disappointment to my mother because I could never get my addictions under enough control to be a good daughter. I let my boyfriend's measure of me be my measure of myself. And I was too embarrassed by my addictive lifestyle to remain close to my sister even though she had come to mean a great deal to me.

I also felt a great deal of guilt over my addictions. Guilt can wreak havoc on us in so many instances, and it does an especially good job of keeping our cravings at a high level. I felt unable and unwilling to stop drinking and felt guilty for letting my family down. The more I drank and used, the guiltier I felt. The guiltier I felt, the more I drank and used. I was caught in the vicious cycle of addiction. As my guilt would intensify, so would my cravings. I was only able to stop drinking after it became very important *for myself*. I couldn't stop because of my family's pressure. It had to come from within me.

In many cases, the more you resist or try to overcome a craving with an external solution such as a meeting, a phone call, or intense prayer, the stronger the craving will be when it returns. And it *will* return! The solution in this case is to go within and listen to what your body is trying to tell you. Is there some part of your life in which you are avoiding taking action? Is there a person you need to confront? Or a problem you need to deal with? Try to look at every aspect of your life and determine where you are not being true to yourself. If you are going through a major transition such as death, birth, divorce, and so on, some pain and trauma is to be expected. In this case, just be kind and gentle and good to yourself until the situation eases. Don't hesitate to give others who depend on you an opportunity to fend for themselves while you take care of yourself.

Responding to cravings with love means answering the hunger cry from our soul. It means letting our inner self feel important and listened to. Many times we have an intuition about something but refuse to act, instead shrugging it off as fanciful or unrealistic. We need to develop the courage to listen to our intuition because it represents our soul trying to connect with us. If we ignore our intuition too often and for too long, it will begin to come out in the form of cravings in order to get our attention. If instead of grabbing for the first addictive substance we can find, we can instead relax, listen, and go within, we will hear the message.

When I became engaged to be married at age twenty-nine, I was in a relationship with a man whom I loved deeply. However, over the course of time we had begun blaming each other for all of our personal unhappiness and the relationship had become stale and lifeless. Although I still wanted to get married, I had not stopped to reflect on what kind of relationship we would have if things continued on the same course. I was denying, avoiding, and ignoring all the pain I felt about our relationship. I was also avoiding and denying my secret desire to live alone and without any sort of intimate relationship in order to work on and develop my spiritual side. At the same time, I was expending so much energy denying and avoiding that I had started experiencing intense cravings. This was rather surprising at first because at the time I had experienced a long period of food abstinence.

I didn't connect the pain and unhappiness I was feeling with the cravings. Finally, the pain became unbearable. I broke the engagement, secured an apartment on my own, and moved out. Without even knowing exactly what I was doing, I was doing the very best thing *for me*. I was finally honoring my voice, my inner authority, my intuition. The cravings didn't automatically go away. In fact, I began using food again for a short time. But this time around, as I slowly and more confidently began to expand my inner world and connect with my own personal version of my Higher Self, my cravings lessened in intensity and eventually left me altogether. This slow process of waking up involved letting go of everyone else's definition of God and finding Him/Her for myself. In the process I discovered that He/She was within me. The external, male God was only a limited view of the universal loving energy, and someone else's view at that. I began to discard beliefs I was taught that I found did not fit me. As I healed myself in this way, my relationship with my ex-fiancé began healing. We began to recognize how much we had blamed the other in order to avoid taking responsibility for our own behavior. We were able to heal so completely that we finally did wed, and this time it was in perfect love, perfect trust, and perfect accountability.

I also began to view my addiction in a different light. By not battling my addiction but instead giving in to it, I got in touch with a lot of the shame that surrounded my addictive behavior. I understood how it was that my shame had kept me battling addiction. By continually feeling unworthy, I was letting an unhealed wound fester within me. And this unhealed wound manifested itself by dragging me back into addictive behavior. I was very ashamed of bingeing and purging again, which was how my addiction had manifested itself this time. I was finally seeing that it was *the shame inside me* that kept drawing me in toward situations, such as active bulimia, that caused me to feel shame, therefore validating the inner belief. I don't think I would have been able to recognize and heal this negative belief had I not encountered it one more time in the process of active addiction. But, this time I did not judge or condemn myself for having an addiction. I merely allowed it to be okay and let this help me through a very stressful period. I, in no way, encourage anyone to use addiction as a way to deal with stressful periods of your life. However, *for me*, it allowed me to see how my belief in my own shame was still running my life and it gave me a chance to finally acknowledge that and heal it. Having done that—healed the negative belief—I have since had no desire to use food addictively. I was finally able to learn the lesson my addictions were trying to teach me.

For me, with my food addiction, relapses were a necessary part of my recovery. When I stopped using alcohol and drugs, it was with complete abstinence. But the food addiction, as my last holdout, took a bit more work to heal. I realize it may be a very unorthodox view to allow relapses, and for someone in a relationship with an addict, his or her using may be very black and white. "If you use at all, I can no longer remain in this relationship," is an acceptable boundary to require of an addict. In this way, any relapse at all is intolerable. In fact, I am currently facing precisely this dilemma with someone in my own life. If this person uses again, is it acceptable if they are truly trying to stop? I think the answer lies in their intentions. If they truly are on a healing path, and are trying their best to come to grips with their addiction, relapses may occur. However, relapses become unacceptable to me personally when they repeatedly occur with little or no regard by the addict to the consequences of the behavior. However, each person can draw their own boundaries and if relapses are part of an addict's recovery but are not acceptable to you personally, then you have to say so and be willing to take the steps to follow through if your boundaries are violated. Patience and love can be crucial to an addict's recovery if he is truly trying to help himself, but he must be willing to go it alone if necessary. Our responsibility, as an addict, lies in accepting the consequences of our behavior. To accept responsibility and try to do everything one can to overcome an addiction is a very different approach than to simply vow to never use again and then take no proactive steps to see that this is the case. You have to determine which camp your addict is in and decide what is acceptable to you. My heart goes out to every person who is in a relationship with an addict who is actively using. The answers are not always clear.

There are other cases in which cravings stem from simply being caught in the vicious cycle of active addiction. This form of craving is different from cravings we have in sobriety. Cravings that you experience when you are caught in the cycle of addiction are much more difficult to resist. When the spiral of active addiction has you in its grip, you are very unlikely to truly break free until it becomes extremely important to do so. Until that time, relief will be fleeting. Threats from your family or an employer may not shake you, continued humiliations are meaningless, losing a job may not even matter when active addiction has you in its viselike grip. Getting a handle on cravings when in active addiction is a tough road to follow but it can be done when you finally decide that you are really ready.

There are many complex components to active addiction. One is the body's nutritional imbalance and possible malnourishment. It is estimated that 80 percent of alcoholics are malnourished. Alcoholism tends to cause excessive highs and lows in blood sugar, which can create and maintain cravings. Without alcohol, addicts often become addicted to sugar and caffeine, which maintain the sugar imbalance and prolong cravings. A wonderful book by Dr. Joseph D. Beasley, *Food for Recovery*, outlines a program of holistic and nutritional approaches to use when recovering from different addictions.

The cycle of active addiction is vicious in that it seems to hold you prisoner. You seem to be blind, deaf, and dumb to any healthy alternatives when the urge to use strikes. The urge to use is likely to strike you at any time and any place and your capacity to resist is likely to be very low. Giving in to the craving means guilt and remorse, which precipitates a future addictive encounter. When you are in this phase of active addiction, it is not so important to try to go within and listen to your inner self. It is important, however, to try and do things that make you feel good about yourself. The low self-esteem that is the inevitable result of active addiction will only serve to tighten the vise of the addiction. Starting a project you have been putting off for a long time, setting some new goals, ending a painful relationship, healing an abusive pattern, discovering and uncovering your childhood wounds and healing them, all these things may boost your self-esteem. The important thing to focus on is what it is about your life that is making you feel so unworthy, depressed, angry, etc. that makes you unable to let go of the unhealthy lifestyle of addiction.

Again, only when it becomes of paramount importance to quit using are you likely to find any long-term success with abstinence. Many times, addicts say they really do want to quit using more than anything but they still subconsciously or consciously want to reserve the right to flee back into their addiction at the first sign of discomfort. One of the reasons A.A. works so well in helping many people achieve short-term sobriety is that people become so desperate for a solution that they will try anything. The dependence and conformity expected by authoritative twelve-step programs is a perfect answer for many. By giving themselves completely to the program for the solution, however, they are giving away the power for their lives. This method does work; however, true healing cannot occur without eventually finding and listening to your own inner guide. Many use A.A. as their guide, and finding that it works in the short run, they never turn within and connect with their own wisdom. The parent-child relationship inherent in the twelve-step model, where A.A. is the parent and they are the children needing guidance, remains the one they use for the remainder of their lives. It is not necessary to be dependent upon this model forever. True healing can occur by moving past the A.A. model and forging your own path. By doing this it is quite possible to recover completely from the disease of addiction and to no longer need to label yourself as "in recovery" for life.

For many addicts fearful of being unable to stop on their own, the dependent model seems to be the perfect answer. While A.A. and other twelve-step groups will help you achieve short-term sobriety or abstinence, continued reliance upon a fear-based dependency model will hamper long-term personal growth. To achieve long-term personal growth requires moving beyond the twelve-step group to become responsible for all levels of your life. This means deciding upon your own guidelines for living your life and no longer looking toward an external system to tell you what's right for you. Just as the young adult must leave home to continue his growth, we must stop asking for a parent-child model to fix us.

8

On Responsibility

ALL THE "EXPERTS" on addiction, it seemed, wanted to let me off the hook. The disease model of addiction told me I had a progressive disease over which I was powerless. Psychology experts told me I had a wounded inner child within and that my behavior was the result of a dysfunctional family. I even had an expert tell me, after only several minutes of interviewing me, that because of my eating disorder, I had obviously been sexually abused by my father, an absurd charge. I had other experts confirm that my addiction was a perfectly reasonable response to a patriarchal, male-dominated society. Everyone wanted to let me off the hook and I was actually being given great encouragement to look outside myself for someone or something to cast blame upon.

But if I was really going to get well again, I learned that I was going to have to ignore all the expert, well-intentioned advice. That meant taking full responsibility for my "disease," full responsibility for my childhood, and full responsibility for any and all responses to living in a patriarchal, male-dominated society. As long as I continued to blame anyone for *my* addictive behavior, complete healing eluded me. While I may actually have a disease, or a wounded inner child, or anything else, I am not powerless over how I respond to these things.

In order to truly heal, we need to start viewing our life's circumstances in a different light. We can no longer get away with thinking we are all simply pawns in some great divine play with no control over what life hands us from day to day and year to year. The truth, and every sage worth his weight realizes it, is that we are each and every one responsible for *all* that shows up in our lives. We are not tossed about in life like a ship in a storm. *Our thoughts, beliefs, expectations, and assumptions create everything we experience.*

One of the very hardest concepts to grasp is how we can be responsible for everything that shows up in our life. We can all single out specific circumstances, instances, or situations that we are certain we had nothing to do with. We developed a serious disease in our life, were laid off at work, we were in a hit-and-run accident or experienced any kind of accident, the bus was late, the check bounced, a stranger picked your pocket or stole your purse, your boss continually overlooked your work and belittled you, etc., etc. The list can go on forever with all the situations and experiences we hitherto have seen as outside ourselves and subsequently outside of our control. But the truth is that we are not the victims of the random circumstances that occur in our lives.

"We create, promote, or allow everything in our life," author Peter McWilliams writes in his best-seller *Life 101*. An example from his book is useful here.

> When looking for areas of accountability (areas where you created, promoted, or allowed it) please don't start with the biggest disaster of your life. Start with the daily slings and arrows that flesh is heir to. Pick a simple "it happened to me" event—misplacing your keys, the plumber not showing up, running out of gas—and see how you might have had something to do with creating, promoting, or allowing it to happen. Helpful hints:
>
> 1. Go back in time. (If you can be honest with yourself) you see that you promised yourself to always put your keys in the same place but didn't, the plumber was not known for his reliability, and the low-gas indicator light on your car had been on for so long you thought your car was solar powered.

2. What was I pretending not to know? What intuitive flashes did I ignore? "I'd better get some spare keys made," as you passed the hardware store a month ago? "This guy's not going to show," when you first spoke to the plumber? "I'd better get some gas," as you passed the thirty-fifth station since the gas-indicator light came on? We all *pretend* to know less than we really know.

I would add a third point that pertains to being in abusive relationships. If we are getting treated abusively in a situation, what messages did we send to teach the other person that we were able to be bullied by them? As hard as it may be, we must be honest with ourselves in all instances.

Even if we are not ready to accept full responsibility for all that shows up in our life, we can begin by realizing that we are responsible for how we *react* to all the circumstances in our life, especially the circumstances that we don't like. While I may not like the fact that my husband often doesn't get home until after our son is asleep, I can react either negatively or positively. Reacting positively means that I try to see what role I played in his behavior. Perhaps I didn't stress to him how important I think it is that he get home in time to play with his son before his bedtime. Or maybe my *expectation* that he would disappoint me and always be late helped cocreate the circumstance. At the very least, I can respond instead of react and recognize that nagging and blaming him will not solve anything. It will only serve to make him defensive and argumentative. Responding means being responsible. I don't assume responsibility for his behavior, but I do assume responsibility for *my* reactions and *my* response.

It is helpful to recognize that every circumstance in our lives can teach us. Suppose the bus was late. Here is a chance to recognize where our impatience and our rigidity about time may have led us to experience a lack of control about arriving somewhere on time. Intolerance of any condition will tend to manifest that condition in your life. However, I believe it is only there in order to help you seek your healing. If we have a lot of negative people around us, it is because we have disowned negativity within ourselves. If we are put down by people, it indicates that we don't value ourselves.

I think Dr. Deepak Chopra said it best in *Unconditional Life* when he wrote of an ancient sage's wisdom concerning the conception of external and internal.

> As is the macrocosm, so is the microcosm,
> As is the atom, so is the universe,
> As is the human mind, so is the cosmic mind.

In other words, everything that exists outside us exists somewhere inside us. That which we tend to view as external to us, and situations we interpret as randomly happening to us, are simply external manifestations of internal conditions. However, we have trouble believing that because we have experienced enormous societal conditioning to the contrary. Unfortunately, we seem to live in a world of victims and blamers.

"Reality is everyone's personal creation," Dr. Chopra further states, meaning that what we experience as reality in our life is the result of our own thoughts, beliefs, and conditioning. We are not, I repeat not, a ship on the sea being tossed about by the random currents of life. We are indeed cocreators with the Universe. We are actually much more powerful than we ever dreamed. But we can never expect to tap into that power until we accept full responsibility for EVERYTHING that shows up in our lives.

The conditions outside us reflect the conditions inside us. This doesn't mean we are to blame ourselves for attracting less than desirable conditions into our lives. However, we'll never get anywhere with our inner healing until we firmly grasp the concept of responsibility. Teacher and author Parker J. Palmer writes, in *The Institute of Noetic Science Journal*, on responsibility:

> The great insight of our spiritual traditions is that we co-create the world, that we live in and through a complex interaction of spirit and matter, a complex interaction of what is inside of us and what

is "out there." The insight of our spiritual traditions is not to deny the reality of the outer world, but to help us understand that we create that world, in part, by projecting our spirit on it—for better or worse. We share responsibility for creating the external world by projecting either a spirit of light or a spirit of shadow on that which is "other" than us. Either a spirit of hope or a spirit of despair. Either an inner confidence in wholeness and integration or an inner terror about life being diseased and ultimately terminal. We have a choice about what we are going to project, and in that choice we help create the world that is.

As long as we view life (or God) as handing us one challenging situation after another with no responsibility on our part for its arrival, we will miss out on one of the greatest opportunities that life gives us to truly learn to create miracles and empowerment in our lives. We will never heal as long as we need to cling to the illusion that we are victims. Gerald Jampolsky writes in *Love Is the Answer*, "When we choose the illusory world, we believe that what is outside us is the cause. When we choose the world of love, we believe that our own thoughts are the cause of what we see and experience."

The twelve-step model wants us to abdicate our power, admit powerlessness and defeat, and surrender. In reality, the only thing we really need to surrender is blame. When we let go of seeing ourselves as unfortunate victims of disease and can recognize that addiction is merely our soul seeking wholeness and healing, we can move toward true power instead of powerlessness. Remember that we create, promote, or allow everything in our life. But how do you create, promote, or allow the disease of addiction? Perhaps because your soul's desire for healing wanted to get a message to you to awaken to love, and only by putting a God-sized hole in your heart could it get your attention. If we can begin to see things through the eyes of love instead of fear, we can slowly start to see how every situation can be used for good.

One definition of responsibility is "the ability to respond." Learning to respond to every situation in our lives with love is the quickest and surest way to heal. A good way is to watch in amazement as all of your relationships become easier, less stressful, and more harmonious as you simply let go of all your fearful, defensive, attacking thoughts toward another and send them thoughts only of love. Regardless of their behavior, surround them in your mind with love. Do whatever you need to do to respond appropriately to their behavior but at the same time look past the behavior itself and picture the other person as actually crying out for love. Sending this mental love can actually change the composition of the relationship. As you let go of your need to be heard, your need for validation or acknowledgement from them, and your need to be right, and send only love, you alter the very outcome of the situation. Be careful, though, that it is not your *goal* to alter the eventual outcome. This indicates that you're still operating from a fear of not getting your way.

Responding to life with love instead of fear opens the way for abundance to flow into our lives. Responding with fear constricts and blocks the flow of the Universe and brings us only life's crumbs.

With that said, if we are to accept responsibility for all the things in our lives, where does that leave A.A. and other institutions such as churches and government bodies that want to tell us how to live our lives? Are we somehow responsible for their presence in our lives? I believe that, yes, we are. We are responsible for cocreating institutions with rigid, dogmatic expectations and requirements, our "collusion in the system" as Charlotte Kasl writes in her book *Many Roads, One Journey*. In the fear and helplessness of our addictive natures, we created these authoritative, rigid systems such as A.A. and religions in order to be absolved of the responsibility for our own lives. We helped create the system precisely so that it could tell us how to live and we therefore wouldn't have to take the responsibility for finding our own inner voices. We wouldn't have to connect with our internal Higher Selves and be the authority for our own lives and our own experiences. We could look to the system to tell us how to live and then blame it when it let us down. However, the silver lining is that we also helped to create it in order to learn what we needed to learn about the futility of fear and the reality of love.

Again, everything can teach us love and lead us to healing if we allow it. Learning to accept responsibility for everything in our lives gives us the opportunity to improve each and every part of ourselves that we dislike. If we dislike our personal habits, we can change them. If we dislike the way we are treated in relationships, we will never change the situation until we recognize and accept our role in creating how we are treated by others. Being responsible is the first step toward healing and gives us the autonomy to be self-governing in all areas of our life. I like Vincent Fox's words on the subject in his book *Addiction, Change & Choice*. "Personal autonomy is the hallmark of a person who has learned to treat reality as an ally rather than an adversary, a person who as M. Scott Peck advises, welcomes the natural flow of problems because in solving them further growth is achieved."

9

Moving Forward

IF FEAR-BASED LIVING is the way of addiction, and love-based living is the road to healing, what is the difference between them? What would a day lived in fear look like compared with a day lived from the standpoint of love? How does a person's life who lives fearfully differ from the life of one who lives lovingly?

First, I must define "living lovingly." This does not mean a Pollyannaish, overly optimistic approach to life that denies the severity of life's normal stresses and strains. Nor does it mean giving unconditional love to everyone regardless of how they treat you. It does mean accepting responsibility for our lives, our emotions, and our reactions. It means trying to see the good in all things and knowing that every problem has the seed of its own solution hidden within it. It means embracing life, in all its complexity and variety, and accepting that paradox, ambiguity, and contradiction are part of it.

When I lived my life in fear:

- I lived for others instead of myself. I lived in guilt and indecision. I experienced financial insecurity at every turn and I lived for the sake of the ego self.
- I ran away from problems that overwhelmed me and I set myself up for addictive episodes by categorizing everything in extremes and thus ensuring dissatisfaction with my life.

- New situations scared me. Life scared me. I believed myself to be a nothing, a failure, and was a disappointment to myself and others.
- I had never examined the beliefs that ran my daily life to see whether they truly served me or not.
- I thought others knew better than I did about what was right for my life and what wasn't.
- I judged myself positively or negatively according to how willing I was to do what others expected me to do, whether it was the voices of A.A., my father, or any significant others, and regardless of whether it felt right to me or not.
- I had no personalized definition of God and simply adopted the view handed to me.
- I believed myself to be diseased with alcoholism and powerless to control my life.
- I forced myself to perform empty rituals that held no meaning for me, like attending nightly twelve-step meetings and doing moral inventories, simply because I thought "they" knew better than I did.
- I believed in limitation.
- I thought success and sobriety would make me a worthwhile person. I believed that external trappings would overcome my negative inner beliefs.

Today, as I try to live in a love-based manner, my whole approach to life is different. I now live confidently. I see that no matter what the circumstances in my life, I can choose to react with love. I can choose peace instead of fear.

When I live my life in love:

- I live abundantly and energetically. I desire things that are healthy for me.
- Having given to myself and found healing, I am able to give joyously to others. I now know that it's futile to give away what we don't have. I don't give out of a sense of guilt or because

someone said I should give to others to help myself. I give because I am filled with abundance and giving is a natural, joyous act borne of love.

- I try to take responsibility for all the circumstances of my life, and when I experience anger, or pain, toward another I fearlessly turn inward and seek to find out how I participated in the situation.

- I know it does no good to blame others for the circumstances in my life. I don't condone anyone harming another and I remove myself from unhealthy situations. However, I try as much as possible to do so with love instead of judgment and blame.

- I trust the Universe to support me in all I do, and understand that living in fear is no longer necessary.

- I have questioned all the beliefs handed down to me by parents, churches, therapists, friends, teachers, and twelve-step programs and have accepted what worked for me, modified what could work for me, and tossed out what didn't work for me.

- I do not believe myself to be powerless and I have learned how to be powerful.

- On most days I no longer see life as a constant struggle. I see life as abundantly alive with creative possibilities and lovingly embrace them all.

- I have developed a personal relationship with the God who dwells within me and I have connected with my inner wisdom.

- I see myself as being infinitely guided and know that resources are always available to me from spirit and from love.

- I have healed my negative beliefs about myself and now believe in my divinity and wholeness instead of my guilt and insecurity.

- My life is filled with meaningful work and I truly enjoy my purpose in life.

So how do we move to this place of love? How do we start operating from a place of love instead of fear?

First, by understanding the nature of fear and understanding the nature of love. We must do away with all the "shoulds" in our life, such as "We should go to a meeting," "We should do a fourth step," "We should call our sponsor," etc. We need to examine all the shoulds in our life. Where do they come from? Who put them there (teachers, clergy, parents, society)? Are they serving our needs or only perpetuating fear, indecision, and dependence?

We need to determine our own internal set of beliefs, with complete understanding that what our Higher Self guides us to do will always be for the benefit of all and would never harm another.

We understand that there is no *one* right way, except to find the way that's right for us.

We recognize the many avenues of expression that are available to all and we honor diversity. One person may need a support group, regular exercise, meditation, good nutrition, a lot of social interaction, self-help books, and alternative forms of healing. Another may need meditation, no exercise, an occasional angry outburst, and little social interaction. The important thing is to find what is right for you and honor it.

Part Two

THE NATURE
OF FEAR

*At the root of addiction is fear
And at the heart of healing is love.*

10

The Nature of Addiction

I RECENTLY CAME across one of my original fourth steps, the searching and fearless moral inventory. I was surprised to have found one, having dutifully burned most of them after I did the fifth step, reading it to another person. It amazed me at first to see how unflinchingly brutal my analysis of myself had been. I recalled how at the time, not knowing the appropriate way to do the fourth step, I had consulted the Big Book of Alcoholics Anonymous. There I found an example that even gave me a few sample moral wrongs to get the ball rolling. At the time, it seemed perfectly normal, but looking back on it now, it seems so utterly unnecessary for an alcoholic who has finally been beaten down to his very lowest point and then summoned up the courage to start attending A.A. meetings to be given a sample of moral wrongs and told to searchingly and fearlessly inventory his own. Is this not kicking someone when he's down?

My own inventory started with selfishness. How had I been selfish? I drank and used alcohol and drugs although I knew it would hurt my loved ones. I lied to obtain alcohol and drugs, thinking only of myself. This wasn't news to me. I was well aware of the selfish, deviant behavior that went with my addictions. It was part of the reason I continually felt so guilty. Was it a moral wrong? Probably. Was I a bad person because I had been selfish? No, I was truly trying to get better. I knew that my true nature was one of kindness and compassion, not selfishness. I didn't need to be told I had hurt people. I needed to know how to gain access to my positive traits, not focus on negative traits that were simply born out of addiction.

I knew deep down that part of the reason my addictions were so hard to overcome and so ingrained in me was my continual focus on these negatives. The second "moral wrong" I got from the sample in the Big Book. Resentment. I resented what others had, I wrote. I resented those who had good things in their life where I had none. I wanted sobriety and the ability to hold down normal, everyday responsibilities like everybody else around me. Were resentments why I drank? No. They were a *result* of my drinking, not a cause. The alcoholism kept me resentful because it kept me from obtaining what I wanted from life. But I was resentful more toward myself than others. Nonetheless, I was told I needed to come up with resentments toward others as part of my recovery.

I went back to the Big Book. The resentment list they gave as an example was filled with resentments toward others for specific acts, such as "I'm resentful at Mr. Brown because he gave attention to my wife. Told my wife of my mistress. Brown may get my job at the office." (This is an actual example from the Big Book.) So maybe I had missed the point by being too general. I tried again. I'm resentful at my mother for confronting me with my behavior. I'm resentful at my father for threatening to take my car away. I really wasn't, though. I knew that they were *very* concerned about me, saw how erratic my behavior was (an example being my not coming home until ten in the morning), and were trying to help me. I wished they'd lay off, but I didn't resent them. I truly saw that they cared. Also, whenever I was really trying to help myself, they always stood strong and supportive beside me. When I told all of this to the person helping me with my fourth step, he said I was just in denial about my resentments and that any normal person in my situation would feel resentments. He essentially ignored what I said, told me to get with the program, and implied that if I didn't really feel resentment toward others I was just kidding myself. I encountered this attitude a lot in doing my fourth step, the notion that any deviation from the exact way given by the Big Book was wrong. If we didn't have a lot of specific resentments, we were told to come up with them. My problem was my negative feelings toward myself, not others. But that didn't seem to matter.

Until I got to the next section in the Big Book: "Referring to our list again. Putting out of our minds the wrongs others had done, we resolutely looked for our own mistakes. Where had we been selfish, dishonest, self-seeking, and frightened?" Much of my addictive behavior had been exactly that. Selfish, dishonest, self-seeking, and frightened. But, again, it was *because* of my addiction, not a cause of it. All of the destructive behavior that surrounded my addiction was selfish, dishonest, self-seeking, and frightened. It went with the territory. But, take away my addictive behavior and that behavior would vanish. We still weren't getting at any root causes. We were still floating up on top, examining all the external behaviors surrounding my addiction. None of these things were *reasons* for my abusing drugs, alcohol, and food.

I read some more of the Big Book: "Notice that the word 'fear' is bracketed . . . This short word somehow touches about every aspect of our lives. It was an evil and corroding thread; the fabric of our existence was shot through with it." Yes, exactly! Now we were getting somewhere.

But, looking further along, what did the Big Book tell me to do with my fears? Set them all down on paper. Tell another. Pray to have them removed. That's it?, I wondered. Then everything will be fine? Oh, yeah. Practice humility and ask for God's will in my life. No more? No examining the causes of fear, taking action to correct those causes, and transforming our fear to love? Nope. Just pray to have these "defects" removed. And continue to take personal inventory and promptly admit when we were wrong. (Who do I tell when I find some "rights" in my inventory?)

A.A. had finally hit upon a very significant aspect of addiction—fear—only to give it cursory attention and a superficial, pat solution. I give up, I thought. Still I laid down all my "mistakes" on paper, read these to another, humbly prayed to have all these defects removed, and waited. Just as I thought. I felt no better, I actually felt worse because I had somehow been given the message in all of this that my alcoholic, selfish, dishonest behavior was somehow to blame when I really felt it went deeper than that. I was frustrated but knew no other way to sobriety aside from the A.A. way. So I simply stuck it out but continued to look for answers.

I then referred to the book *Twelve Steps and Twelve Traditions*, another indispensable guide to "how it works." I went to the chapter on step four. I had begun to think that the moral wrongs were eerily similar to the seven deadly sins, another parallel between A.A. and religion. I got to page forty-eight and I suddenly knew why I had felt there was a parallel: "To avoid falling into confusion over the names these defects should be called, let's take a universally recognized list of major human failings—the Seven Deadly Sins of pride, greed, lust, anger, gluttony, envy, and sloth." The text then goes on about how to inventory each "sin" and its appearance in our alcoholic lives.

Twelve Steps and Twelve Traditions does a great job of detailing the ways in which these defects, sins, or whatever one calls them, are ever-present in our lives. It gives us specific questions for specific areas, such as sex, money, worry, pride, "When, and how, and in just what instances did my selfish pursuit of the sex relation damage other people and me? . . . Did I recklessly borrow money, caring little whether it was repaid or not? . . . Looking at both past and present, what sex situations have caused me anxiety, bitterness, frustration, or depression? . . . can I see where I have been at fault?"

But here is the problem I had. The program spends all of its time having me focus on *the behavior itself*. Where have we been prideful? Selfish? Lustful? Envious? How and in what specific ways did we hurt others, thinking only of ourselves? How and in what ways did we live for the ego? Etc., etc., etc.

But they never asked WHY. Why were we prideful? Selfish? What about us caused us to be fearful, jealous, envious, lustful? This was the burning question for me. Why? Why? Why?

A.A. just scratches the surface. It is right on track when it says that "by discovering what our emotional deformities are, we can move toward their correction." But they stop short of getting to the heart of the matter. By simply focusing on the behavior, telling us that these "character defects represent instincts gone astray," they never ask the question, "Why did our instincts go astray?" The program implies, especially with the seven deadly sins analogy, that we simply went astray because we were sinful, because "our natural desires have warped us."

The program goes on to say that if we humbly turn our will and our lives over to the care of God, confess our defects, and pray to have them removed, we will be relieved of our disease. By the way, author and founder of Rational Recovery Systems Jack Trimpey writes in *The Small Book* (his response to the Big Book) that "A.A. is in denial about its not being a religion." Given all the religious over-tones I noticed, I happen to agree with him.

A.A.'s fourth step comes so close to the solution. All of these "emotional deformities" *did* relate to my addiction. I experienced feelings of guilt, worthlessness, and shame, which drove my addiction. But by merely focusing on the external behavior these negative beliefs caused, I never got to find out what my real problem was, what these emotional deformities really were. A.A. kept me on the surface, when I needed to go deeper, down to the root, the messages and negative beliefs, not the resulting behavior.

My pride stemmed from *low self-esteem*. My envy stemmed from *worthlessness*, my selfishness from *fear*, my anger and resentment, toward myself or others, from *guilt*. But A.A. didn't go deep enough to show me that. Instead, all my focus on the behavior itself only made me feel worse and showed me what a real jerk I was.

Part of the nature of addiction is its ability to keep us from seeing the truth about ourselves. And A.A., with its pat "turn-it-all-over-to-God-pray-to-have-it-removed" solution, kept me from seeing the truth about myself as well. I was selfish for a reason, I was prideful for a reason, I kept thinking. What were those reasons? I wanted to know so badly; I felt it to be at the heart of my healing. And I didn't believe it was simply because I was a sinner, or because I had a disease I was powerless to control. Nor did I believe that this behavior (pride, selfishness, etc.) defined me in any significant way.

The other problem I had with the twelve-step program related to the disease theory and all the negative messages it sent me.

11

The Disease Theory
and Powerlessness

AT THE CORE of the fear-based belief system of A.A.
is the disease theory of alcoholism. The disease theory, of course,
supposes that we are the recipients of a cunning, baffling, and powerful disease that we are powerless over; it is, therefore, futile to attempt to control it with willpower alone. The disease theory further
proposes that the disease is progressive, that even in remission it will
progress steadily, and that we will have this disease forever. The only
solution, according to the disease theory, is complete abstinence from
alcohol for life.

On the healing path that I was on for complete recovery from
addiction, I found that the disease theory was fraught with danger.
My fully adopting the disease theory without question hindered me
for years without my even having been aware that it did so.

I would like to very briefly outline the ways in which it did so, but
before I do so I want to give due credit to Dr. Stanton Peele for his un-
believably accurate and insightful book *The Truth About Addiction & Re-*
covery. I stumbled across his book just recently and it clarified so many of
the things I had been suspecting about the disease theory for years. My
own experiences are a testament to the accuracy of his insights.

The dangers I found with the disease theory are:

It disregards how your personal problems play into addiction. From the
age of eighteen, I believed that I had a disease I was powerless over.

99

I never once thought to examine my own beliefs about myself, my inner pain, and my sense of inadequacy, the very things that kept me turning to addictive substances in order to numb these feelings. If alcoholism is simply a disease that has nothing to do with personal problems, then why do we crave addictive substances more when we are having problems than when our life is running smoothly?

A variation on this theme is the premise held by some that it is the alcoholism (or other addiction) that *causes* the personal problems. If this is the case, then why in this country are there so many A.A. meeting rooms filled every night with the tales of woe of recovering drinkers? Wouldn't their problems have gone away in sobriety if they were related only to the alcoholic behavior? After sitting through hundreds of meetings myself, and listening to people struggle with their ongoing issues and personal problems, I am well aware that personal problems do not go away simply because one halts the addiction. And personal problems definitely played a very big role in perpetuating my addiction. But the superficial focus on character defects and shortcomings kept me from recognizing and working on the personal problems I had that contributed to my addiction. In Peele's words, "If the labeling of alcoholism as a disease provides welcome relief from the shame of over-drinking, it also prevents people from confronting the emotional tasks they need to accomplish to attain personal wholeness."

The disease theory implies that you are at its mercy and will experience a total loss of control once you begin to use. This is simply not true. We still retain a great deal of control over our actions when using. After receiving a DUI (driving under the influence) citation in my early twenties and spending a weekend in jail, I was later very cautious about drinking and driving and would have others drive me when I had had too much to drink. I could also control where and around whom I binged on food. I could control when and with whom I snorted cocaine and drank alcohol. If alcoholics or any diseased addict experienced a *total* lack of control about their addiction, then addicts the world over would all be knocking over 7-Eleven stores in order to finance their expensive habits when they ran out of money. But they don't. Very few addicts resort to armed robbery to support a habit. But if I was totally out of control, wouldn't I resort to doing whatever I needed to do? This is where personal autonomy comes into play, and addicts have more control over their actions than we give them credit for. I would never knock over a 7-Eleven to support a habit, and I don't know anyone else who would. I could absolutely control the level to which I would sink in my behavior. Although I may sometimes have acted in very demeaning ways, it was still my choice to do so.

The disease theory says you will never be fully recovered. "Once an addict, always an addict." This is so defeatist. I believe that it is thinking like this that causes alcoholism and other addictions to be so hard to treat. We fully expect recovery to be next to impossible and never actually completed to the degree that we are completely recovered. I drank champagne on my wedding day, two little glasses, of which I didn't finish the second. About four months ago, I had a beer with my sushi lunch and a month before that at my uncle's eightieth birthday party I had wine with my dinner. I have no desire to drink today; during the course of a day the thought of a drink or a drug or a food binge does not cross my mind. Dr. Peele recounts story after story in his book of those who were self-cured and now drink rarely or moderately. The authors such as Charlotte Kasl and Jack Trimpey who write about alternatives to twelve-step programs know of the reality of being able to be fully recovered from addiction. There is even a support group call Moderation Management that was founded by a woman who discovered she could easily drink in moderation after healing herself from years of abusive drinking. It is not a fantasy and it is not a form of denial that people can fully recover from any addiction for the rest of their lives. Food addicts prove it every day each time they have a normal, moderate meal.

The disease is progressive. Where does this notion come from? The experiences of a small number of severe hard-core alcoholics in the 1930s? I heard this progressive disease stuff and when in treatment was shown the medical chart, but I believe it becomes a self-fulfilling prophecy for many. "Well, I slipped once. I might as well go whole hog." It sets people up to completely throw in the towel if they've made one small slip—one drink, one line of cocaine, one too many bites of food at a meal. It doesn't give us hope in the power to stop ourselves anywhere along the line. It doesn't even indicate that we have the ability to stop when we wish. There were two times when I have had much more alcohol than I intended to have in the time since I left A.A. Both times it was the *expectation* that I would be unable or unwilling to stop drinking at a moderate level that contributed to my drinking too much. I still believed that it wasn't possible to have only three glasses of wine at a celebratory occasion such as my best friend's wedding. I now know that contrary to what the disease theory tells you, the disease is not progressive for everyone.

It downplays the role of personal power. This touches on all the previous examples I gave and how my belief in my powerlessness actually made it a self-fulfilling prophecy. I wish, when I attended my first twelve-step group at age eighteen, that someone had told me that I had a power within myself that could assist me in my addiction. Too many times, when confronted with a craving, I felt, "Why even resist?" We should be teaching addicts ways in which to increase their sense of power, not take away what little they have by forcing them to believe in powerlessness.

It is a very dangerous belief to teach our young. Dr. Peele has the best words for this one:

> The disease theory forces teenagers to take on the identity of addicts or alcoholics or children of alcoholics. Young people are warned that their substance abuse is a permanent trait, even though we have seen that a large majority will outgrow substance-abuse problems as they mature. Presenting this message to the young can only *prolong* or exacerbate their substance abuse since it denies their own capacity for change and forces them to believe that *any substance use for the rest of their lives will lead them back to excess, addiction, and drunkenness.*

It sets people up for failure. A.A. tells you that you cannot succeed on your own and that if you leave the A.A. fold you will surely drink again and will probably die. The words "Rarely have we seen a person fail who has thoroughly followed our path" from the Big Book of Alcoholics Anonymous, which are read at the beginning or end of every meeting, seem ironic given the fact that 70 percent of those who attend A.A. meetings will not obtain long-term sobriety. Plus, this kind of wording makes it sound as if it is all your fault if the program fails to help you.

Overall, the disease theory perpetuates fearing alcohol or the drug of choice instead of viewing it as simply a symptom of deeper problems. Addiction is not about drugs or alcohol or food. The addictive substance isn't the real issue. It is our beliefs surrounding it, the power we give it, and our own internal dissatisfaction with life. If we resolve the underlying problems, we resolve the addiction.

Dr. Peele recounts an especially profound story in his book about an ex-narcotics addict who was given a four-week prescription for Percodan (a strong and addictive narcotic) following surgery. Although an ex-pill addict, the fellow had no desire to abuse the drug. As he told Dr. Peele, he had resolved his life's problems and drugs had no allure for him. He took his prescription as prescribed and went about his life.

Perhaps the most useful quote I found in Dr. Peele's book is the following:

> One of the beliefs that most contributes to the susceptibility to addiction is the *belief in the power of the addiction itself.* Believing that drugs are stronger than you are means you will become addicted more easily and stay addicted longer. But if you recognize that drugs and alcohol never take away your own responsibilities and capacity to control your destiny—even if you have alcoholic relatives or have had addictive problems in the past—you always stand a better chance of avoiding addiction or dealing with it successfully.

Dr. Peele doesn't seem to have personal experience with addiction himself, and in my opinion these words gloss over the truth a bit. As an addict who wanted desperately to quit, I know it takes more than simply changing our belief systems. But he's on the right track in that all of the rigid, limiting thinking surrounding addiction only hardens our belief system, making it *more* difficult, not easier, to quit long-term.

The tendency to cloak addiction in all this defeatist thinking is not only not necessary, but it increases the difficulty level of those trying to quit.

One of the truths about my own recovery was that once I focused on the seven components I outline in part four, I resolved all of my addictions completely, easily, and effortlessly. And because I was honoring myself in ways I never had previously, it was also a very joyous and fulfilling journey for me.

POWERLESSNESS

Living as an addict whose behavior was out of control for years, I didn't believe I really had what it took to know what was best for me. And in the beginning of my sobriety, I probably didn't. This was the time when A.A. really had a lot to offer me just as a parent may know in a child's youth what is best for the child. However, as children grow older and become more experienced, they will need to make their own decisions and their own mistakes. The twelve-step model did not encourage me to ever leave the fold. It wanted me to remain forever in the nest, dependent and fearful—fearful of drinking again lest I stop attending meetings, and dependent upon the model to tell me how to live; and although the intention was not to keep me dependent and fearful, that was the result.

Was I really powerless, I questioned, as I slowly let myself miss more and more of my regular twelve-step meetings? Am I really so disconnected from my own self that only by doing things that don't feel right for me will I heal? At every meeting I attended I had to rotely pledge my allegiance to the powerlessness concept, "We admitted we were powerless over alcohol." It was as if I needed to be reminded at every meeting of my powerlessness in case I had forgotten or in case I just didn't quite accept or believe it.

The truth about powerlessness is that we don't need to embrace it as a requirement for our sobriety. Although it works, and works well for many, it will not serve everyone. I achieved freedom and total release from four addictions (nicotine, alcohol, food, and cocaine) without giving up my personal power. In fact, it was only by *embracing* my power that I truly began to live free of all cravings. As long as I remained mired in the model of powerlessness, I was never certain when a craving would strike. I also always felt a little uncertain as to whether or not this Higher Power would see fit to relieve my cravings. There were so many times when He didn't relieve my cravings, leaving me stuck with weeklong stretches of cravings; the best solution I was given for this was to go to more meetings and call my sponsor.

So although I may have been sober, and although I may have been abstinent, I still felt no sense of empowerment. Instead, I felt as if all my sobriety hinged upon my willingness to attend meetings, my willingness to believe that I was powerless, my willingness to share in meetings, my willingness to lead meetings, call sponsors, continue to do personal inventories, admit wrongs, pray to have defects removed. None of it felt harmonious to me. It all felt like work. Work. Work. Work. Work.

However, the model of empowerment I discovered did harmonize with me. It blended my needs with the areas in which I needed to heal. It activated my inner resources and left me feeling more complete and whole than did the powerlessness model. It even made me a little grateful that I was an addict in the first place because it left me a much more powerful person.

The requirement for powerlessness also has an element of fear-based thinking to it. Fear is afraid of how powerful we really are. Fear is much more comfortable with the status quo arrangement of having someone else have all the power and decision-making capability for our lives. For those addicts who were continually given messages of unworthiness growing up, and who have never asserted themselves, a requirement of powerlessness may only serve to perpetuate a childhood wound. "See, you still don't know what is best for you. Let us and God decide for you" is the inherent message. These people will find the greatest healing in becoming empowered, by becoming powerful.

What does becoming powerful entail? Becoming powerful means accepting full responsibility for all of our life's problems. Many painful childhood wounds can be cleared away forever as soon as we accept full responsibility for *all* of our problems, whether they stem from our childhoods or not. We release all parties from blame, including ourselves. We are not to view accepting responsibility as finding fault with ourselves instead of others. By accepting full responsibility, we recognize that our soul was simply trying to get a message through to us that we needed healing in a certain area and was drawing attention to those issues in a way that was sure to get our attention.

Every circumstance in our lives has the ability to heal us and energize and empower us if we see it through the eyes of love rather than of fear. Addiction can be a very positive experience if we find true healing as a result of it. Becoming powerful means taking the reins of our lives instead of consecrating ourselves at the feet of an external authority. This doesn't necessarily mean stopping going to meetings, but it does mean stopping letting others run your life. You can clear everything with your own sense of inner wisdom, and when something resonates with you, you can follow it. Churches and twelve-step groups offer a great many positive opportunities for growth if, in the process, we do not allow ourselves to be overshadowed. By remaining aware of what does and doesn't work for us, or feel right for us, we can become the power center for our own lives. Our wings no longer have to remain clipped. We can learn to fly.

12

The Dangers of Slogans and Labels

IN FEAR'S DESIRE to keep me separate from myself and my feelings and other people, slogans and labels served a useful purpose. Slogans can cut people off from their feelings, invalidating and shaming them. Labels compartmentalize people, and reek of bigotry, superiority, and hierarchy.

I remember watching a telling scene one evening after an A.A. meeting. A particularly fragile young woman was sharing her feelings with her sponsor about her pain and anger at having been molested. The sponsor's answer was to tell her that she needed to let go of her resentments and let God. Overhearing the conversation, I winced at her sponsor's advice. With one fell swoop, the sponsor had unknowingly invalidated all of the girl's pain and anguish. By essentially telling her to get over it and leave it in God's hands, she wasn't giving her any positive reinforcement with which to embrace her anger and resentment. The young woman wanted someone to empathize with her pain, despair, frustration, and grief.

The best way to move through our emotions is simply to feel them. The A.A. slogans such as "Let go and let God," "Don't take their inventories," "Don't blame," however, have a way of trivializing emotions that we are struggling to bring to the surface after years of denying and repressing them. Making matters worse is the A.A. requirement to admit all of our wrongs, defects of character, and shortcomings. I was well-aware of all the harm and carnage that lay in the wake of my using. It was partly due to the enormous amount of guilt I felt over my behavior that I continued to be caught in the cycle of addiction. What I really needed was *not* a systematic deflation of my practically nonexistent self-esteem, backed up by A.A. party lines, slogans, and labels. I needed some positive reinforcement that I was a worthwhile person, whether I was drinking or not.

On the subject of slogans, Vincent Fox, in *Addiction, Change & Choice*, writes:

> Don't drink, go to meetings, and read the Big Book. Believe and don't ask questions that can't be answered by over 200 slogans such as "Utilize, don't analyze," "Take the cotton out of your ears and put it in your mouth," "Let go and let God." The A.A. program is one of indoctrination, not education. As they say in A.A., "K.I.S.S!," an acronym for "Keep It Simple, Stupid!" The statement is ill-advised, impolite at best, and offensive at worst. People seeking self-esteem don't need to be called stupid.

Another troubling aspect for me was when I was struggling, after a long period of abstinence, with cravings. Of course, the cravings were a signal that something was going on with me that I wasn't dealing with. My sponsor's advice was to go to a meeting and to do a fourth step, the "searching and fearless moral inventory," superficial answers for a very real problem.

Slogans seem to me like putting a very small Band-Aid over a very large wound. It gives only cursory attention to a problem that deserves real attention. Slogans ignore the individuality of the person. By giving me pat answers, I never felt as if I were really being heard or acknowledged. It became much easier for me when I began hearing and acknowledging my own problems and issues rather than continually turning to the superficial support of A.A. and its members. I needed to rebel.

I was told all my life how I needed to do this and needed to do that. That was part of my problem. And the A.A. slogans felt like more of the same. Someone felt as if they knew better than I did what I should do with my life. It was time for me to take responsibility for my having asked others to provide me with the answers, and time for me to start deciding for myself what was and was not best for me.

Tied in with the use of slogans is the tendency of A.A. members to quote passages from the Big Book when responding to specific issues or problems. However, much of the language used throughout the Big Book assumes that everyone feels the way the original writers felt. It negates those of us who had experiences very unlike those which the original Big Book authors write about. An example used by Charlotte Kasl in *Many Roads, One Journey* refers to the passage from the Big Book, "It was only through repeated humiliations that we were forced to learn something about humility. . . . A whole life-time geared to self-centeredness cannot be set in reverse all at once."

This passage assumes that we have been very self-centered and now need to be knocked down a few notches and learn the lesson of humility. Kasl writes, "I thought of all the women (or men) I have known (and not known) whose lives were crippled through being geared to other people's needs. These were the women (or men) for whom self-centeredness and rebellion were a first breath of their own lives." I agree with her words. If low self-esteem and unworthiness have plagued us all of our lives, or for those people wrestling with issues of co-dependency, we need to *build up* our self-esteem through positive, loving reinforcement, not continue to humble ourselves at the feet of other people, groups, or institutions. In fact, learning a bit of *healthy* self-centeredness, in the form of stopping doing for others what they need to do for themselves, may be our first step toward freedom.

Labels are another manifestation of fear. Labels separate and compartmentalize people instead of joining them. At first glance, the requirement to label yourself as an alcoholic in order to begin your process of recovery may give you a sense of bonding, a sense of belonging where before you felt none. However, the term "alcoholic" or "addict" has the connotation that you are diseased and somehow less of a person than the nonaddict. It is much the same as a church's requirement that you admit that you are a hopeless sinner in order to repent and gain salvation.

Labels smack of superiority. In A.A., sober people are seen as better than people who are actively addicted. This viewpoint is similar to the Christian one in which repentant souls are much more pleasing to God than unrepentant sinners. The truth is that we are all worthy. I was still as worthy of love and healing when I had my head down a toilet throwing up as I am today.

I also do not agree with the view of relapse as something awful to have happened and something to be avoided at all costs. I made myself very miserable by struggling with cravings day in and day out. They dogged me every day and were sometimes so overwhelming I seemed unable to accomplish anything. I do not recommend that you give in to your cravings and use recklessly; however, the times I did give in to my cravings at least afforded me a release from the pain. In a way, it was my way of nurturing myself. I would feel better for having experienced a respite from the cravings, but because of the overwhelming guilt messages I received from A.A. and society regarding relapse, I also felt extremely guilty.

At the time, I did not know the healthy, healing way to deal with cravings, which is to determine what is causing your desire to escape and what it is you are wanting to avoid. I simply knew I was in pain. As long as we continue to see relapse in a negative light, we will not give people the complete freedom to come around to love when they are ready. You cannot force the various stages of healing. They must come in their own time. My own awakening was very slow at times, and little "slips" and "relapses" at least eased the pain a bit. Being taught that they were bad merely reinforced the message that *I* was bad. I rebelled at this idea and needed to reaffirm for myself that just because I used again, I was *not* a bad person. As a matter of fact, every time I would slip or relapse and let it be okay, the need to do so again in the future would lessen and lessen, until it was no longer a temptation.

In the final days of my bulimia, as I had finally learned to let it be okay to relapse, to occasionally slip back into my old binge-purge behavior, I had unwittingly stumbled upon the solution to stopping for good. Every time I had "slipped" or "relapsed" in the past, I had beat myself up with guilt and remorse, not realizing that I was just setting the stage for another addictive episode, the future addictive episode being fueled by the guilty feelings I had suppressed because of slipping. My efforts to control my behavior had always failed but, ironically, when I let a binge be okay without judging it, and most important, without condemning myself, the desire to binge again lessened considerably. It was as if I just needed to *accept* my addiction, not try to control it and especially not beat myself up, to be released from the struggle.

13

Character Defects and Limiting Beliefs

I SAT IN an A.A. meeting one rainy night silently hoping for some new insight into myself. The speaker was talking about how he knew that if he ever stopped attending A.A., his only options would be jails, institutions, or death. How many times in the years of attending A.A. had I heard that phrase? "Our only options were jails, institutions, or death." Suddenly, it struck me that this was a very negative, fearful way to maintain sobriety. It further dawned on me that the speaker undoubtedly expected his own "true" nature to be that of a hopeless drunk who wouldn't know what was right for himself, and left to his own devices would surely wind up in a jail, an institution, or dead. How bleak! Was my true nature really so self-destructive? I wanted to believe that my *true* nature was a bit closer to the divine. I wanted to believe that my true nature was the one made in the image of God. But fear wanted me to be distrustful of my nature and so told me I was a "sinner" and an "addict" and that this was my true nature.

Dr. Chopra offers some very insightful words regarding our true nature:

> As he walks a tightrope between the evil strength of alcohol on one
> side and the saving grace of a higher spiritual power on the other,
> the addict's true inner nature remains unknown and perhaps even

irrelevant . . . We are not emotionally or spiritually neutral, nor are we equally inclined to do harm to ourselves as to do good. Our true, inborn orientation is toward what is good for us and away from what is harmful. There is no real need, therefore, for an attitude of constant vigilance against the dangers of alcohol, or anything else.

Fear didn't want me to see the truth about myself: that I am a powerful, creative, loving, and vital being, as we all are. Fear didn't like me rocking the boat by asking questions, wanting to know why I had to do this or that, and by standing up to its authority. Fear loves the status quo and wants things to stay exactly as they are. Fear wants to continually remind me of how limited I really am and fear also wants me to focus on my character defects. By keeping my attention diverted to working on overcoming my character defects (and A.A. is quite happy to provide us with examples lest we should be unable to come up with them on our own), I missed the boat of true living. I have sat through so many meetings in which people were just talking about their character defects and how they were trying to overcome blaming, judging, or resentments and be a better person. While this may be a good thing, the superficial level the discussion remains at will not serve in truly healing at the deepest levels.

The fourth and fifth steps of A.A. are: 4) "Made a searching and fearless moral inventory of ourselves," and 5) "Admitted to God, to ourselves, and to another human being the exact nature of our wrongs." What happens to many in working the fourth and fifth steps is a continuation of the guilt and shame that may be the core reasons for their drinking in the first place. If I drink because I have unresolved feelings of guilt and shame, it will not lift me out of my addiction to sit down and make a list of all the horrible things I have done and caused because of my drinking. In fact, it is my intense focus on how guilty I am that perpetuates my addictive cycles. Kasl writes,

On the other hand, it may be counterproductive for oppressed, depressed, or ordinary people to immediately look at their faults before they have affirmed their intrinsic goodness, strengths, and power.

Most people, particularly the oppressed, tend to blame themselves for their abuse—"How could I have let them do that to me!"—and this step (Fourth Step) often reinforces self-blame. *We are obsessed with guilt and shame in this culture*, and spend very little time affirming the magic, wonder, and beauty within us and around us. Thus this step is very unbalanced. [emphasis mine]

Step six of the program, which states that we "Were entirely ready to have God remove all these defects of character" uses the imagery of holding certain parts of ourselves as apart, separate and undesirable. It is only by embracing *all* of our qualities, good and bad, that we can be released from the more "negative" aspects of our self. In fact, it is our *nonacceptance* of negative traits that binds them to us like glue. Step six encourages us to label, to point out certain parts of us as not desirable.

Fear is certain that deep down we are unworthy and less than. Fear *wants* to find certain parts of us that can be labeled as bad and undesirable. That gives fear the chance to say, "See, I was right. Right here, you have judgment, resentments, blame, greed, insecurity—blah, blah, blah." It tends to reinforce fear's message that we are intrinsically at fault or faulty.

Love wants us to embrace all parts of ourselves as worthy. Love doesn't judge. While not condoning or justifying particular actions or behaviors, love nevertheless sees them merely as a cry for love. Where love is not, there is fear. Therefore, to love and accept all parts of ourselves frees us from the hold of the "negative" qualities.

My own experience is that I tend to be judgmental. Because of the inner work I have been doing, I can now recognize that what I am judging about another simply represents what I do not accept about myself. And on my better days I can even recognize where within me that trait is. However, the more I beat myself up for being judgmental, or do not do the inner work necessary to transcend my judgmental thoughts, the more entrenched they become. When I leave the power and responsibility for my judgmental behavior in the hands of an external, authoritative God, I notice that I tend to feel guilty when I feel a judgment welling up. A part of me tries to convince me that I didn't pray right, or pray enough (to have my character defects removed). Or perhaps God didn't find me submissive enough, or worthy enough, or simply not humble enough to remove my character defects. But when I simply accept that I am judgmental, and refrain from making it worse by judging myself for judging, then I move closer to wholeness. And I also notice that as I can embrace and accept my "negative" qualities, their presence in my life lessens.

It is my view that the sixth step parallels the "worthy in the eyes of God" message that I grew up with, that God likes us better without character defects and shortcomings. And I have had to struggle all my life to overcome the message that God likes us better when we are being good. Most of my years of rebellion were because of this very message. I wanted to believe more than anything that I was worthy with or without character defects, shortcomings, or even in the midst of addictive behavior that was wildly out of control. Love finally gave me the ability to be able to accept myself just as I am.

LIMITING BELIEFS

Why on earth would we want to argue for limitation? When a child has dreams of growing up and becoming this or that, a policeman or doctor or lawyer perhaps, do we sit the child down and explain to him how he certainly *cannot* become anything he wishes to be? But that's essentially what we do to ourselves with limiting beliefs. If we have a problem with alcohol or drugs or food, it's because we have temporarily accepted that role for ourselves. If I believe A.A. is the only way I can achieve sobriety, then that is probably what I will find to be true for myself. However, I no longer wanted to fit all my potential and ability into a box. I ached to stretch the boundaries of what I could be and could achieve.

I wanted to stare all the limiting beliefs in the face and say, "Who says so?" Because someone or some group has had these certain experiences does not make it carved in stone for everyone else. We need to "substantially update" our view of the world. We can now do all sorts of things we couldn't do just twenty years ago. I certainly couldn't have sent an E-mail message to a friend in Malaysia twenty years ago by the press of a button on a computer. Why do we expect the system of behavior and thought that worked fifty years ago to be so relevant in today's world? I would like to quote a passage from Charlotte Kasl's book that is particularly fitting.

> While the emergence of twelve-step programs and *Alcoholics Anonymous* were highly significant occasions that did at one time shed new light on alcoholism, without substantial updating this institution falls into the category of Vaclav Havel's words (the leader of Czechoslovakia): "It no longer provides new, spontaneous, and effective evidence of things hitherto only guessed at." The twelve-step approach purports to be for all people, but its literature lacks knowledge of most people. By continuing to define people who are alcoholic or partnered with an addicted person in a narrow, stereotypical way, omitting discussion of women, minorities, drug addiction, and cultural influences, it indeed "falsifies the real world."

However, to move beyond the limiting beliefs requires more than a desire simply to do so. We must work in conjunction with what feels right for us personally. While I encourage those who need and desire structure and guidance to seek help in A.A. or other twelve-step groups, those who have embraced the parent–child model and are ready to move beyond it can begin by examining all their limiting beliefs and deciding internally whether they really feel right for them any longer.

In many cases, we simply accepted a belief without questioning it and later found that it didn't really suit us. Or we may have been provided protection and relief by the use of certain limiting beliefs and we are now beginning to outgrow them. Don't feel compelled to stay loyal to the same beliefs just because they worked for you before. Fear, remember, in striving to keep us safe doesn't want us to change the status quo. Love, on the other hand, supports affirmative action. When we move forward in a state of love and trust that the Universe will support us and that we are doing what feels right to us personally, we can blast through our limitations in ways we never imagined. The only way to truly get at our inner truths is to let go of our tight hold on beliefs that want to limit us and keep us fearful.

14

The Role of Ritual

I ATTENDED A WORKSHOP on healing in which the speaker was questioning an audience member about his jogging habits, asking, "Do you jog every day? Is it a sort of ritual for you? How do you feel on those days when for some reason you can't jog?"

The audience member admitted that on the days he couldn't jog he was very irritable, would snap at his wife and kids, and would later regret his behavior. "You are locked into a powerful ritual that you need to be careful about. Is it serving you or are your rigid demands that you *must* jog every night making you serve it?" the speaker commented. The audience member chuckled as he admitted that there were many nights when he forced himself to jog even when his body was begging for a break, and he wound up feeling worse after the jog on those days. "I'm sort of a slave to it at this point, although it no longer relaxes and benefits me the way it once did."

Rituals have a way of providing safety, comfort, and security in a world seemingly filled with chaos and confusion. We may have a particular dinner ritual we perform every night with our family. We even look forward to it during the day. One spouse cooks, the kids join us, and we all discuss our day. Afterward, everyone returns to their various activities, one to watch TV, one to clean up, the kids to play. The ritual reenacts itself every evening, and although it is without fanfare or glory, it is comforting and predictable.

It is the nature of rituals to offer us comfort. They appeal to our need for predictability. However, rituals can become rigid systems of behavior that can be counterproductive to our continuing personal growth. One can become so dependent on the ritual that he or she is afraid of anything upsetting its occurrence.

The fear of going outside the bounds of the ritual can be paralyzing or, at the very least, unhealthy. When rituals become charged with a great deal of fear, they have become too rigid and dogmatic. Thus, instead of comforting us, we begin to be a bit obsessive about adhering to the ritual.

Rituals in this sense are not the big rituals such as marriage, funerals, bar mitzvahs. I am referring to the smaller, more mundane rituals we all have. In my experience, addicts are especially prone to being fearfully attached to rituals. The twelve-step meeting itself is a ritual. Go to a twelve-step meeting anywhere in the world and you'll see the exact same thing. Every meeting begins with the reading of the introduction, followed by the twelve steps, then the welcoming of newcomers. There may be a bit of variation, but very little. At one particular O.A. clubhouse I attended, it took at least fifteen minutes to get through just the preliminaries. All the members together read each twelve step and tradition out loud. I used to get so angry that it took so long. Why the twelve steps *and* traditions, and why out loud, and why *every* time when they've already asked if there are any newcomers and we can see that there aren't? But try to change this ritual and people would become very upset.

People cling to their rituals as desperately and fervently as they cling to their limiting beliefs. When I asked, in my O.A. group, "Why don't we change this? It seems a little foolish to go through the whole thing every time when we are staring around at the exact same faces from the meeting the day, or week, before." I got back only an illogical answer: "We have to read all the steps and traditions every time in case there is a newcomer," which was an illogical answer because we had already asked if there were any newcomers (there weren't), and the meetings were so small that a newcomer would be spotted right away anyway.

Don't get me wrong, rituals can be very healthy and can encourage healing. But rituals can also play another role, they can feed off people's fears. People want structure and order so badly that they will give away their power for the sake of the continuity of the ritual. You see this in the church, in twelve-step groups, and also in many of the New Age schools of thought. "Do a thing this way, every time, without deviation," a ritual demands. There is no room for flexibility or individuality, and there is no room for growth.

In the first scary and unpredictable days and weeks of achieving sobriety, A.A. rituals offer a safe haven for the addict. This safe haven can cause people to stagnate if they allow it to become too dogmatic and unchanging. You know a ritual has become dangerously close to this unhealthy stage when you feel you can't deviate from it at all.

I personally became very interested in examining many different New Age schools of thought, and I was surprised to discover essentially the same tendency. Many of the New Age books I read were adamant about meditation as a necessary, absolute, essential requirement to achieving higher states of awareness. Even Deepak Chopra, whom I greatly admire, proposes meditation for all those who wish to heal at deeper levels. I believed this for a while, and then discovered it simply wasn't true. Many times I prefer to find a higher awareness by the use of the mind/intellect instead of "letting go of all thoughts" as meditation stresses. I like using my imagination to create a higher awareness within myself. I find it to be a limiting statement to assume that one cannot find higher awareness without meditating.

Remember, there are no limitations other than those we place upon ourselves. If I can find healing and wholeness without the rigid use of rituals, I have done what feels right for me. And doing what feels right for you is the barometer. If using rituals works for you, by all means use them. However, if you find them too limiting and confining, then by all means honor that, too.

Be aware that rituals can be a receptacle for our fears of venturing into the unknown. Rituals can play on these fears very skillfully. Knowing we desire healing and wholeness, rituals beckon us with promises of relief and recovery. However, they can become like a Venus's flytrap. Once inside, the jaws close around us, and fear tells us to not go beyond the rituals. There comes a time, if we are to continue to try and find our own voice and chart our own path, that we must question whether our rituals are really working for us in a healthy way or whether they are holding us back. Many times, those who argue the most strongly for the perpetuation of the ritual are those who are comforted by remaining in the parent-child model. They become afraid when any aspect of the ritual is challenged. When rituals can be flexible, open, and yielding, they are more likely to feed our long-term growth.

The definition of whether a ritual is best for you or not lies in whether it's a fear-based ritual or a love-based ritual. A fear-based ritual tends to tell us what to do without asking for our input, much the same as a parent to a child. We are not asked what feels right for us, what clicks with us internally. Fear-based rituals simply say, "This way, every time. Don't question. I know best." Who is the "I" who knows best? A fear-based ritual doesn't really have our best interests at heart. A fear-based ritual has its own continuity at heart.

A love-based ritual, on the other hand, wants to lovingly give us comfort and security through predictability. I like knowing that every evening, after my children are asleep, I can curl up and read a few pages of my favorite book. It's part of my evening ritual. And I like looking forward to spending every Friday afternoon with my children and one of my close friends and her child. It's comforting to know that that will be there for me, every night, every week, for as long as I wish it to be.

Love-based rituals are open to change, to suit the changing needs and desires of the participants. A love-based ritual is not unyielding, rigid, or authoritative. It instead supports our highest growth by being exactly what we need, when we need it, for as long as we need it. We can take what we want and leave the rest.

Sometimes I notice that fear has taken meaningful aspects of my life and turned them into empty rituals that no longer have my pleasure or comfort in mind and instead simply demand adherence based on guilt. I don't know how many times I've attended a meeting based more on guilt (the "I *should* go") rather than a true desire on my part to attend. Somehow, pleasure gets mixed with guilt, with the result that I feel as if only the unenjoyable tasks of my life are the ones that benefit me, and as if pleasurable activities could never actually be good for me.

15

Pleasure and Guilt

OUR SOULS LONG for pleasure, we need joy and pleasure in our lives. However, many of us grew up in households either devoid of joy or fraught with guilt-ridden pleasure. We weren't taught how to experience meaningful pleasure. Instead we were taught, by example or directly, that pleasure is bad, somehow sinful. Many churches hold to this view, without really meaning to, and send the negative message to children of a vengeful, judgmental God who views pleasure as a sin. It is somehow grouped with lust and greed.

The teaching that pleasure is bad feeds into the fear-based message many of us carry around that says that *we* are bad. Therefore, in responding to our inner urge for pleasure, we must be bad. This results in our unconsciously seeking pleasure in ways that make us feel guilty. Deepak Chopra makes a very astute observation regarding guilt and pleasure. From his book *Unconditional Life*, he writes:

> Addiction "solves" this problem by permitting pleasure while at the same time insuring that the pleasure is furtive and guilt ridden. [Addicts] are hooked on the alluring combination of enjoyment and guilt. Often it is pleasure itself that they find shameful, therefore, they have no alternative but to seek pleasures that have built-in dissatisfaction . . . A guilty pang accompanies the jolt delivered by the

drug, and without the guilt, the jolt would lose its allure. . . . At the heart of addiction, I would propose, lies a deep nostalgia for pleasure that echoes a legitimate need. Despite what our conditioning might tell us, to seek pleasure is not bad. . . . Addiction is basically the result of a mistake. The addict is caught in a circular trap of his own devising; he cannot get enough pleasure to finally abolish his guilt; he cannot suffer enough guilt to keep him from the next fix. Rather, the two impulses circle each other in an endless dance.

One of the tendencies of fear is to keep our pleasure from us, or to at least accompany any pleasure we do experience with feelings of guilt and unworthiness. We have never been taught that life is meant to be savored and enjoyed, with us as fully alive and aware. Instead, many of us grew up with the view that life is to be endured and is full of suffering, so we might as well get used to it.

We need to examine our childhood for messages regarding pleasure: Did we see examples from one parent that pleasure was bad and sinful while we watched another parent seek pleasure addictively? Or have we internalized the message that pleasure is only achieved as a result of a great deal of work and stress? What message did our parents send us about pleasure?

Whatever message we did receive, in most cases we have now internalized it and unless we consciously work to change it, this internalized message will subconsciously color our ability to experience pleasure. I grew up with the dual message that pleasure is bad and a sin, and that life is suffering. The best you could hope for was to muddle through the best you could and hope to achieve salvation after death. What a bleak picture! However, I had a deep need for pleasure, and without consciously being aware of what I was doing, early on rebelled at the notion of pleasure I received growing up. I acted out the scenario described by Dr. Chopra. All of my pleasure was guilt-ridden and furtive. Seeking pleasure in this way validated the message that pleasure was bad and also meshed with my internal message that *I* was bad.

The innocent child part of us knows that life is not a chore to be endured and suffered through. The innocent child part of us has a very strong need to experience pleasure. As children, we are well-springs of joy and pleasure, but if we grow up with societal conditioning that tells us pleasure is bad, we will begin to seek out guilt-inducing ways to experience pleasure. If we were never taught anything about pleasure, we will most likely insist on taking pleasure wherever we can find it, whether it hurts another or not.

Many addicts discover early on that their addiction serves as the only pleasurable part of their lives. Having never been taught positive, healthy ways to experience pleasure, they are simply responding to their internal need for pleasure the best they know how. And the more society shuns or shames their addictive behavior, the more guilt-ridden the addict will become. This places them on the wheel of addiction: Addictive pleasure causes guilt, which then causes a desire for more addictive pleasure in order to escape the pain of guilt. On and on the cycle goes. Because of the trauma caused by this vicious cycle, many addicts are the spiritual equivalents of the walking wounded. However, their need for pleasure offers them very little hope for escape.

Love rescues us from this circular trap. Love offers us pleasure without guilt. Love teaches us healthy, positive ways to experience pleasure without guilt and without suffering. Love wants more than anything for us to be true to ourselves, therefore love understands that our guilt-inducing behavior was simply our way of responding to our inner cry for pleasure.

I believe that in many ways addicts are more in tune with the way things ought to be than are the nonaddicted. Our wild and erratic behavior is merely our way of trying to right things in a world full of societal pressure and strict moral codes of right and wrong that addicts refuse to be stifled by. That's simply my point of view, but perhaps others may agree with me. I try to shy away from all this need to focus on wrongs and negatives. Simply put, our society needs to learn positive ways to encourage children to have high self-esteem and healthy ways of feeling good.

Love says we have a right to experience pleasure, and love validates our need for pleasure. Think of the joy you experience when you are doing something to help another. Or the rush of excitement you feel when you are beginning a new project. Or the pleasure of exhilaration you feel when you cautiously step forward in faith to follow a gut instinct that proves to be right on track. The more you open yourself up to new, positive ways to experience pleasure, the more ways will present themselves to you.

Try to be aware when you are operating from rigid codes of conduct that dictate your behavior without regard to your personal desires or wishes. We can learn to fulfill our inner need for pleasure without it harming us or those around us. *Follow Your Bliss* is, in fact, the title of a best-selling book by Hal Bennett that describes how to create healthy, revitalizing pleasure in every day of your life by finding the work you are most suited for and thereby get paid for doing what you enjoy.

Once I saw how my need for guilt-inducing pleasure was a trap for me, I needed to discover these healthy, positive, pleasurable activities. At first, it was very hard for me to honor my need for pleasure without feeling guilty. My early religious upbringing would kick in and try to tell me that I was being selfish or sinful or irresponsible. It is probably very similar to the "Catholic guilt" I hear my friends talk about, that little voice that chirps in whenever something is really enjoyable and fun and tries to turn it into something negative. "All the good things in life are supposed to be hard and involve lots of self-sacrifice" was what my own particular little voice said to me.

But, knowing myself as I do, I knew that for any recovery to work for me, it would have to be pleasurable and involve pleasurable activities. I was determined to break the cycle of "life is suffering, pleasure is bad" that plagued my consciousness. One of the first ways in which I allowed myself to enjoy pleasure was in my long sojourns at a bookstore. Sitting in a cozy, overstuffed chair with books all around me, I often felt guilty for not "being productive" or for not being at my office working. But it was time to do something, anything, that I really, really wanted to do without continually giving in to those little voices of guilt and doubt.

I slowly learned to tune out those negative voices as my soul cried out in joy that I was finally doing something just for me. The nightly meditation group I attended at the time was also another way in which I experienced healthy pleasure. Immediately after I began with this group of people, I noticed I was much more relaxed and calm the day after a meditation. This feeling gave me the encouragement to seek out more pleasurable activities. I gave myself permission to break dates occasionally if I really didn't feel like going. I was so used to always thinking of the other person's feelings that I would never put my own needs first. Although breaking dates is not very respectful of other people, it was an important test of whether I could honor my own needs before the needs of others for a change.

Out of all these things, it was my solitude from which I probably got the most pleasure. I was spending time with myself, getting to know myself, discovering what I truly liked and didn't like, free from the expectations of others. I took long walks. Took myself to the movies. Spoke with friends on the phone, read. I was examining all the things and beliefs in my life that didn't serve me and slowly letting go of them. And I was trying to honor those things that did work for me and did feel good to me.

It is becoming an outdated concept that our work and our lives have to be filled with cheerless tasks and thankless drudgery. We can experience positive fulfillment on all levels: work, play, family, solitude. When we discover modes of positive pleasure, we are taking care of ourselves with love and not fear. And when we do that, we are lifted far above our addictive cravings. When we are meeting our need for pleasure, the addictive cravings have no reason to bother us with their demands. We have transcended our addiction.

16

Achievement Addiction

I AM AT my most vulnerable to falling into the trap of achievement addiction when my *self-destructive* addictions are under control. Being sober, having food abstinence, being free from any of these cravings leaves me full of energy and drive. Suddenly, my inner feelings of worthlessness are offered a solution: I *can be* worthy. In fact, I'll prove to others how worthy I am by achieving these goals right here. So I steer off on a course of goal-setting, work, and achievement, not knowing that what I'm really doing is still giving in to my feelings of worthlessness by trying to overcome them with the external trappings of success. When I am seeking approval, recognition, awe, envy, respect, or jealousy from other people, my achievement addiction is in control. The tricky part about achievement addiction is that it masks itself as a positive trait and can be the same thing as workaholism. Our culture is obsessed with the outward signs of success, and because hard work and perseverance are highly encouraged in our society, achievement addiction is not always recognized as such.

The family of an achievement addict may feel the loss in the number of missed family experiences that are explained away by the excuse of mommy or daddy having to work. An achievement addict can also get away with his behavior much longer than an alcoholic or drug addict because rarely does society put any pressure on us to work less.

In fact, cellular phones and computer commercials encourage us to work anywhere, everywhere, all the time, around the clock. An achievement addict may also be held less accountable for his actions.

While the pain and devastation caused by alcoholic and drug-addicted behavior is very obvious, the pain caused by the achievement addict may be much subtler and less obvious. This is partly due to the seemingly positive payoffs of an achievement addict—he or she may bring home a bigger paycheck. However, owning a larger house or having more discretionary income is hardly worth it when our children begin to emulate our behavior by detaching from their feelings, seeking to win at all costs, and believing bigger is better, money is power, etc.

Our society would be benefited much more by our raising children who are compassionate, wise, kind, and believe in everyone working together to achieve something instead of defeating weaker opponents in order to feel like a winner.

My achievement addiction, while quieting my feelings of worthlessness, also masks a fear of intimacy. It is much easier for me to chase outward success than it is to face my inner fears and demons. The driving force behind an achievement addiction is the message that we aren't enough and that if we are vice-president by age thirty-five, or are the highest producer, or whatever our measure of success is, we will be worthwhile and thereby lovable. Achievement addicts feel unworthy and unlovable, though they may be the last to recognize this as what drives them. They may be so obsessed with their quest for success that they never stop long enough to feel the pain they hold inside. The singular quest for achievement is their way to avoid the pain and emptiness within.

I was very moved by Dr. Wayne Dyer's personal description of his belief that if he had his Ph.D. degree, he would be somebody. That didn't do it. So then he thought his first book would do it. That was a hollow victory as well, so he told himself his first best-seller would make him feel worthwhile. After he had exhausted himself achieving greater and greater levels of outward success and still felt hollow inside, he was forced to admit that no amount of outside achievement could quell his inner dissatisfaction.

Some A.A. members, and members of other twelve-step programs, having achieved sobriety, become achievement addicts. Still unable to face their real issues and problems, they feel that alcohol or drugs was their main problem. After achieving sobriety they still feel a vague, or not so vague, sense of disquiet and dissatisfaction. Having sobered up, they are now ready to pursue their goals with renewed vigor. They are probably not even aware that this compelling drive to achieve is fueled by the same spiritual dilemma that caused them to use in the first place.

I felt as if I had to make up for lost time after I achieved sobriety. I felt that I had wasted too many years just bumbling about life with no direction. With my newfound sobriety, I had energy, I had goals, I had a positive, clear-thinking head. It was only after achieving a number of my goals and noticing the hollowness of the victory that I began to really question my motivation. I discovered that although my intentions were good in wanting to make up for lost time, unless I really dealt with the underlying issues that were driving me, I'd wind up using addictively again. It was tough to admit that I had really just switched addictions. I realized that I had simply given up the addictions that society so frowned upon and adopted ones that were more socially acceptable. But it was only by accepting myself as okay just the way I was that my internal messages of unworthiness began to lessen.

Fear, as usual, wants us to believe that we are not okay just the way we are. Fear wants us to continually look to others for examples of how to live our lives. Magazines are full of suggestive images of how we should look, feel, and behave. The same magazines also offer numerous stories of those at the height of success who realize the hollowness of external success. Fear wants us to believe that external things will satisfy our inner longing.

Another aspect of this is the tendency in A.A. to forever be working on oneself, as if self-acceptance awaited us as soon as we could be free from all our character defects and shortcomings. The step that is probably at the heart of this tendency is step ten, "Continued to take personal inventory and when we were wrong promptly admitted it." This step, along with the overall A.A. focus on moral wrongs and defects, had me continually focusing on my faults instead of just living my life, imperfections and all. Step ten also implies that our personal inventories will surely include only wrongs. It doesn't tell us what to do if we find a whole bunch of "right" behavior in there. Do we promptly admit our "rights" as well, or are we supposed to just keep quiet about those?

Love, on the other hand, wants us to connect with our inner purpose. Love wants us to examine and heal our childhood issues so that we may realize that we really are worthwhile and lovable just as we are, whether we are a down-and-out drunk or a CEO on Wall Street. Love takes us beyond all the societal messages of worth and helps us to discover inner meaning for ourselves and inner direction for our lives. Love sends us help in the form of intuition and gut instincts. Love gives us the courage to follow our bliss every day of our lives, whether we are working on raising productive, responsible, happy children, or selling insurance to those in need, or simply building a better life for ourselves by taking responsibility for everything we create.

17

Judgment

JUDGMENT IS ONE of the toughest issues I struggle with. Although knowing in my heart that I shouldn't judge people, I tend to find myself doing so more often than I should. Because I noticed that the issue of judgment came up a lot for me, I began reading everything I could about judgment, trying to get an understanding of why I am this way. I came to see that judgment is a way of avoiding what I dislike and have disowned about myself. Judgment shows me the areas in which I need to forgive and heal instead of condemn and blame. The judgment I feel toward another is really a judgment against myself. I am seeing in another some part of myself that I have disowned and deemed unacceptable, irritating, or downright repulsive.

So my judging another for having a limited belief system simply mirrors back to me that I am the one who still has a limited belief system and in my inability to see this part of myself, I disown this trait and project it on to another and I then judge that person unfairly.

Knowing what I now know about judgment, it is very limited of me to think that I could possibly know another person well enough to know what their motivations are for their particular actions. So my judging their outer behavior just shows how limited my own thinking is. One can never completely know another person's inner motivations, fears, and drives, and I can't judge another simply because they operate differently in the external world than I do.

I can, however, offer understanding and compassion to others instead of condemnation when I notice myself judging. In this way, I not only help the other person, I help myself because I am sending out love instead of separation. Quantum physicists and other scientists are now telling us that everything in the Universe is connected. It is judgment that separates us, not physical matter. At the subatomic physical level, everything is energy, an energy that is all encompassing and connected. Just as judgment separates, it is love that joins us.

Fear uses judgment as a way of separating ourselves from the truth. The truth is that our reality as we experience it is exactly what *we* have created. So, if my life is filled with a lot of judgment, I am being offered an unparalleled opportunity to grow and love. My quest for self-knowledge was showing me how this principle operates throughout my day without my even being aware of it. As an example, suppose I board a plane one day. On this plane I see a husband and wife bickering over some triviality. I may judge them for fighting in public and for fighting over such a trivial matter. I can overhear their conversation and I notice that the wife is blaming the husband for not filling up the gas tank on the way to the airport. She is telling him what a nuisance it is going to be to get gas when they have returned from their trip and are tired and ready to get home. She is certain that this is all his fault and is being very critical and judgmental. I think she's being too hard on her husband and should lay off. I have a sense that he's probably a good guy, but gets a lot of criticism from his wife. In fact, he's looking a little overwhelmed and distraught because of her anger toward him.

What the principle of judgment teaches me is that the *judgment* I feel toward the wife in this situation, that she is being too critical and hard on him, is exactly the same feeling I have about myself yet am not aware of it. By being judgmental toward others, I am finding fault not only with external people and situations, but with my inner self. Some part of me is looking at some other part of me and being critical. Yet this all occurs at a subconscious level, where I am unaware of it. The higher part of me wants to heal, wants me to accept and love all parts of myself as okay. However, fear jumps into the game and distracts me from going inward and resolving these issues by keeping me focused on things external to myself.

Fear is afraid that if I go inward and begin looking at these splintered parts of myself I'll discover that my childhood messages of guilt, shame, worthlessness, etc. are really true. So fear is trying to protect me, once again, from venturing into the unknown. By keeping me focused on judging and criticizing external things, fear has effectively kept me from turning inward.

Love, on the other hand, knows that the inner negative messages I have about myself simply aren't true. Love beckons me to stop looking at outer signs of dissatisfaction and heal my inner dissatisfaction. "Look inward and discover your beauty and wholeness," love gently beckons. Love wants to heal me and show me that my negative messages are as but shadows that keep me in darkness. They are illusions built on nothing. Love draws me toward the light and the shadows all disappear.

Many times it is so hard to recognize how a judgment is reflecting a disowned and disliked part of myself. It's so easy to judge a man who is a drunk, doesn't take care of his family, stays out late, and spends his money on alcohol instead of the family. We look at that and say he's no good. He doesn't take care of his family. He's irresponsible, and so on.

However, by our placing a judgment on him instead of sending him love and forgiveness, we are doing the same thing with our inner lives. We are being irresponsible by thinking critically of him; he is a child of God and worthy of love just like everyone else. We may fail to realize he grew up in a home with no father, a drunken mother, and was sexually molested by her boyfriends. He is trying to escape his pain in the only way he knows how, even if it means drinking every night. He is terrified that his wife will leave him and is also terrified of becoming a child abuser just like his mother's boyfriends were. Yet he is unable to come to grips with his fear and so drinks himself into a stupor. This man will heal much more quickly if we offer him help and forgiveness. Healing is not something you are worthy of or not worthy of. *Everyone* deserves it. By offering this man forgiveness and love, even if we do it in the form of a silent prayer, we are creating a legacy for our children. We are examples for our children, and when we judge, we create children who judge. Thereby, we are taking no better care of our families spiritually than the man who spends the family money on alcohol.

Every time you feel a judgment, picture the person you judge as an innocent child. Picture this innocent child as looking around for love and finding none available. Picture this innocent child all alone in his crib and crying. The behavior we judge may be a direct result of this adult never having been shown love as a child. The behavior doesn't make the person. The *lack of love* created the behavior we judge and condemn. The giving of love and understanding will heal the need for the behavior to exist. As we love all people, regardless of their behavior, the unacceptable behavior no longer needs to exist. I don't encourage tolerating violence or crimes against people, but we can say an act is unacceptable and take steps to correct the behavior without putting a negative judgment on the person. Perhaps if the person we judge had been given loads of unconditional love and acceptance, was brought up with daily doses of encouragement and positive role modeling, and was taught to feel valued and worthwhile, the negative behavior would never have manifested. This doesn't mean people aren't responsible for their behavior if they're brought up in a dysfunctional home. If we are brought up in a dysfunctional home, it is up to us to be responsible for learning how to heal the pain caused by a traumatic childhood.

However, being judged does nothing to heal. Judging adds more energy to the collective energy of fear. Releasing judgment, offering love and peace, at the very least in our thoughts, heals the need for negative behavior, heals "us" internally, and adds to the collective energy of love, making the world a more loving place.

As more and more people choose love instead of fear, forgiveness instead of judgment, we are leaving a much richer legacy to our children. We are teaching them not only acceptance but kindness, compassion, and responsibility. Being brought up with examples of nonjudgmental acceptance, our children will surely be able to go farther than we have in helping the planet evolve peacefully.

Another reason to let go of judgment is the law of karma. Each time we judge another, we add to our karmic burden. And as we judge another unfairly, we ourselves will be judged or treated unfairly by another in order to balance the universal scales of karma. This can also work in a positive way. As we extend love and forgiveness to another, we will be offered love and forgiveness in return, perhaps not from the same person we are giving our kindness to, but our graciousness will be returned to us in a manner similar to that in which it was given. The more we can respond with understanding and acceptance to one another, the more quickly we help the planet to evolve, as well as heal ourselves. And healing is exactly what we need in order to transcend our addictions.

18

Shame and Guilt

SHAME AND GUILT work hand in hand in keeping us sick and addicted. Many of us experience internal messages of shame, coupled with guilt, that we aren't even aware of. After having achieved sobriety in A.A., I spent a good deal of time turning back the clock and reliving all the times someone important in my life shamed me or made me feel guilty: the taunting I received as a child for being pudgy, the way my boyfriend scolded me for not being responsible, the messages I got from my parents about my lack of worth. I thought these people were the cause of my shame-based thinking. It wasn't until many years later that I realized these people in my life were simply responding to my *internal* messages of shame and guilt. They were there to show me my own erroneous messages, but I didn't realize it. My fear kept me judging them and blaming them.

I believe that each of us comes into this particular soul journey, or lifetime, with a prepackaged set of issues that we hope to resolve in this lifetime. We may have been struggling for several lifetimes with the same people and keep drawing them into our life in order to heal our anger and hatred. We also may have built-in issues of shame and guilt, which we want to resolve. Our Higher Self knows that love is available to us to guide and heal us. Our Higher Self also knows that we have everything within us to take responsibility for

141

these issues and heal ourselves, without needing to cast blame on ourselves or others.

If shame is something we struggle with, our childhood is likely to give us many clues as to the origin of our shame messages *in this lifetime.* We may not have received much support or recognition from our family of origin. Or we were teased or made fun of. Or perhaps we were made to feel worthless and given the message that we were a burden to our family. I believed I was a burden to my mother. I always felt as if I were a chore she would rather not have to deal with. I can remember the firm way she set her mouth and how this made me feel unwanted and in the way. I cannot heal if I blame my mother for this. I can look deeper and see that she was all alone during the day (my father worked long hours and was on the road a lot), trying to raise three children the best way she could. Her focus was on providing us with a home in which to grow up and she was over-whelmed by the enormity of the task. Given her lack of outside as-sistance, she did a great job with what she had. But I came prepackaged with internal messages that said I was unworthy. Some-where long ago, fear convinced me that I was not especially lovable or worthwhile. Not knowing better, I believed fear's message. So I cocreated, with the role models in my life, situations that echoed my sentiment that I was unworthy. I became an underachiever and was very self-conscious. I can now see how shame was lurking beneath every negative behavior trait I had.

It is critical to get to our deeper internalized messages and see how they drive us if we want to heal ourselves and our addictions. Our desire to escape facing these supposed demons is what keeps us sick. The "demons," however, have a wonderful surprise waiting for us. We can discover the beauty lying below the negative belief if we dare to go inward and heal ourselves.

There is a children's story I saw on PBS that demonstrates what fear leads us to believe about ourselves. In the story, a small boy living in the country lost his father. Being the oldest child, he informed his ma one fine, bright morning that he was going to go to town and get a job in order to help support the family. His ma, seeing the resoluteness on his face, helped pack his knapsack and saw him off to town. At the end of the first day, having walked all day, the boy picked a spot along the side of the road to make camp for the evening. He was enjoying a can of beans beside his fire when an old man came from the field behind him. The boy asked the man to join him and offered him some beans. The old man gratefully accepted and sat down to chat. The boy told the man what his plan was, to go to town and earn some money for his family. The old man then told the boy about a house nearby. He said the house was believed to be inhabited by a mean, vicious ghost and that the owners no longer lived in the house. Wishing to be rid of the house, the owners said they would give the house, along with a trunk filled with gold and jewels, to the first person who could spend an entire night there. The boy, seeing his opportunity, excitedly asked for directions to the house. Upon arriving at the house, he cautiously mounted the front stairs and made his way inside. He felt a little uneasy, but he noticed that mostly he felt hungry. He didn't see any ghosts, so he made his way to the kitchen. He had opened another can of beans from his knapsack and was heating them on the stove when he jumped at a loud vicious voice coming from behind him. "GET OUT" the voice screamed. The boy felt terror, but he also felt concern. Who was this mean ghost who wanted to run everybody off? Instead of fleeing, the boy said, "Who are you? Let me see you." At that, the meanest, ugliest face he'd ever seen began to materialize in front of him. Swallowing his fear, the boy said, "What is your name?" The ghost nearly yelled, "You must leave! I am Lothar, the keeper of this house." "Why are you scaring everyone off?" the boy said, and courageously stood his ground. "I have done nothing to you. In fact, I want to see the rest of you." With that, the rest of the ghost materialized. Much to the boy's surprise, the rest of the ghost looked nothing like the head. The body of the ghost was soft and billowy and emanated a beautiful purple hue tinged in bluish white. As the boy was marveling at this, the ghost began to speak, although this time in a much less angry tone. "I want to thank you," the ghost said. "You see, I have been trapped here in an invisible body. Until someone requested me to materialize, I was forever invisible. My fear made me very angry and so I scared everyone away. Because everyone approached me in fear, I came to believe that I was hideously disfigured in some way, but I can see now that I'm not." "No, you're beautiful," said the boy. With this, the ugly face of the ghost disappeared and became as radiantly beautiful as the rest of the body. "Thank you so much for seeing past my fear and anger and loving me. You have released me from bondage and I can join my family in heaven now," the ghost said. With that, the boy watched in astonishment as the apparition disappeared from view. His beans were starting to boil over on the stove. The boy, in gratitude, sat down to eat them. By and by, the boy's family received the house and the trunk filled with gold and jewels from the grateful owners. Through his childlike innocence, trust, and courage the boy had given life to his family and freedom to the trapped ghost.

Healing our guilt and shame operates on much the same principle: Where fear says, "Do not tread," is exactly where we need to go in order to discover our inner beauty. When we take care of our inner spiritual life with love, peace, understanding, and acceptance, we are released from the bondage of shame, guilt, fear, and unworthiness, as well as the need to be addicted.

More Guilt

As addicts, we are prone to feel guilty for all of our previous indiscretions. However, the guilt we continue to feel for our pasts will cause us to use again until we recognize it and heal it. Just as you are able to forgive another for his transgressions, realize that you yourself have made mistakes in your striving to find wholeness within. Addictions and the destructive behavior that accompanies them are simply our erroneous ways of responding to our spiritual hunger. Looking within to the cause of the hunger relieves us of our need to feel guilty.

The person with an underlying feeling of guilt needs positive encouragement and the validation that he is okay just the way he is. Those of us who struggle with feelings of guilt have been *overinvolved* with our wrongs, defects of character, and shortcomings. That is part of what kept us caught in the cycle of addiction. We need to learn to love all aspects of ourselves and trust life when it begins handing us one wonderful thing after another. There is a great quote used in his inaugural speech by Nelson Mandela, who attributes the words to Marianne Williamson:

Our deepest fear is not that we are inadequate.
Our deepest fear is that we are powerful beyond measure.
It is our light not our darkness that most frightens us.
We ask ourselves, who am I to be brilliant, gorgeous, talented,
    fabulous?
Actually, who are you not to be? You are a child of God.
Your playing small does not serve the world. There is nothing
    enlightened about
shrinking so that other people will not feel insecure around you.
We are all meant to shine as children do.
We were born to make manifest the glory of God that is within us.
It is not just in some of us; it's in everyone. And as we let our
    own light shine, we
unconsciously give other people permission to do the same.
As we are liberated from our own fear, our presence automatically
    liberates others.

Love sees no one as being guilty. Love holds everyone as being worthy of love because love sees everyone as they truly are, innocent children of the Universe. Could you ever picture judging a three-month-old baby by his behavior or see him as unworthy of love? The Universe sees us all as being as innocent as a newborn baby. Society must hold people accountable for their actions, but we need not judge a person as unworthy of love. Guilt wants us to see ourselves and others as unworthy of love. Guilt wants to say some acts are worthy of love and others are not. Parceling out love in this manner ensures the perpetuation of guilt. Love sees everything as either an expression of love or a cry for love. Acts that society deems as negative, love sees as a cry for love. Where there is no love, there is fear. Fear and guilt cannot exist where there is love. Therefore, to heal guilt is to feel love and to see ourselves as innocent.

19

Choices

EVERY MOMENT of every day we are offered choices. We can choose fear, intolerance, judgment, blame, and anger, and remain addicted to our need to escape from life. Or we can choose love, peace, tolerance, compassion, acceptance, and understanding, and choose to live fully alive, aware, and conscious. By choosing love instead of fear, we allow our splintered parts to heal.

Addiction is the result of our being splintered. There are certain parts of ourselves that we cannot accept, or love, or even look at. So we break off from these parts, splintering our personalities, and then watch in horror as these unloved, disowned parts of us are reflected back to us in our life situations.

Fear would have us remain separate and keep us sick. Love says, "There is nothing to fear. All is valid, everything needs only love to heal."

The next time you are experiencing a craving or an addictive impulse, try to go within and connect with the part of you that you are denying, or the pain from which you are trying to escape. Have you been letting your life become too regimented and controlled? Have you been dictatorial with yourself, or others, or allowed others to run your show when you felt rage at being told what to do? How are you not being true to yourself? What part of you needs attention and love?

Perhaps at this time you need a support group or outside assistance with your addiction. What do you feel inwardly that you need to do? Every moment offers you a chance to choose. Do you choose love and give yourself the freedom to do *whatever* it is you need to do, knowing that whatever you do, it's okay? You may even relapse for a time until you finally stop being so hard on yourself and imposing too many rigid requirements on your poor body. If your soul doesn't feel it's being heard because you are imposing rigid, controlling expectations on it, you *are* likely to use again.

Rigid, controlling expectations have fear as their basis. When I insist on things going exactly as I would like them to with my rigid expectations, I set myself up for disappointment and resentment. The disappointment and resentment I feel further increases my need to have things go just as I would like, which sets me up for more disappointment. Love, on the other hand, accepts and allows all behavior, knowing everything works together for good. I had to let it be okay to binge on food occasionally before I was finally able to let go of this behavior. Once I let this occasional bingeing be okay, it no longer needed to control me. I have a quote I got from a book a long time ago: "By valuing all things equally, by giving equal right to all things to exist, experiences that we do not want will never come. We can simply learn to trust life, with all its variants. Face your fears, if and when they come up, and send them Love."

Another good way to put it, which was in Richard Bach's book *Running from Safety,* is the following, where he is describing the definition of "is."

EVERYTHING "IS"
- is okay
- is perfectly valid
- deserves acknowledgment
- wants love

Love wants to assist you and is surrounding you right now with its healing arms. Love simply needs a request from us and then the gates of heaven can be flung open and abundance poured forth. The request can be as simple as "Give me the willingness." But be open to whatever way in which love wants to come. Our judging how we want to receive love's bounty will only open us up to receive it in ways where we still hold judgment, for where we hold judgment, we are in need of love's healing balm. For example, we may suddenly have a lot of angry people around us if our own anger is where we need to experience the most healing.

I quote from *Your Sacred Self* by Dr. Wayne Dyer:

Even [negativity] will be part of the divine order because you know that the moment will arrive when you are totally free of the addiction, as long as you stay focused on purified thinking. Your thoughts are the most important thing you have in the battle to discontinue addictive behavior. Your thoughts are in the invisible realm where your higher self is found.

I have outlined in this section the many ways in which fear wants us to remain afraid and weak.

Fear doesn't want us to look inward and heal our pain or resolve our issues. Fear wants to keep us focused on external things. Fear tells us that addictive behavior will ease our pain. When we become ready to be rid of our addiction, fear then feeds us a model replete with powerlessness and rigid requirements that focus on defects, wrongs, surrender, and limiting beliefs. Fear wants us to keep the power for our lives in things outside ourselves. In case we do desire power, fear tells us that control is the way of power. Fear tells us that we are separate, and fear labels some things as acceptable and others as unacceptable. Fear tells us that we can have justified anger, and fear blames others for our problems and labels us as victims.

Fear doesn't want us to experience the positive side of life in a pleasurable way. Fear tells us that our natures are not to be trusted, so we must seek guidance and direction from outside, external authorities who know better than we do how to live our lives. Fear imposes moral codes of conduct, and fear judges us when we don't live up to them. Fear tells us that we are not worthy of being loved unless we *earn* love through right action. Fear tells us to give to others before we have ever given to ourselves. Fear doesn't want us to look around for other, better ways to live our lives and so fear convinces us that living in fear is the best way.

Love, on the other hand, offers us forgiveness. Love offers us empowerment and the freedom to make our own choices about our lives. Love shows us how connected we all are and how a judgment on my brother is really a judgment on me. Love wants to clear away and heal all of our pockets of resentment, anger, and pain. Love understands that we didn't mean to hurt others or be hurt by others, we were all simply doing the best we could with the limited information we had. Love understands our inability to accept its awesome power and our inability to accept our own personal power. Love wants to show us that we can create lives of purpose and meaning and that this creates better environments for our children, for by leaving them a better planet, we leave ourselves a better future. Love wants us to surrender blame but is patient when we cling to it with justified anger and resentment. Love wants to hold our hands as we walk through our pain, and love wants to guide us to our beauty and wholeness.

Love infuses each of us with inner guidance through intuition, and love wants to tell us we can always trust the Universe if we are taking affirmative action. Love wants to turn even our mistakes into positive opportunities for growth and healing. Love encourages us to trust ourselves, connect with our Higher Selves, and take responsibility for creating the best life possible for ourselves. Love guides us to always seek the "highest and best for all concerned" when we are taking an action we are not certain about. Love wants to handle all the details of our lives. Love wants us to transcend addiction and experience healing on all levels.

Every moment, we can choose either love or fear, and if we don't like the choice, we can choose again. A good example of how daily life affords me opportunities to choose love or fear is in my relationship with my husband. Every time my husband and I disagree and I can sense a fight coming, I now know I can withdraw from the situation until I've calmed down. I then try to picture love surrounding the situation and I also try to determine how I am responsible for what's going on, how the incident somehow reflects one of my internal messages of guilt, shame, blame, etc. I do not focus on how I can blame my husband even if my limited self perceives that he has done me an "injustice." As I hold love as my intention and try to understand my role in cocreating the disagreement, the energy surrounding the situation changes every time. Many times my husband will call to apologize right about the time I was about to pick up the phone to call him. With love as our intention, we can both offer forgiveness to the other and acceptance of our own roles. I am amazed every time at how suddenly the situation changes on the other end when I begin to clear my own fears and insecurities out of the way.

Thus, though love may sometimes be the toughest choice, it always leads to healing, happiness, and wholeness if we follow it through to the end.

In situations where choosing love is the harder choice, it may be because we feel caught in the fear and the negative energy is starting to suck us in. In these cases, all we need to do is cry out for love to enter. And love will rush forth from all corners to assist us. Situations can change *instantly* when love enters. Thoughts may suddenly enter our minds about various options we can choose in order to avoid a negative behavior. *Take them.* The Universe supports affirmative action. The same forces that balance the solar system and designed something as intricate and miraculous as the human body are available for our use any time we need them. It is our choice.

Part Three

THE NATURE
OF LOVE

. . . at the heart of healing is love.

I LOVE READING BOOKS. For the entire time I was soul-searchingly trying to make peace with my addictions and find a solution that worked for me, I read. I read everything that looked interesting and many things that didn't. The subject areas I covered were New Age, inspirational, self-help/personal growth, autobiographies, religious and spiritual topics. Many times an entire book would click with me and its messages spoke straight to my heart. Other books had only a few bits of wisdom that resonated with me. And others had nothing whatsoever to offer me. But it was mainly through books, coupled with my personal experiences, that I grew in wisdom.

I would take the words that offered me hope, inspiration, strength, and courage, and use them to assist me in my quest for healing and empowerment. I had also embarked on gaining knowledge through personally examining different religious schools of thought. I attended Catholic masses, Mahakari (a Japanese religion) sessions, Buddhist lectures, and for quite a while attended nightly meditation sessions based on a Hindu belief system. Now that I no longer had to fit everything into a prescribed doctrine, such as a religion or a twelve-step program, all schools of thought were open and available to me.

I examined Deepak Chopra's Vedic system of healing, Dan Millman's *Way of the Peaceful Warrior*, and The Enneagram. I threw out that which was ritualistic and dogmatic and embraced that which spoke to my heart. I allowed myself to question everything and allowed myself the complete freedom to construct my very own personalized belief system based on what felt right to me and what harmonized with my own experiences. It was an empowering and exciting time for me. My heart and spirit felt as if they were being quenched after a thousand-year thirst and I felt truly alive and stimulated by life itself instead of by external trappings, of which I had very few at this time anyway. During most of this time I was living in my own apartment, and having published my first book, was doing my consulting work for international firms.

One of the most enlightening books I read was one by Lee Jampolsky titled *Healing the Addictive Mind*. This book defines addiction as stemming from fear-based thinking and its insight definitely applied to me. It helped me to see where my fear-based thinking ruled my life, and clarified the points I spoke of in the previous section. But it was the book's focus on living in a love-based system as being crucial to healing addiction that struck me the most forcefully. Mr. Jampolsky defines recovery from addiction as being "the process of awakening to love. Opening the heart to love is the highest human experience, and is what undoing addiction is about." Very wise words.

I took the author's insights and applied them to my own life. I examined where I needed to be love-based instead of fear-based and in doing so, my healing was greatly accelerated. My inability to question authority, my "blaming the parents" stance, my resistance to the "life is suffering" notion—I reexamined everything in the light of love to see how it applied to me.

This section outlines the areas in which I most needed to transform fear into love, dependence into independence, and conformity into freedom. It begins with my questioning everything.

20

The Universe Supports You

THE LOVE-BASED SYSTEM that I was discovering encouraged me to think for myself. It encouraged me to decide what was right for me personally. I began letting myself be the authority for my life. I also realized that what works perfectly for *me* may not be what another person needs. But the general principle of letting *yourself* decide what is and isn't right for you is helpful to everyone. Life offers us an abundant number of choices in all things.

In a love-based system, we learn to live by our own internal authority. This does not mean mentally justifying what the ego may say is right for you. Neither does it mean irresponsibly disregarding the external authority in your life. I have found that your own internal authority will always lead you to what is of the highest good and is best for all concerned. It would never lead you to harm another although others may not like your new behavior or may be threatened by your positive changes. This will especially happen when you are breaking away from old ways of being that have been destructive to you. It might be that others are counting on your being fearful, weak, or dependent, so your newfound independence and confidence will temporarily rock the boat. However, rest assured that you *are* taking things to a higher level and that all who come along will benefit. Be prepared for some people to drop away from your life, some perhaps quietly, others not so quietly.

So exactly how do you go about thinking for yourself? You begin by getting in touch with your gut and what it tells you. Have you ever felt "in your gut" that something wasn't right for you? You just knew it deep down inside, but you were not willing to act on that hunch. One reason for its being so hard to act on our gut instincts is because logic steps in. Logic will wreak havoc on gut instincts. "But how can this make sense?" logic queries. "No one has *ever* done it *this* way!" logic nervously goes on. "What will people think?" "No one will understand." "What will the family think?" On and on, logic fearfully, and sometimes tearfully, tosses up one justification after another in support of the status quo. "But what will happen if you do it this (new) way?" logic offers as its final, tearful plea. I JUST MAY DISCOVER A BETTER WAY OF LIVING! And become more empowered in the process! And more loving, too! And more self-assured! Most important, you will become better able to trust your gut instincts the next time around.

Logic is a very useful and necessary part of our ability to function in this world. However, logic can stymie us, and can prevent us from taking action where we may need to take action the most. Logic, like fear, wants to keep us chained to only what is predictable and controllable. Logic wants us to stay in the status quo, and if we do attempt change, for the change to be in a controlled, predictable, familiar environment.

Thinking for yourself means cross-checking everything you are told you *should* and *must* do with whether or not it feels right to you. And feeling right to you may not necessarily mean you *want* to do a particular thing. I may not want to work in my office every night after the baby has gone to bed, but it feels right to me that I share a portion of our family's financial responsibilities. For everyone, there are many things we must do in order to be responsible adults. However, there is a whole realm of externally imposed rules and regulations that we blindly follow or follow simply because we are afraid of doing things differently. There is safety (and stagnation) in conformity.

Thinking for yourself does not mean ignoring the rules of the road.

Thinking for yourself means allowing your inner wisdom and inner voice to have a say in your life. It means "substituting knowing and trusting for doubting and fearing," as Dr. Wayne W. Dyer writes in *Real Magic*.

As I slowly began thinking for myself, I was continually asked to step forward with my new faith into the unknown. If questioning institutions and authority brought me new realizations about myself and about life, I would still not move forward until I tested these new insights. And that is when I discovered one of the basic truths of living in a love-based system of thinking. I discovered that as scary as these unknowns may have been to me, the Universe always supports affirmative action. The Universe wants to guide us toward our highest good and can take whatever raw material we have and use it for good.

Leaving A.A. was especially scary because I had no guarantee that I would be successful on my own without someone such as a sponsor, or a twelve-step group, to monitor me and keep me out of denial. I had no game plan, just an intuitive sense that I was doing the right thing. And as I trusted this inner voice, I was guided to exactly the things and people I needed to be guided to. Simply my intention to courageously trust the Universe was all the impetus needed to ensure that I received exactly what I needed. Today, I trust more easily in the process, but I still sometimes fall into the trap of fearful thinking. This usually happens when I am experiencing a lot of indecision.

When the problem of indecision comes up in my life, I am usually fearful of something. I often find myself trying to decide between two seemingly trivial courses of action. Should I go to the grocery store first or the gym? Should I have sushi for lunch or a salad? Should I go out with my friends tonight or stay home and work? Fear uses indecision to keep us from taking action, to protect us from going into the unknown. In my case, I usually am fearful of choosing the "wrong" action. I seem to be able to come up with endless mental lists of pros and cons favoring any particular action and an equally compelling set of pros and cons for an alternative action. Knowing I must choose one or the other often leaves me paralyzed. I seem to have some sort of inner insecurity that I will choose the wrong course.

The reality is that either course of action will be just fine. In fact, it is precisely when either course of action suits the situation that I find myself the most paralyzed. Surely, one action is "better" than the other, I argue with myself. Some part of me has a hard time fathoming the fact that two courses of action can both be just as good for me, especially when it involves the big issues in my life, such as should I stay with this person or not? Should I have another child or not? Should I pursue this line of work or not? Because of the unlimited power of the Universe, any action can be used for good. The Universe can take even the most bleak or the most violent situation and use it for a higher purpose. Perhaps some will learn to experience forgiveness or love where there was none before.

Whatever raw material we hand the Universe, if we have good intentions, we can be certain that the Universe will support us. And we will be absolutely amazed at times to witness this unconditional support. One of the primary factors in enlisting this support is our intention. When embarking on any new course of action or going into any unknown situation, we can simply ask for "the highest and best for all concerned." We may still remain uncertain as to whether we have chosen the wisest path, but to the Universe all paths are the right paths. If we have good intentions, our Higher Self will see that our highest good will be done no matter which path we are on.

The very stuff the Universe is made of is Love. I read a description that describes it perfectly: The energy that holds atoms together is Love. This means that the energy of the Universe is Love. The energy that supports your body, guides your heart to beat, your mind to think, and your body to grow is Love. Love is the pervasive force of the Universe. There aren't two diametrically opposed forces of good and evil. There is only good. Some may call this poppycock, but it is the wisdom of the ages.

Dr. Deepak Chopra talks about the field of infinite possibilities. This field of infinite possibilities is Love. With love, anything and everything can be healed. So-called evil can be transformed into love. Hatred, violence, and war can be used to incite positive growth. The world and its billions of people are slowly becoming more and more

conscious of personal growth and personal evolution. Bookstores today are crammed full of books that tell people how they can master
the forces of the Universe and control their own destinies.

The Universe works with us in cocreating our highest good. If
our intention is to heal, we may be shown within ourselves many
pockets of anger, resistance, judgment, and resentments. We need to
heal in these areas if we are to be free from our pain and addiction.
If we take the very tiniest step toward creating a higher good for
ourselves, the Universe will surround us with mighty forces of assistance, guidance, support, and love, because the Universe is made of
Love, and our very bodies are held together with Love.

By seeking our highest good, we are connecting with our Higher
Self. Our Higher Self is the God within us. Jesus said, "The kingdom
of heaven is within you." For me, the Higher Self represents that
kingdom. "On heaven as it is on earth" means that we can experience
the wonder and power and joy of heaven *right here on earth*. Seeing
God as external to us is only part of the process. God is also *within* us
and *is* us. We all have the power of God within us, accessible to us.
We have been conditioned by society, by repression, by rigid, authoritative institutions, and by fear to believe that God, with His
awesome power, is an immense father figure outside us.

My personal version of this is to call the external power that exists
outside me the Universe. This very same power is within me and is
my Higher Self. All that goes on outside me also goes on inside me.
Therefore, my inner intention for "the highest and best for all concerned" is a link to the compelling power of the Higher Self and the
Universe and can literally move mountains of obstacles away with the
wisp of the wind.

Knowing that the Universe supports affirmative action allows me
to venture, fearfully or courageously, into unknown territory. It allows me to test limiting beliefs to discover whether they are true for
me. It also encourages me to step outside judging how "the highest
and best for all concerned" is supposed to look. It may come to me
clothed in intolerance and anger. However, the Love that binds the
Universe together gently encourages me to go even where there is

intolerance, hatred, and anger. For Love wisely knows that to go there in peace and acceptance will literally transform these negative traits into Love itself.

There can only be the duality of good and evil, right and wrong, love and fear at the lower levels of awareness. For at the highest levels, there is only Love. Love sends itself out and returns to itself. All the world is a journey in which love seeks to go where it is not and heal itself. We can each do this individually with our own lives and our own physical bodies. To go where love is not, fully supported by the Universe, we heal.

21

Surrendering Blame

A RECENT TELEVISION talk-show program went
something like this: A forty-five-year-old woman who appeared
overweight and poorly dressed was bemoaning her life. She lived in
a trailer, her grown kids were "irresponsible" and always hit her up
for money. Her husband was unreliable, drank too much, and simply
lay on the couch in front of the television set every night. Wanda
(not her real name) was certain that if she could get her "kids" (who
were really of adult age) to behave the way she felt they should, and
if she could get her husband to stop being such a ne'er-do-well, her
life would be better and she would finally find the happiness that
eluded her. At one point, as she continued her litany of woes, the
talk-show host said, "Well, Wanda, who do you blame for your unhappiness?" "Why, my kids and my husband! Ain't ya been
listening?" "But isn't it true," the talk-show host asked patiently,
"that *you* are the creator of your own happiness or unhappiness, not
your husband or your kids?" "Well, yeah, I guess so. . . . But things'd
shore be a lot better if they'd all just shape up!" she said and snorted.

I'm sure there were a lot of people in the television audience who
could see that Wanda's dissatisfaction was obviously the result of her
focus on everybody but herself. There is nothing stopping her from
enrolling in self-improvement classes, joining a fitness group, taking
a brisk walk in the evening, reading a book about self-improvement,

attending a spiritual or religious meeting, etc. The answer to her unhappiness lies *within* her, not in anything external to her. As long as
she keeps the cause of her unhappiness outside herself, she will never
find permanent, true happiness. The grim truth is that we all do the
same thing in one way or another, sometimes without even realizing
it. We have all become a nation of blamers, whiners, and victims, all
too happy, when we get the chance, to pass the buck to someone
else for our troubles.

I flipped the channel and found a documentary program on the
downsizing of corporate America. The segment was showing an interview with a man who had just been laid off from his assembly-line
job in the auto industry. All of his bills were overdue and the bank
was about to foreclose on his house. He was very agitated and angry
over having been laid off. He had quite a few unprintable words to
say about his former employer.

"Who do you blame for this?" the interviewer asked. "Well, General Motors, of course. They closed our plant and now seventeen
hundred of us are out of work! What are we supposed to do?" The
sad reality is that he probably will lose his house because he is unable
to see past his anger and blame to the solution to his problem. Of
course, it is unfortunate that he lost his job, but there were many
indicators along the way that he would, and he chose to ignore them
all. Layoffs and plant closings have become routine in the auto industry. His own plant had been rumored to be closing for eighteen
months prior to its shutdown. By updating his skills or perhaps ac-
quiring new ones while he still had a steady paycheck, he could have
been ready to reenter the job market in a new and perhaps better
area. Or he could have begun looking into other places to live that
offered more reliable work. At the very least, he could have begun a
small savings account in anticipation of the worst. Any number of
solutions could have been possible with an open mind and an eager
heart. Life continually offers us challenges. He could have viewed this
as an opportunity to improve his lot, but because he chose to remain
a victim, he will never see positive solutions to his problems.

Our nation's leaders are even demonstrating models of blaming, name-calling, and general finger-pointing. When the government shut down in December 1995, the Republicans (led by Senator Robert Dole and House Speaker Newt Gingrich) all blamed the White House and President Clinton. Clinton, in turn, blamed the Republicans for not bringing him any reasonable solutions to the budget dilemma. The truth was that the writing had been on the wall for a very long time that the government would be shut down if budget agreement wasn't reached before the deadline. But instead of actively seeking positive solutions, with each side taking responsibility for fixing the budget problem, both sides chose to wait until the last minute and then argue about who was going to sit where at the budget meetings.

No one wins as long as we choose to blame. Only when you take *full* responsibility for everything (yes, everything) in your life can you then see through to the solution.

Think about what sort of message is being sent to our children when they see all the adults around them complaining and blaming. "It's the government's fault, it's your father's fault, it's my boss's fault, it's my secretary's fault, *it's the other guy's fault!*" Do we really want to raise our kids to be victims and blamers?

I will admit that blaming is very easy to do. It can be energizing in a negative sort of way. You can get a real charge out of blaming. You feel your heart rate increase and you can feel the surge of adrenaline. It's especially gratifying if you've got an active participant. "Yes, and can you *believe* that X actually did that to me!" On and on goes the litany of blame.

Because medical experts told me I had a genetic tendency to addiction, and because the psychological experts told me my dysfunctional childhood (which wasn't even dysfunctional) contributed to my addiction, I naturally blamed my parents. Because they gave me the inherited gene for alcoholism and because they didn't hold me and rock me as a child, I'm an addict, I thought for many years.

This kind of thinking is so counterproductive to true healing. I'm now reading a book by George McGovern, *Terry*, in which he describes his daughter's struggle and subsequent death due to alcoholism.

He was devastated by her death, and had lovingly tried to help her for years, paying for treatment, attending family sessions, offering unconditional love. In reading her journals after her death, he realized that she had never gotten past blaming her childhood upbringing for some of her problems. All the countless high-priced experts she saw for years unknowingly stunted her ability to heal by keeping her mired in blame under the guise of helping her to make peace with her past.

As I now know, my parents did the best they could. We had a roof over our heads, never lacked for a single material thing, and my mother bent over backward to shuttle me to every new interest I had, from soccer, to basketball practice, to softball, to parties, to trumpet practice, etc. I don't know that I could have done as good a job.

As a parent myself now, I'm quite sure I'll drop the ball at some critical point in my children's development, to the point at which they can point a finger at me in their adulthood and say, in all honesty, "You weren't there for me." *No one* comes out of childhood without at least a few of these incidents. My big lesson in all of it was not to discover where I could point to some supposedly pivotal happening in my youth, but to forgive all and let go of blame. I'm not a perfect parent any more than my parents were. Releasing blame is the key that opens the door to healing. For as I do so, I am available to love my parents in the way nature intended.

Blaming is not empowering. It will get you no closer to a solution. It feeds off negative energy. While many of our problems are very complicated, and there may seem to be obvious targets for us to point fingers at, we must realize that no solution will be found by continuing to blame.

What is much harder than blaming is surrendering the blame and accepting full, not partial, but full, responsibility for the events and circumstances in our lives. This means being brutally honest with ourselves much of the time. We don't want to admit that, okay, yes, maybe we did suspect that a certain event might happen and we took no positive steps to avoid it. Or, all right, I'll admit I could have walked away from this situation when it started to become unhealthy.

It can be especially hard when we must venture into a completely uncertain future. A woman who is continually battered by her husband and chooses to stay is not a victim. She is a participant. There are shelters and nonprofit groups in *every* major city where she can get help. You often hear women say they are staying for the children's sake or because they have nowhere else to go. What kind of message does it send the children when they see mom continually abused and verbally degraded at the hands of a violent man? The children will get the message that women are to be treated this way and they will grow up to be either wife abusers or wives who are abused. It would send a much more powerful message to children if they saw mom taking charge of her life, seeking help, breaking free, supporting herself, and gaining self-confidence, self-confidence that can then be passed on to the children, thus allowing them to assume responsible roles in society.

It's very scary for a woman to take responsibility for her life, declare that "I will not tolerate this," and move out with perhaps no place to go but a shelter. Remember that the Universe *always* supports affirmative action. I have left an abusive relationship with nothing more than the clothes on my back. I had nowhere to live, no money, and no job. All I knew was that I had to get out. In this relationship, I had lost every bit of self-respect I had. It was the most frightening thing I had ever done to move out with no place to go and no future prospects. But I trusted, I literally forced, the Universe to take care of me. This trust was imperative. Within one month I had a decent place to live, a job, a small amount of money, and all the self-respect a woman could ever ask for. I was so energized and empowered by the way I had taken charge of my life and the marvelous way in which the Universe had taken care of me that I felt I could accomplish anything. It was the most enlightening and empowering time of my life.

Sometimes it seems as if the more we are willing to completely walk into an unknown situation, trusting the Universe to provide for us, the more bounty (and self-esteem) we are given. You will find that as you move from victim to responsible participant you are able to see your life's circumstances as challenges and opportunities instead of crises and problems.

We cannot heal ourselves as long as we choose to be victims. Surrendering the blame allows us to heal. It allows us to open our hearts to love and to see how everything in our lives is there because we either created it, promoted it, or allowed it.

As we surrender the blame, we move from victim to active participant in our future. We become cocreators with the Universe in shaping our destiny for the betterment of all. More important, we allow love to find its rightful place in our lives.

THE TRUE NATURE OF POWER

I was recently engrossed in a story, written by James Herriot in his book *All Things Bright and Beautiful* in the 1940s, that involved a little neighborhood boy who was apparently the town bad boy. At the young age of ten he busied himself carrying out one cruel prank after another. He scrawled on people's cars, he threw firecrackers in mail slots. It seemed as if he pulled every mean trick he could think of. The author of the story had reason to go to his house one time and was not surprised to find that the house was in the poorest part of town. He was, however, shocked by the absolute squalor he found once inside the house.

The boy's mother, very fat and unkempt, was seated at a filthy kitchen table scattered with dirty dishes. A cigarette dangled from her mouth as she thumbed mindlessly through a magazine. The husband, who was not the boy's father, lay in a stupor on the couch, reeking of alcohol. It was very easy for the author to see that the child was not an "imp from hell" but was a neglected child. It is so easy in this situation to judge the mother. Reading the story, I wanted to reach back in time and shake this mother and tell her to stop neglecting her child, to take care of herself and her family, to quit living in hatred.

However, I realized on reflection that this mother, whom I could so easily want to blame, is a product of exactly the same sort of neglectful treatment that she is giving to her child.

Her son doesn't feel loved and valued; therefore he acts out in negative ways. When the mother was a pure, innocent child, she herself was not loved and valued. Her father was abusive and neglectful and her mother was an alcoholic. Coming from a neglected home doesn't relieve the woman of the very real need to take responsibility for her life and stop the cycle of neglect and hatred. However, it does allow one to see that no one is really to blame. Blaming does no good. Her father's family had never loved or cared for her father. There is probably a vicious cycle of neglect going back for generations.

At some point, we all must stop blaming and judging and simply say, "Love didn't exist here and no one in this family has been able to find it within them to love each other." Having never received love from the family of origin, each succeeding generation lacked the ability to give love to their children. The result is a history of drug abuse, alcoholism, sexual dysfunction, and criminal behavior.

Very few addicts probably feel as if their childhoods were filled with love, positive encouragement and support, and validation. We all have areas in which we wished we had received more love. But the answer to a lack of love does not lie outside us. The answer lies within us. Love lies within us. We have the power, right now, to clear away the debris of our past, to stop hurting ourselves with addictive behavior, and simply to start trusting love.

The true nature of power is love. Love heals *all*. Fear is the antithesis of love. Dr. Gerald Jampolsky writes in *Love Is the Answer*: "[Fear] will do everything it can to make us afraid of love and to block us from forgiving ourselves [and our families], loving ourselves, accepting love, and giving love to others." We need to trust in love, not fear. There is no power in living life from a fearful standpoint. Fear closes us down, restricts us, and causes our denied need for love and healing to surface through addictive impulses and cravings.

We need to go within, acknowledge our need for love, and learn to give love to ourselves. We need to give unconditional love to ourselves, as we do, we will then slowly become able to give unconditional love to those around us. Coming from a place of love allows us to see that no matter what the circumstances, love can exist there. If we can hold the thought of love in our minds in the stickiest of situations, the negativity will begin seemingly to vanish and we will eventually be able to see how all things are working together for the good.

Man has been afraid of his own inherent power since time immemorial. Early man turned this fear outward and thus used domination and fear as a way to control others. He built temples of power and wealth to mask his inner feelings of inferiority, and he waged wars that reflected his own inner, unconscious struggle. Man, in denial of his own inner fear, has always projected it outward. We now have whole societies that exist based on this fear.

The truth is that we have nothing to fear. As long as we fear fear itself, it will always have power over us. The solution is to stop feeding the fire of fear. Go within and find your love. Love yourself. Listen to your inner guidance, your intuition. If you let your inner wisdom be the guiding force in your life, then you are truly operating from a powerful place. Love would have us harm none, blame none, and shun none because love knows that as long as we fear, we will experience illness, unfairness, violence, and addiction because our fear really stems from an inner fear, a fear that we are not lovable or valuable.

Love knows the truth. We are lovable and valuable. The homeless man who begs quarters so that he can buy cheap wine is lovable and valuable. The poor mother who neglects her child is as deserving of love as you or I. In fact, it is because she *didn't* receive love that she is as she is. As long as we hold the notion that some things are more lovable and valuable than others, then our society will continue to churn out Jeffrey Dahmers and Unabombers. Everyone needs love, no matter how despicable their acts. People commit despicable acts *because* of a lack of love; therefore, as we love each and every one equally and wholly we will eliminate the presence of violence and hatred in our society. I am, of course, not condoning violence and criminal behavior. We can send a person love without condoning the behavior. Every person must be responsible for his or her own behavior. However, we need to refrain from seeing these people as separate from us and as not deserving of love.

If we could all hold love in our minds and mentally send love out to each and every person who irritates or disgusts us, then we could magically heal those dark places within us where we don't love and accept ourselves. And it is our denial and suppression of these shadow areas within us that contribute to our sickness and addiction. So sending love to others helps us to heal ourselves.

22

Life Is Not a Toll Road

MANY ADDICTS MAY THINK their *addiction* is what is making their lives empty and devoid of meaning, and that their lives would instantly be meaningful if they could only quit using addictive substances. I contend that it is *because* their lives feel empty and devoid of meaning that they drink and use other addictive substances. Using was the only way I could temporarily escape the pain that was my life. After achieving sobriety in A.A., many people never stop to reflect for very long that their lives may still be empty and devoid of meaning. The people, the meetings, the sense of belonging, the ego boost that comes from helping newcomers, all these things can create a superficial sense of purpose in one's life. But it is not until we stop living our lives according to the adopted and approved beliefs of those around us that we will truly experience the wonderment of life on all levels. The courage required to live your own life, and be your own authority, will take you farther than you could ever have imagined.

Life is not meant to be a series of struggles and hardships with a few successes scattered in. Each and every day can be lived fully—fully empowered, fully loving, and fully living.

I remember in my late twenties struggling with overwhelming food cravings after a long period of abstinence. Some days the cravings were so intense, I searched for anything to read that might help and inspire me. The only thing I could get my hands on was a devotional book that had page after page of how to make it through suffering. I thought excitedly, Oh, good, this is what I need. This will help me. But the solution the book offered me was that suffering is part of life and *must* be endured. "Suffering purifies us, and we must expect suffering to always be in our lives because of our sinful natures. It's healthy and will cleanse us of our impurities," one of the messages of the book read. This sounded pretty heavy-handed to me, but I was desperate, so day after day as the cravings intensified, I lay on the floor, prayed, and read more of this "life is suffering" philosophy.

One day, I finally had it. "Enough of this crap!" I shouted. "I can't force myself to take this medicine anymore. I don't believe it. It doesn't feel right to me that we should not only endure suffering *but expect it to always be present in our lives!* And it is not helping my cravings at all!" I threw the book away and was forced to resolve the issue that was making me crave in the first place. In my searching for relief from my cravings, I had fallen back into the trap of forcing myself to believe in something that didn't feel right to me simply because I thought "they" knew better than I did.

Dissatisfaction is another way in which the "life is a toll road" mentality can quietly creep into our lives. I have spoken to many people with years of sobriety who still felt a vague sense of disquiet about their lives. They knew they were living "right" because they were going to meetings and living up to all the requirements of the program. But something just seemed to be missing in their lives. Until we go within, and heal that inner sense of bleakness, until we learn to create lives filled with purpose and meaning, we will continue to be an eight-cylinder engine that stays in first gear.

Living is all about using all eight cylinders. No one benefits by our needless suffering and striving. Fear keeps us from living up to our full potential by:

- teaching us that life is suffering
- that good only comes as a reward for hard work and sweat
- that life is hard and a struggle
- that our addiction is what is making us miserable

As we follow the path of our hearts' desires, we are following our bliss. We do not need to feel as if all of life is drudgery. We can feel alive and filled with purpose. Work can take on the characteristics of play. Love wants us to do what feels meaningful and important to us. And love wants to guide us to our specific purpose in life, our bliss. As we follow what we want to do, life becomes lighter and flows more easily. Stop making excuses for why you can't have what you really desire and go after it. As you do you will experience what Gary Zukav describes in his book *The Seat of the Soul* as "a richness and specialness to the lifetime of that personality that is recognized and honored by its fellow souls."

Sometimes it is our early childhood experiences that teach us that life is suffering. We are led to believe that good things come only after much (unenjoyable) hard work and striving. We were never taught that life itself is happiness—not things or other people.

An old theme from Christianity teaches us that life is suffering. The idea of suffering was introduced when Emperor Constantine made sweeping changes to the words and meaning of Jesus' original message. To tell his followers that they were to expect suffering was one way to discourage the masses from seeking any individual power of their own. The church leaders wanted to consolidate all their power among themselves and leave the masses with fear and the expectation of suffering as a way of life.

We were taught to trust in things outside ourselves, to trust God to know what was best for us, to trust that life was not necessarily meant to be enjoyed. Love, on the other hand, doesn't ask us to give up the power for our lives or admit wrongs, defeats, or shortcomings. Dr. Wayne Dyer has an excellent discussion in his book *Your Erroneous Zones* in which he describes how by attempting to forcefully change a behavior by focusing on the negative part of it, we weaken ourselves. The trick is to focus on our strengths, our power, and our inherent wholeness, our divinity.

Love tells us that we can have happiness just by being true to who we are and by honoring our path. Love puts no prerequisites on our happiness. If we are here on earth, alive, that's good enough for love.

The road of love is truly the joyful road. As we clear away our old garbage, life begins to take on a pleasure and meaningfulness we didn't really anticipate. Every moment offers us the opportunity to choose love or fear. To choose love often takes a great deal more courage; however, the payoffs are enormous.

The Universe is filled with so much abundance. We need only get in touch with our souls, heal our addictions, and begin to receive some of this abundance for ourselves.

Our inner messages of guilt, shame, blame, abandonment, unworthiness, etc., which all stem from fear, keep us from our true birthright, which is zestful, happy, aliveness every day.

As we heal our negative beliefs, we learn that we really are okay just the way we are and that we are good enough just the way we are. We become able to let life be our canvas and we start painting it exclusively as we see fit.

23

Looking Within

I WAS GOING THROUGH some old notes recently and ran across a statement I had written toward the end of a year devoted to finding my spiritual path. It read: "Each man (or woman) must find the truth that is right for him (or her). I don't believe there is a specific kind of knowledge one must adopt to be able to find their good within."

Thinking back, I remembered why I wrote this. I had just spent a great deal of time and energy trying to find some sort of external guidance or belief system that really worked for me on all levels. I had discovered that Christianity did not give me the sense of personal empowerment I was seeking. It helped me in some ways but felt rigid and forced in others. I used A.A. as my spiritual guide for a while but ran into the same shortcomings as I had with Christianity. I had to find a way to connect with a power *within* me, not external to me.

Many practitioners of Eastern religions, as well as many New Age devotees, use meditation as a primary way in which to connect with their inner wisdom. I meditated for a while and did enjoy many benefits; however, I still felt resistance to being told I *had* to meditate in order to connect within. It felt like another limited belief, another must that said, "In order to find your inner self you *must* experience the silence within." I wanted to be able to gain access to my inner wisdom without having to be dependent on an outer ritual in order to do so. My intuition was telling me that what I desired was possible.

Many religions, along with many facets of the human potential movement, make it seem as if it is going to require rigorous devotion and practice in order to connect with our Higher Selves. However, I had the distinct inner impression that this was a bit like a fish looking for water while all the time he was floating and breathing in it. That is the way we are. We exist, live, and breathe in the very divine essence that so many people are ardently searching for. The trick is to give up the search and just bask in our own divineness and the divineness of others. It is all around us; we simply have to have the intention to see it.

However, I had yet to discover this simplicity, so I kept searching. I read a slew of self-help books, personal growth books, went to workshops, attended creativity groups and meditation groups. From each of these, I came away with a few more pearls of wisdom and a few more convictions of what did and did not feel right for me.

The answer slowly and surely began to dawn on me. An analogy that sums it up for me is to view life as a Baskin-Robbins store. There are thirty-two different flavors of ice cream, six or seven different kinds of yogurt, including soft-serve, low-fat, lite, and sugar-free. There are a dozen or so different dry toppings and a dozen or so wet toppings. There are cups, cones, shakes, and a host of splits, delights, parfaits, and special-order cakes. You can have whatever flavor, topping, serving size, or specialty order that you desire. Have a little of this and a little of that if you please. Get a cup of mint julep and pecan praline with hot fudge topping and nuts, or a simple scoop of vanilla in a cone. As you go out the door, no one is going to judge your order and make assumptions about your character based on the ice cream you prefer.

Life offers us infinitely more varieties than a Baskin-Robbins store. We should all feel free to take what works for us and leave the rest. Many of the books I read advised me to do just that and, consequently, they were the books that had the greatest impact on me. No one should judge others because of their beliefs, and we also shouldn't force others to see things as we see them. Our experiences, needs, and personalities are all infinitely different, and life is accommodating enough and the world big enough that we can each find what works best for us.

Some may find that a great deal of structure works best for them, particularly those who had no structure growing up. Others may need to make up their belief systems as they go along. Today's world is more accommodating, more open to variety than it has ever been. In fact, I recently saw a clip on *The Today Show* about a 600-year-old play in Great Britain that now features a woman playing the role of God (to the dismay of more than a few old-timers who prefer the traditional male God).

Booksellers' shelves are bulging with all sorts of books that cover everything from past-life regression therapy to body work to tarot cards to Buddhism to Native American practices, etc. One of the largest sections at the Barnes & Noble bookstores is the self-help section. This bookstore also carries a good number of New Age books. Twenty years ago bookstores were much different, much more middle-of-the-road. However, the bookstores of today are simply reflecting the needs of society. We are all searching for meaning, searching for a connection.

To look within means to connect with our Higher Selves. And the best way to connect with your Higher Self is to let your intuition guide you, hold love as your intention, and be open to whatever comes your way. Life is a very personal, very unique journey for each and every person. Even in families, where the basic structure is the same, each individual's needs can vary greatly. Let life be your guide. Believe that the Universe supports you. Try to recognize when you are operating out of fear and when you are operating out of love and check to see if that feels okay with you.

As you open up to life, your instincts and intuition will grow stronger and you will feel more confident and will experience less indecision. You will know when something doesn't feel right for you and you'll be able to say, "No, this isn't right for me." Standing up for your own needs will give others the courage to do so for themselves.

Our inner life seeks to work with us and wants desperately for us to search within and connect. A quote from John Fischer in Peter McWilliams's book *Life 101* says it well: "The essence of our effort to see that every [person] has a chance must be to assure each an equal opportunity, not to become equal, but to become different—to realize whatever unique potential of body, mind and spirit he or she possesses."

We heal our addictions as we heal ourselves when we honor our soul's journey. To look within and use your thoughts, feelings, hunches, and desires as your guide will do much to heal your soul, heal your pain, and heal your addiction, even if your intuition seems to be guiding you in the opposite direction for a short while. Allow yourself to do that which you really want to do. I remember that in the beginning of my journey I just wanted to sit in a bookstore all day and not work at all. I couldn't see how this would ever contribute to my finding a way to make a living, but I did know that my soul was starved and that I had to do something to honor myself or I would use again. All the meetings in the world couldn't do for me what following my heart did.

As long as we view addiction as a disease to be overcome, we won't stop to hear the message the addiction has for us. We need to allow our addiction and the pain it covers up to be heard. Go within and seek your answers in the way that feels right for you. You can heal completely and you will find yourself filled with life and purpose and fulfillment. Living a purposeful life frees you from the cycle of cravings, binges, remorse, and more cravings.

24

Prayer and Letting Go

"LET GO AND LET GOD." Many of us are all too familiar with this slogan. It's plastered on A.A. meeting room walls across the country. But what does it imply, and what does letting go really mean?

The A.A. version of "let go and let God" implies a passive letting go and turning everything over to God, including our power to take action. A more functional and empowering version of letting go entails a proactive approach. Letting go in this way means doing as much as you physically can and then letting your Higher Self take you the rest of the way. It is a surrender only after the initial willingness and work has been done on our part to start the process in motion. We then let go to allow the process take us where it will.

Letting go also means suspending judgment of how our good will come to us. As Charlotte Kasl describes it in her engaging book *Many Roads, One Journey*:

> My image is of a cooperative union between the power of the Universe and my own will. I ask for the Universe to energize my will. Instead of praying for God to take care of me, I ask for the strength to take action . . . The power of the Universe is everywhere, in all living things. It's not "out there."

And in her description of letting our good come to us in its own way, she writes ". . . while we can take action, ultimately we can't tell a gift how to come."

Letting go and letting God in A.A. implies that we pray to an external God to change or to help us tolerate a person, place, or thing and we then surrender ourselves to His will and assume our position of powerlessness from there on out.

I agree that letting go involves prayer; however, I tend to view prayer as Ms. Kasl does: "I ask for the strength to take action" and "a cooperative union between the power of the Universe and my own will." Napoleon Hill in *Grow Rich with Peace of Mind* echoes this theme:

> Prayer . . . is to be based on a real need for help to accomplish something of constructive value. In true prayer one asks for help only after he has proved, *by his own efforts*, that his own powers are not sufficient to enable him to accomplish his purpose. The person who prays *should not assume* he gives over his own individual freedom of action, but rather should know he is to co-operate with the helping agencies he cannot see [emphases mine].

Therefore, letting go actually means working in conjunction with our Higher Selves and our unseen guides. (I believe we each have unseen spiritual guides who seek to help and assist us.) Letting go is not, then, a turning over of everything to an external God or Higher Power simply to seize the issue back again when we don't receive our answer the way we wanted to or the way we thought we would.

On the subject of how our good (or our answer) comes to us, remember that our intention for "the highest and best for all concerned" means that anything that comes to us can contain our good. Often our good comes to us wrapped up as a challenge or a problem just to see if we are paying attention. If we're thoughtful enough and patient enough, and willing to face the challenge or problem instead of running away, we will discover the treasure contained within. Norman Vincent Peale described it eloquently when he wrote about the tendency of life to wrap up its most precious and beloved gifts in the middle of a problem or challenge. Meeting the challenge head-on and solving the problem with love and patience allows us to discover the wonderful, beautiful gift waiting for us inside. If we view everything in terms of good or bad, then we don't allow the true light of love to emerge from seemingly horrible, negative situations.

It is especially important in the beginning to let go of how our good comes to us. From the time when we first state our intention to heal, one by one (or all at once) our negativities and fears will emerge from the depths in order to be recognized and healed. When I first became serious about my own healing, I had so many positive intentions and so many positive experiences occurring in my life. But I also noticed a lot of negative emotions, such as judgment, fear, and intolerance, coming up that I thought I had already overcome. Actually, I had just buried these emotions instead of dealing with them. Now they were rising to the surface, in order to be healed. I dealt with each one as it came up by first accepting it as a part of me and then worked on releasing it as a no longer necessary or desirable part of my life. If we can remain open and hold love in our hearts, we can allow the butterfly to emerge from within the cocoon of our fears. We will notice our negativities rising to the surface if we suddenly see that we are attracting the same situation over and over in our lives If we keep attracting angry people to us, we can be sure that we are holding anger within ourselves. Turning within to heal the anger will release the need for these angry people to show up in our lives.

Letting go means living in the present, free from the bondage of the past and free from worrying about the future. As long as we cling to our former misdeeds and continue to identify with them, we will remain chained to the past. Similarly, our fears about the future will send negative energy forth to achieve the very thing we fear happening. Fears about the future imply a lack of trust and faith in the Universe and in our ability to take care of ourselves. Clinging either to the past or to the future keeps us from enjoying and making the most of the present. The entire energy of the Universe is contained within this precise moment. We can use it well or we can squander it. Letting go allows us to receive the bounty the Universe and our Higher Selves are wanting to send us. Letting go allows the Universe to take care of the significant others in our lives and frees us to take care of ourselves. The best way to take care of others is to take care of ourselves first. If our cup is empty, it's impossible to give. We must first fill our cup, then we have something to give.

I often notice as I'm trying to work on a particular task that my mind is wandering to a million things: "I wonder what my husband meant this morning when he said he was so depressed. I should call him and make sure he's okay and make sure he doesn't need anything." . . . "I wonder if I should leave my son with a sitter while I work on this book." . . . "I wonder if I hurt my sister's feelings last night by what I said." . . . "I wonder what I'll fix for dinner tonight." . . . "I wonder how I'll pay for the new fax machine." My mind is so focused on taking care of things that I can't take care of the task at hand. This is a form of mental escape. I keep escaping from the present moment. It's as if I'm afraid of this moment, afraid that if I totally let myself go into this moment none of this other stuff will get taken care of. (But the truth is that all this stuff I was worrying about takes care of itself the minute I let go of it.)

Words themselves often offer insights into their deeper truth. The trick about the present moment is to view it as a great, big, unopened *present* that the Universe wants to hand us. Contained inside is a bountiful amount of beauty, joy, aliveness, love, peace, and bliss. But our fears see the present being offered us as a big, unknown risk. And we've discussed how fears despise the unknown and are frightened silly about risks. So fear is scared silly that this big, unopened present is filled with disappointment, pain, and suffering (because in our fear we reenact past disappointments over and over again until we heal them and release them).

So fear, in its infinite attempts to care for and protect us, distracts us from the present with trivial, fruitless concerns about the past or the future. When we allow fear to successfully distract us in this way, everyone loses. We lose because we miss out on the great, wonderful present the Universe created for us and the trivial things we're so preoccupied with lose because they aren't given the chance to take care of themselves. Love asks us not to be afraid of the present. For love knows that the present will never harm us. Love knows that the present will only bring us good and truth. As we awaken and let go into the present, the big, beautiful gift from the Universe unfolds and wraps itself around us with beauty, joy, wholeness, and love. Ask to be given the trust to relax into the present and let go.

25

Why I Fired My Sponsor

SPONSORSHIP IS a double-edged sword. In many cases, especially in the early stages of recovery in A.A., a sponsor is a very useful person. He can guide you and explain the steps while you are going through a very confusing and tough time. I remember the first time I stepped through the doors of an A.A. meeting. I had brought a friend along who also felt he had a problem with alcohol. After the meeting, everyone was very kind to us and gave each of us a Big Book to take home. I took it home and began reading it. I read the entire Big Book and was no closer to understanding what it was all about than when I had begun. It was a long time before I went to another meeting, but when I finally did, I stuck with it a bit longer. Long enough for someone to suggest I get a sponsor.

For many, the sponsor's assistance and guidance is critical in the beginning of recovery. A sponsor can explain the steps to you, answer your questions, calm your fears, and offer much needed encouragement and support. However, after early sobriety is achieved, the dependent bonds of sponsor-sponsoree are usually well formed. Many sponsorees do not allow their relationship with their sponsor to grow past the parent-child model into one of equal footing. The sponsor, in many cases, becomes more of a parent than is necessary. In telling the sponsoree *how the program works*, they often cross the line into telling the sponsoree *what to do*. You often see sponsors who will

187

require their sponsorees to attend a certain number of meetings a week and call them every single day. They virtually dictate every aspect of the sponsoree's recovery.

I've heard so many people describe with *pride* how they had a "Nazi sponsor" in the beginning who really laid down the law with them. Many recovering alcoholics and addicts seem to need this sort of dictatorial relationship. It helps them to not have to chart their own recovery, but to let someone else do it for them. However, I've never been able to tolerate someone telling me what I'm supposed to do, when I'm supposed to do it, and so on. I've always rebelled at the notion that I have to follow someone else's instructions to the letter or else. I prefer finding my own way, with a bit of useful "how-to" guidance, but according to my own timetable.

One of the main flaws in the sponsor-sponsoree relationship is that it many times does not encourage the sponsoree to find his own voice and his own wisdom. I can recall struggling with a particular issue regarding my then fiancé (my husband now), whom I loved dearly, and discussing it with my sponsor. In first building the relationship with this sponsor I had opened my heart to her and had shared my innermost secrets. I trusted her. On the occasion when I was struggling with the issue between my fiancé and me, my sponsor told me that she had given it much thought, and had heard me share many times before about our struggles, and that she really didn't feel he was the right guy for me; she went on to question why I would even want to marry him. I was appalled. I was hurt, and I was never able to trust her again. In my opinion she had overstepped the bounds by deciding what was or wasn't right for *my* life. It's one thing to offer useful advice and empathy regarding recovery; to tell me what to do with my life was another matter altogether. And especially to hand down such a scathing judgment on a relationship (my fiancé's and mine) that meant so much to me. Because I looked up to her (which was my choice and my responsibility), I was crushed. I was merely seeking assistance in how to work through some issues with my fiancé. To flat out tell me that in her opinion he wasn't the right one for me was the end of our sponsor-sponsoree relationship. I had to take responsibility for having let the thing go too far. I had put her in the role of adviser but had also willingly turned my power over to her. This was apparent in that she felt she could decide what was and wasn't right regarding a decision as personal and important as who I planned to spend my life with. In the beginning of the sponsorship, I needed a good deal of validation and support and compassion. Having someone there for me whom I could always count on was very important and helped a great deal.

However, there is no encouragement in A.A. for the sponsorship to come to a conclusion. Sponsorees fall into a childlike relationship with the sponsor as the parent in the beginning of the relationship and it continues along these limited lines for months and even years. It doesn't develop into a more equitable arrangement.

A healthier way would be for sponsors to encourage sponsorees to find their own voices and become the authority and strength for their own lives. This would include a mutual agreement to bring the role of sponsor-sponsoree to a close and move the relationship into one of friendship and equality.

Unfortunately, many sponsorship relationships are co-dependent. The sponsoree becomes afraid to make any major moves without the counsel and approval of the sponsor. The relationship thus stays mired in fear and dependence, similar to the way in which many members of twelve-step models are stuck in fear and dependence.

Or the sponsoree continually seeks external validation for every move he makes. This is especially detrimental because one of the symptoms of addiction is continually seeking outside ourselves for direction and fulfillment. So to mask the addiction behind the pseudo-guise of sobriety has not really cured the addiction if the addict has simply shifted his behavior to that of a co-dependent.

Truly healthy relationships are those in which each person is encouraged to think for himself, to become the creator of his own destiny by following his heart, and is allowed the full expression of himself.

Co-dependent, fearful relationships are those in which one person is continually seeking to please the other, often at the expense of his or her own personal development.

If you have achieved sobriety, and no longer need the direction of a sponsor, it is time to think about firing your sponsor. Perhaps the best way to do this is simply to be open and honest about your need to become your own counsel and your own authority. Express gratitude, if indicated, for the sponsor having been there for you, and request that you now both simply have an equitable friendship based on each person honoring the other's path, whatever it may be.

It is very difficult to truly find your own path within the confines of a sponsorship relationship. Validation for honoring your own path is really not part of the deal. The whole idea is that the sponsor knows better than the sponsoree. So, of course the sponsor will encourage the sponsoree to follow the path that worked best for him, whether or not it is appropriate for the sponsoree.

Suppose the sponsor is one who in the beginning of his program, when he was a sponsoree, needed a lot of firm direction and a no-nonsense "Nazi sponsor" to tell him his every move, right down to how many meetings he was expected to attend. A sponsor who received this type of treatment as a sponsoree is very likely to repeat the same process with all of his new sponsorees. He may, however, have a sponsoree who has never been encouraged to find her own voice, who has always done things to please others at the expense of her self-esteem, and who needs lots of room to find what works best for her instead of being told what to do. The sponsorship relationship in this case is likely to be more harmful than helpful. Without regard to what is best for each individual, personal growth and true healing are thwarted.

I will concede that in the first phases of alcohol or other addiction withdrawal a person is not always capable of knowing what to do and what is best for him. Here is where sponsorship is truly helpful. It is a beacon of light for many who cannot think very clearly yet and are confused about how the program works. A good sponsor can show you the ropes and answer your questions. He doesn't, however, ever need to *tell* you what to do. Part of the reason many of us remain addicts for so long is that we've never really grown up. And many sponsorship relationships simply echo the twelve-step, parent-child theme. The implication is that the sponsor (or the program) knows best, and the sponsoree would be wise to heed that fact.

A healthy sponsor is simply someone who is there in the beginning and answers questions and explains the meaning of the steps and how they work. Beyond that, a sponsor does not know what is best for each individual. True healing and true empowerment only come when we are willing to take full responsibility for our lives, our decisions, and the urgings of our souls. No one but me can know where my heart is leading me and what path is truly right for me.

Part Four

The Seven Components of My Freedom

26

Healing My Pain

AUTHOR CLARK VAUGHAN WRITES in his book *Addictive Drinking,* "I discovered that I drank for very real reasons and until I healed those reasons, I would continue to drink addictively." A Harvard Medical School conference speaker on addiction said, "Once we can find out what needs the drinking satisfies, then we can eventually help people find something to replace it with." And psychologist Caroline Myss writes in her new book, *Anatomy of the Spirit,* "healing begins with the repair of emotional injuries."

Wise words. But at the time I was trying to chart my own course of healing, I didn't have any of these pearls of wisdom to assist me. I was sort of drifting out there without a rudder, trying to steer a course through cravings and feelings and confusion. But as I allowed myself to attend fewer and fewer twelve-step meetings in order to get a real handle on my addiction, I began to feel the increasingly familiar tug from my intuition.

"Do what feels right to you, Marianne," the small voice seemed to say. Not knowing what was right for me, I started working with the things that *didn't* feel right to me to see if I could get a clue as to what *was* right for me. Being told to take a moral inventory that included only my moral *wrongs,* to take a good, hard look at my character defects, to pray to have these shortcomings removed—how did these things really make me feel? Like a failure, a jerk, guilty, ashamed. But this was the way to heal my addictions, right?, or so I was told. Because doing the moral inventory and focusing on my character defects made me feel even worse, I asked others how they felt after doing their fifth step (reading their inventory to another person). *All* of them, without exception, stated how wonderful, how relieved, and how unburdened they felt afterward. Me, I just felt as if it were a continuation of the "you are a failure, you are nothing" theme I had been berating myself with for years. But because I was willing to do whatever I needed to do in order to get sober and abstinent, I went along with the program. I had heard it said enough times in A.A. that "We were never helped until we were entirely ready to do *whatever* we were told." Sounds a bit cultish, but okay, I'm game, I thought at the time.

But it didn't work for me and I could no longer continue doing what felt wrong. As my twelve-step attendance started dropping off, the first thing I felt was wrong with the program was its focus on moral wrongs and defects of character. Could someone perhaps help me become a better person without focusing on my wrongs? I wondered. Becoming a better person by focusing on my wrongs seemed a bit like hitting a child because he hits his little sister. It inadvertently perpetuated the problem by sending a mixed message. The way to become a better person would naturally involve focusing on what was right about me, I brilliantly concluded.

Okay, now that I've got the initial barrier to my recovery (focusing on my wrongs) out of the way, where do I go from here? If I were to truly get to the core of why I drank and abused substances, I would have to look past the disease model of addiction as well. It seemed to me that the disease model, by placing the entire responsibility for my behavior on my disease and my powerlessness over my disease, encouraged me to look no farther, to not look for any real reasons beyond the fact that I had a disease. It led me to believe that emotional problems, injuries, and pain were *because* of my addiction, not a *cause* of it.

It's interesting to me that so many of the authors I read today who write about addiction agree that we drink for reasons—escape, fulfillment, etc.—that go beyond those which the disease theory espouses.

So, out goes the disease theory, along with the belief that I'm powerless. The powerlessness concept goes hand in hand with the disease theory and served only to weaken me, not strengthen me. So out it went. Now I've gotten three things out of the way—the need to focus on moral wrongs and defects of character, the disease theory, and the belief in powerlessness over my behavior. I was really getting somewhere now. My intuition was right. Getting rid of what didn't work was really clearing the field to help me see what could work.

All these great insights were occurring in my life during the period after I had broken off my engagement to my fiancé in order to live on my own and "find myself." I think it is no coincidence that I was receiving more clarity and insights than ever before. At this point in my life, healing myself was my primary focus. When I first moved out on my own, away from Bill, my fiancé, my first book, *Selling to America*, had already been published and I had already begun receiving requests from overseas to do market research consulting work. Because the apartment I moved to was too small to accommodate an office, I started out working on the floor, with my computer keyboard in my lap and papers strewn all around me. When a friend offered to share her office space with me, I no longer had to work on the floor. Although the consulting work was important to me, my healing was my primary concern. But working for myself was great in that it offered me lots of opportunities to further explore myself, my real feelings about myself, and whether I had what it took to follow my dreams. I was realizing that although working for myself had always been a dream of mine, the outlet I had chosen may have been dictated more by my desire to please my father and my fiancé than something *I* really wanted. It was such draining work. I wanted so badly to do something that felt inspirational, that motivated me, challenged me, and recharged me.

The very fact that I used to take entire mornings off to sit in Barnes & Noble with a stack of self-help books was very telling, as was the fact that a whole day of doing my consulting work made me want to binge on food when I got back to my apartment at night. What was going on? Why was my work so painful? Why did I resist it so much and have to force myself to do it? And why was my favorite thing to do in the whole world to read book after book on self-improvement, healing, and personal growth? There seemed to be some things I loved to do and other things that were such drudgery. Having the complete freedom to examine the why behind all this for the first time in my life, I began to do so.

One reason consulting work was so hard for me, and one I resisted so much, was because it was where I had placed all the definitions of myself, along with all of my expectations, my father's expectations, and Bill's expectations, whether these were really their expectations or not. For all I knew, my father would have been just as happy with me if I had pursued a career in acting. But because his expectations of me from twelve years of age on had been about business, I had come to define myself with the same limiting parameters, to the point where I no longer knew where his expectations stopped and mine began. They were all the same now. I had internalized them and made them my own. When I got into my relationship with Bill, I naturally assumed *he* wanted me to be successful in business as well. So there was a lot riding on whether or not my consulting business was successful. If it failed, it meant *I* was a failure. The stakes were high.

No wonder it felt so draining. For one thing, the work wasn't really me. It didn't harmonize with me, although I felt that it should. After all, I had spent four years of college studying business, and two more years of graduate school getting a master's degree in business. By God, business was what I knew and what I wanted, I told myself, not knowing that inside me was a small voice aching to be heard, and a heart that longed to be tended to. But I couldn't just stop working; I had to support myself. So I worked hours that were reasonable to me, even if that meant only four hours a day because that was all I could stand, and I allowed myself the time my soul was crying out for.

Standing in the place I am now, with complete freedom from my addictions, I see so clearly how everything then was playing itself out, but at the time, much of the underlying motivation for my behavior was not really known to me. I was simply responding to what felt right to me and trying to honor that for the first time.

On the days when work was particularly draining, I felt like binge-ing on food at night. Alcohol was no longer a desire of mine, and hadn't been for years. I had even quit smoking the same week I moved out of the house I had shared with Bill. Food was the only addiction that had any appeal for me. I had by now given up completely on Overeaters Anonymous meetings being able to help me, so I was utterly on my own. The only real friends I had at the time, except for the woman I shared office space with, and my sister, were the friends I had made in A.A. And even though I no longer attended A.A. meetings either, these people remained with me. But I didn't express to them what I was going through. In fact, none of them even knew of my bulimia. So my support network as regarded my recovery consisted of me and me alone. Was I up to the task? I felt instinctively that I was and felt exhilarated by the prospect of getting to do things my way in *every* area of my life.

So back to my healing. Why did I feel like bingeing at the end of a hard day at work? The answer, as it revealed itself later, was due to the fact that although living on my own, I was still living for others. I still felt deep down as if I were less than, a nothing, and I was unable to honor my own desires without experiencing overwhelming guilt and shame. But I didn't know all this then, I just felt an inner ache, an emptiness, and longed to both escape from it and at the same time fill it. So I binged.

But for the first time in my life, I did it consciously. I was learning all about how to live in a love-based way from all the reading I was doing, and I was beginning to get in touch with my real feelings about myself. Why did I continually feel that I had to prove myself to others? I asked, and found that by succeeding I would prove to myself and others that I was worthy. The low self-esteem I had been struggling to overcome my whole life was finally rising up from the depths of my subconscious, where I had buried it long before in order to be done with it once and for all. And my desire to binge was partly due to this—I didn't want to deal with it.

I began looking back. I had been giving myself messages of unworthiness and guilt all of my life. I was always looking to what was lacking in my life, to what others had that I didn't have. As I tried to get what others had, and continually fell short of the mark, I concluded that I must simply be unworthy of having these good things and, therefore, that I was somehow guilty. After years of putting myself down, I eventually felt unworthy of having anything good happen to me; and when it did, I felt guilty about it and unable to accept it. My whole life I had never felt lovable for just being me. I was still seeking approval, like a little child from a father who wasn't there for her emotionally and would only love her if she lived up to his expectations of her.

I also saw that I had a lifetime issue of shame. I was pudgy as a child, and felt shame about that. I wasn't the perfect child the way my older sister was. I was promiscuous in high school because of both my shame about myself and my longing for love and affection. And my bulimia was born out of my shame. Having bulimia was by far the most shameful secret I had ever carried. Early in our relationship I told Bill about it because I felt he had a right to know. But for years I told no one else. In fact, it wasn't until my sister, one of my closest friends for years, asked to read a copy of this manuscript that I finally told her about it. She was naturally hurt that I hadn't told her years before, and wanted to know why. Because I was ashamed, was all I could say. It had nothing to do with whether or not she would have understood because she undoubtedly would have. It was me. *I* was ashamed.

So these were my "emotional injuries," as psychologist Myss terms it, the reasons for my addictive behavior, the "needs the drinking satisfies." My painful negative beliefs about myself. My feelings of being a failure, wanting to prove I was somebody, feeling like a nobody, wanting to feel special, being told I needed to be humble. Unworthiness. Guilt. Shame. The three bugaboos. My Achilles' heel.

The fuel that fanned my addictive flames. The repressed feelings I had sought to escape my whole life.

Could I now face them, with courage, and with faith, and with love? It felt as if I would be consumed whole if I really faced these inner demons. "What if they were right?" fear said to me. "You'll discover the truth about yourself and you'll be crushed for life," fear tried to convince me. But that was just more of what I had been telling myself my whole life. If we just do more of the same, we'll get the same results, I remembered hearing. A small, almost unrecognizable voice said, "Trust me. You do have what it takes, Marianne. You've wanted to believe it your whole life. Now is the time to put your money where your mouth is. We'll be there for you." Love took my hand, saying, "I'll lead the way."

HEALING

One morning I rose up off the bed, which was actually more like a mattress on the floor in this small and cramped apartment I had rented, and asked myself, What today? Do I drive to the office to do more of what I hate? Can I be kind to myself today? What if I do a little of what I don't want to do (work) and a little of what I do want to do (Barnes & Noble, cappuccino)? Slowly, I was learning to be gentle with myself, to stop my senseless pattern of categorizing everything in my life by such extremes—I hate this, I love that. I was trying to find healthy balances now, and I was starting to feel better.

A large painting of water lilies that the apartment owner's mother had painted hung on the wall across from the bed. It's interesting when I look back on it now that at night when I went to sleep on the mattress on the floor, with all the lights out, and only the lights from the city shining in the room, the painting changed, because all you could see were shadows. Instead of water lilies, there was a very distinct portrait of a woman, a very graceful, peaceful-looking woman with her eyes closed and a look of complete serenity on her face. The whole image was of only her face. But the look was of such peace and grace. When I first noticed it, it scared me a little. But eventually I grew to see it as sort of a sign that I was being watched over. The face came to symbolize an angel's presence watching over me, praying for me, and protecting me. I later told the owner about her mother's painting and asked if she had ever seen a woman's face in it at night when all the lights were out. No, she said, and she thought it a little strange that I could. Yet before she began renting her apartment, she had slept in that *same* fold-out bed with the mattress that rested on the floor and looked at that same painting *for twelve years* without ever seeing the image that was so clear to me. It's my guardian angel, I concluded. I'm being watched over and guided. Love was guiding me, healing me.

Now that I knew what my three main negative beliefs about myself were—unworthiness, guilt, and shame—and now that I knew what didn't work, the next step was to discover what *did* work for me and then do it. I knew at this point that to delay facing the inevitable would just mean more food binges and more unhappiness. This is where all the reading I had been doing, and my guardian angel, really came in handy. As it turned out, all my endless hours spent at the bookstore were now beginning to pay off.

The first thing I had to do in order to heal my feelings of shame, guilt, and unworthiness was to allow myself to feel them, really feel them. I had unknowingly been running from them all of my life, and thus implicitly validating them. Every time I ran away from dealing with them by using addictively, I sent a message to myself that said I truly was guilty and worthless and shameful. Now was the time to use everything my experiences had been trying to tell me about what I *really* needed to allow healing to occur.

When I finally did allow myself to feel these feelings of guilt, unworthiness, and shame, I resisted very strongly at first. "But I'm *not* guilty, I just got taught that by people who didn't know any better themselves," I thought. "I'm a child of God, I don't need to feel ashamed. That was just an erroneous message." That's when it all clicked into place for me.

My inner messages of shame, guilt, and unworthiness were all

ERRONEOUS! It was simply my fear that they were really true that caused them to manifest as reality for me. I began to recognize that I really was a child of God. I really was special. If not in anyone else's eyes, I could learn to be special *in my own eyes*. By fearfully running away from myself all of my life, I had disconnected myself from the very divinity I carried within me. And it was my desire to heal my negative beliefs that bridged the gap between my fearful feelings of guilt and my inherent beauty, wisdom, and wholeness.

I had never realized this simple truth before because I had implicitly believed that my negative beliefs were the truth. I hadn't *wanted* them to be true, but my addictive episodes seemed to indicate that they were true. And A.A. reinforced the message that my horrible deeds needed to be rehashed again, as if my deeds had anything to do with my worth as a person, and that I needed to be humbled instead of always striving to feel special. So it was no wonder I had never questioned these inner beliefs about myself. To do so would have meant not only questioning the very foundation of my belief system, but the authority of A.A., the authority of my church, and all of my influences growing up.

But love gave me the courage to stop denying my *real* feelings and to allow the spark of my divinity to begin showing through the darkness of my negative beliefs. As I saw that all these beliefs I had been carrying around for a lifetime were erroneous, I was freed. Freed to create whatever beliefs I wanted. Freed to discover my real beauty. Freed from the bondage of escaping from myself with addictive behavior. And freed to accept myself just as I was, without having to prove my worth to anybody.

Acceptance and love is that bridge that takes us from where we are to where we want to be. Ever since I was a child I had wanted to believe that I was worthy of love regardless of anything I did, said, looked like, or felt like. I was now beginning to discover that God doesn't put any conditions on our acceptance of ourselves. We do.

The next step was to focus on what was *right* about me. As I focused on what was right about me, I discovered that I was a very valuable person after all. And as I nurtured these new feelings of "rightness," I became less fearful of examining the painful negative beliefs I had about myself. I saw that I was lovable and worthwhile whether I was "being productive," whether I was bingeing and purging, or whether I was meditating and exercising. My external behavior had nothing to do with my internal worth. It had taken so much to discover that. I wish we had all been taught that truth as children.

Ask your intuition for guidance on how to speed up your process of healing, ask to be led to the methods that will work the best for you, and be open to whatever comes your way. Some use writing in journals, others write letters to various parts of themselves. One recommended method is to write affirmations. Do what feels right and empowering for you. Allow yourself all the time you need. The struggle will eventually lessen until you have completely healed the inner message and transformed it into a message of love, joy, power, and wholeness.

I had to return again and again to release and change these messages. I had been giving them validation for years, so it is no wonder that it took more than one day to replace them. Once you have identified your core messages, though, you will more readily be able to recognize them when they show up in your life. You can then respond to them with love instead of fear, acceptance instead of avoidance.

A word of caution here. One of the tendencies I saw in A.A. was to forever be working on yourself and your problems. A friend still discusses her abandonment issues with the same fervor she did seven years ago. She still allows her pain to have power over her instead of the other way around. "We need to get over our pain, not market it," as psychologist Caroline Myss writes. She has a great example of this in her book *Anatomy of the Spirit*.

> She was thoroughly entrenched in her wounds, so much so that she converted her wounds (incest) into a type of social currency. She felt she was owed certain privileges because of her painful childhood: the privilege of being able to call in sick at work whenever she needed to "process" a memory; financial support from her father

because of what he did to her; and endless emotional support from all her "friends." True friends, according to Mary, were people who understood her crisis and took over her responsibilities for her whenever they became too much for her.

I believe that we can all become stuck in the "I'm in recovery" phase and not recognize that the bulk of our healing needs to take place with us as active participants and then be completed. We don't need to advertise our "dysfunction" in order to feel valued or pitied. Nor do we need to work on healing our issues for the remainder of our lives. Again, Charlotte Kasl, in *Many Roads, One Journey*, writes of "recovery narcissism," in which people become obsessed with recovery perfection, ridding themselves of character defects and shortcomings, and constantly analyzing their behavior.

We need to do the important healing work on ourselves and then get back to living our lives. I would much prefer spending the rest of my life trying to grow personally and spiritually than forever be "working on my stuff." Life is for the living. Heal and get back in the ball game.

My life was beginning to be filled with incredible joy in so many ways as I healed these painful negative beliefs that had been haunting me my entire life. The air seemed to be sweeter, songs on the radio seemed more inspiring, I looked forward to my days in ways I never had before. My relationship with my significant other was now moving into a new phase, a healthy phase, as we stopped blaming each other and as I stopped trying to live up to the expectations I had imposed on myself. The guardian angel over my bed seemed less like a silly notion and more like a true manifestation of spirit in my life. And the next step on my journey of healing was unfolding, which is honoring intuition.

27

Honoring Intuition

~~~~ HOW DOES OUR HIGHEST GOOD come to us? How are we supposed to know what is best for us and what isn't? If listening to the voice of fear is not the answer, and using rigid models of behavior is not the answer, then what is? Learning to live by your own internal authority is the second step to complete freedom. And we have a built-in guidance system at our disposal. It's called our intuition.

"What does honoring intuition have to do with healing from addiction?" I asked the program speaker at a workshop on healing I attended in Atlanta. "One reason our intuition is so useful in helping us to heal from addiction is because our suppression of it, and our disconnection from our own wisdom and power as provided to us through intuition, is one of the contributing factors in addiction," the speaker responded.

When we lose touch with our intuition, we lose touch with a very important part of ourselves, that part of ourselves that knows precisely what is right and wise for us personally. Intuition is like a unique, completely customized guidance system which, when used properly, can steer us through the roughest of waters.

Much of my addictive behavior was a result of my having denied my intuition and my inner power. As Dr. Wayne Dyer says: "If prayer is you talking to God, then intuition is God talking to you." I had been ignoring this wise part of me for long enough. I felt so relieved as I gave myself permission to step away from everything everyone else had taught me and begin listening to "the heartbeat of my soul," as author Rosemary Altea wisely describes it in *The Eagle & the Rose*.

It turns out that my intuition knows far more about me and what is right for me than institutions and organizations and people outside myself. These programs could point the way for me. But long-term personal growth must include the encouragement to think for yourself, establish your own workable belief system, and operate from love instead of fear (fear of using again, fear of painful feelings, fear of others, fear of ourselves, fear of life letting us down, etc.). And as I saw how my pattern of always seeking answers outside myself was part of my problem, I was even able to attend twelve-step meetings occasionally and enjoy the *people* rather than judge or blame the program. There are many people who through A.A. and other twelve-step groups find their first taste of true spirituality and I encourage them to follow this program if it is what feels right. However, what felt right for me was to follow my own path and begin to establish a relationship with my intuition, which is a direct link to my God within.

CONNECTING WITH INTUITION

When man roamed the land many eons ago, he had a vastly developed intuition. He had no society imposing strict guidelines on what he was supposed to do and how he was supposed to act. Early man sought food when he was hungry, fought when he was attacked, copulated when he was so inclined, and slept when he was tired. Of course, his instincts were only concerned with basic survival. Our world is far more complex, we are much more evolved and have a vastly different standard of living. But since mankind arose from the basic survival stages of early years, we have been building more and more elaborate systems of behavior with which we expect people to conform. Much of this has a positive intention. With so many people on the planet today, it is essential to have standards of conduct for individuals or people will just run amok. But one look at a newspaper today will tell you that people are running amok anyway. And this is at least partly due to the rigidity of our governments and institutions. The more we attempt to impose rigid rules of conduct on people without regard for their individuality, the more violent will be their response when they finally break free.

Addiction is one result of what happens when we allow our own voice to be stampeded by the voices of control. We don't always need society to impose its rigid and demanding expectations on us. Many times, we'll do it to ourselves. Whenever we get too far away from our own inner voices, we will be denying a very important part of ourselves, a part of us that offers wisdom, insight, and helpful assistance. Stifling our intuition in many cases causes us to act addictively. The pain of denying or ignoring this important and vital aspect of ourselves is overwhelming.

Reconnecting with our intuition takes a good deal of practice at first. Probably the first tendency we have is to follow any little gut instinct that arises, with possible horrible results. I find that I may jump the gun and wind up acting on secret desires instead of true intuitive feelings. So how does one distinguish between secret desires and true intuitive feelings? The quickest way is through experience. When you feel a gut instinct, which you recognize as either a secret desire or a true intuitive feeling, follow it. See where it leads. The answer will become clear. And as you experiment more and more, you will become much more attuned to your real intuition and will easily be able to hear it when it speaks.

It helps to keep in mind that your intuition is your Higher Self acting through you. It is how our Higher Self, our God within, speaks to us most often. As a wise old sage once told me, intuition is our direct link to God. Your Higher Self would never lead you to harm another. This is a good guideline when trying to sort through true intuitive feelings and secret desires. For instance, you may dislike your husband, and with your newly confident self, decide that because of your dislike, your intuition must be guiding you to divorce him.

However, what you are not aware of is that he is simply a projection of all the disowned parts of yourself that you refuse to accept. Therefore, your divorcing him would only cause these same disowned parts of you to show up with the next guy, or perhaps in your career, or at the worst, with your children.

Intuition knows that love heals. Intuition wants to guide you to your highest good with love and acceptance as your assistants. The voice within us is the wisest voice we have, yet our whole society is geared toward listening to the voices of others. From early on we are taught to listen to our parents, then our teachers, then, as we grow up, our governments and our religions; even big business wants to guide us in how to think as they seduce us with their ads. Taken to an extreme, we are even supposed to believe that tobacco doesn't cause cancer and that nicotine isn't addictive, or so the tobacco industry has told us.

The world we live in today places great value on logic and man's use of his rational mind. It is no wonder we have denied and lost touch with our intuition. As author Shakti Gawain writes in *Living in the Light:* "Our rational mind can only operate on the basis of the direct experience each of us has had in this lifetime. The intuitive mind, on the other hand, seems to have access to an infinite supply of information. It is also able to sort out this information and supply us with exactly what we need, when we need it."

If we combine the power of our intellect, our rational mind, with the wisdom of our intuition, we create a guidance system that will take us directly into higher states of awareness and an expanded way of living.

It is the combination of these two elements, our intellect and out intuition, that works best. However, in the beginning it is necessary to recognize that you will probably have a tendency to override any incoming intuitions with the use of the rational mind. Lacking the faith that the gut instincts you feel will actually lead to your highest good, you will fearfully come up with rationalizations to oppose the intuition. Recognize these defenses simply as fear's way of keeping you from venturing into the unknown. The only way to ever begin to trust that your intuitions are leading to your highest good is to act on them. As you begin to see how correct your intuition is, you will have greater faith in following its course in more areas of your life. You can be certain that there will be times when your intuitions will go directly against acting in ways taught to you by churches, family members, old belief systems, and other external forces. On intuition, Shakti Gawain writes:

> You might say, "Intuition, tell me what I need to know here. What do I need to do in this situation?" Trust the feeling that you get and act on it. If it is truly your intuition, you will find that it leads to a feeling of greater aliveness and power, and more opportunities begin to open up for you. If it doesn't seem right, you may not have been truly acting from your intuition but from some ego voice in you. Go back and ask for clarification. . . . As you grow more sensitive to this guidance from the intuitive feelings within, you will gain a sense of knowing what you need to do in any situation. Your intuitive power is always available to guide you whenever you need it. It will open to you as soon as you are willing to trust yourself and your inner knowledge.

In the bestselling book *The Aladdin Factor,* by Jack Canfield and Mark V. Hansen, contributor John Prieskorn gives a good example of how he honors his intuition:

> I was going through some personal problems about twelve years ago and I began asking questions of myself out of frustration because nothing else was working for me. I had read something about building a relationship with my inner self, my inner mind. I knew nothing about that and thought it was a little kooky at first, but since nothing else was working, I decided to start trying, As I began getting some success from that, I decided to quit drinking after twenty-five years. Using this process of asking my inner self, I was able to stop drinking by myself—alone and unsupported, without outside resources. That was a very big success that rooted me in the process. I've come to the conclusion that it is my job—the conscious mind—to ask the

questions. The inner self or my inner mind then provides answers. The third step is for me to put the answers into action in the outside world. And then I can go back and do another reflective process with my inner self and mind.

He is describing perfectly how the best process is to use both the rational (conscious) mind and the inner (intuitive) mind.

In today's world we are offered many different avenues to help us understand our addictions, what they are about and how to overcome them. There seems to be no end to the "expert" opinions on the subject. But people drink or act addictively for many and varied reasons. It is not possible for one explanation or theory to fit all. There are also many different options for healing: conventional medical treatment, psychological counseling, support groups, cognitive behavioral therapy, inner child work, holistic treatment therapies. How does one decide what is right and what isn't? Simple. Use your intuition.

I found it very helpful to examine many different avenues—different treatments, different religions, meditation, alternative therapies, vitamin therapy, traditional counseling, etc. I learned to take from each what felt right for me, what resonated with me internally. We are very lucky to live in a world that offers us so many different options. Take from each what you need and leave the rest. It is as if we are each offered a buffet, the buffet of healing and understanding. With the empty plate of an open, nonjudgmental mind, select a little of each dish that looks appetizing. I ran across a book at my local library entitled *Addictive Drinking*, by Clark Vaughn, that was written by a man who healed his addictive drinking by using exactly this approach. I found a passage that sums it up very well.

I didn't know what I was doing at first but by trial and error I finally learned how to stay dry long enough for my thinking to begin to function better with more complicated ideas. I began to understand what had really happened to me to turn me into a drunk, and I began to see what I had to work at to get myself sorted out and really well. To do this, I found I could take advantage of a great variety of specialized facilities and therapies I hadn't even known were there, as long as *I* was able to figure out what it was that I needed from each, so that *I* could use it at a *time* when it made sense to *me* and in a *way* that made sense. Nobody could tell me this. I was the only person in a position to do it, because I was the only person who knew exactly how I felt and what I could accept at any particular stage in my recovery. It worked. I have become convinced that no single therapy is broad enough to assure or even offer almost total freedom from dependence of any kind, but judicious use of a variety of facilities, therapies, and certain ideas can. [emphases mine]

And it is intuition that will guide you safely through the smorgasbord of "facilities, therapies, and certain ideas."

Another good way to utilize your intuition is when you are reading something, say a self-help book or even this book. Do you feel a resistance inside or do the words harmonize with you? If you feel an inherent sense of rightness, even in the face of logic, trust that feeling and follow it.

I struggle to understand, and I search my heart, and I pray for clarity. I have learned not to deny my feelings when things don't feel right to me. And as I have learned to honor that resistance when I feel it, I find that it leads me to greater and greater insights about myself and about life. One of these is to honor the fact that everyone's path can be different. What works for you may be different from what works for me; the highest truth is to honor the fact that there is not any one true path but many varied paths. Your intuition is your guide to what works best for you; for many that intuition says to follow the A.A. way. However, encourage yourself to follow a different drummer if that is what you feel.

I was very fortunate to be able to read a prepublication copy of *Proud Spirit*, the second book by bestselling author Rosemary Altea. A paragraph in it touches upon this topic: "Should I discard other men's words, other men's truth? But there are many wise words, written by many wise and knowing men and women, of many different 'religions,' so rather than discarding all that I read, I will keep that which my heart acknowledges as good."

Growing up we are not taught to think this way, that we need to honor the resistance we feel inside to certain things. We are taught that when we feel resistance to something, we need to push on through anyway. We are taught to buck up, or that we don't know what is best for us. "Your best thinking got you here," we are told in A.A. It is for this reason that we've gotten so out of touch with ourselves, with what we really need, with what out bodies are really trying to tell us.

But who among us hasn't said about something, "You know, this just doesn't feel right. I think I should do something different," and in the face of all logic we follow through on that gut instinct only to find that it was unerringly correct. A friend of mine barely averted a horrible traffic accident because something in her told her not to turn, even though she had the light and the intersection she was about to turn across was clear. She sat and waited anyway, thinking that this was crazy. A split second later, a car sped through the intersection, running the traffic light and smashing into an oncoming car. My friend said a prayer of thanks, and now has a different viewpoint about gut feelings.

Our feelings are a vital part of us. When we continually override them, suppress them, or ignore them, we are headed for trouble. Our feelings are the gateway to our hearts. If we continually deny our feelings, we will experience the pain of addiction. We need to teach ourselves, gently, how to honor our feelings, for they hold the key to our intuition. They tell us when things are right, and when they are wrong. And our feelings have the great advantage of being able to operate free from logical distractions. Have you ever met someone for the first time and instantly not liked them? There was just something about them, not anything in particular, mind you, just a strange feeling you had; later you learned that they were really bad news. Without any logical basis, your intuition was telling you, through your feelings, that this person was not trustworthy.

This may be a bit simplistic because we've also met people who really were trustworthy and our *fears* told us that they were not. So getting in touch with true intuition and being able to differentiate it from fears is important. And that comes through experience.

At first it is very scary to begin trusting our intuition. For those who are used to letting others tell them what to do, it is easy to feel as if you are being selfish when you start taking care of yourself and taking time for yourself. Perhaps your intuition will encourage you to do less for those around you. You do not serve anyone's highest good when you are doing for them what they should be doing for themselves. Allow the Universe to take care of them. Give them the chance to find their own power just as you are finding yours. Both people lose when one spends time co-dependently focusing on the other: The one being taken care of is kept from having to do for himself and being accountable for his own actions, and the other is distracted from focusing on his own issues.

Be courageous as you begin to follow your intuition. Listen to your still, small voice, ask for the highest and best for all concerned, and then plunge forward with the faith that the Universe will support you and will support those around you.

Honoring intuition means stepping out in faith and trust. For you can be sure that intuition will ask you to do things and act in ways that have no logical basis. If we have a notion that the Universe is a friendly place, and that we are always supported with much spiritual assistance, our tiny notion will soon become an unshakable certainty as we are shown higher and higher possibilities for living. This teaching does not apply only to healing from addiction. It affects our whole approach to life.

28

Finding My Inner God

"THERE IS NO GOD up in the sky, or down below the earth or the sea. 'The Kingdom of God is within you.' If we are to find that kingdom, therefore, we shall have to seek inside to find it, for that is where it is," Joel Goldsmith writes in *Parenthesis in Eternity*.

I have been taught since birth, as most of us have, that God is an all-powerful, all-knowing, all-seeing male entity outside ourselves who holds the key to whether we get to heaven or not. We are seen as less than God when religions and twelve-step programs encourage us to place all of our power in and turn our will and our lives over to Him and He will then direct us in all our ways.

I want to say, for the sake of clarity, that I am not an agnostic. I believe very fervently and deeply in God and have a very personal relationship with Him/Her. However, I believe that God is also within us and IS us, and that to focus solely on an external portion of God is only half the picture. My healing from addiction advanced by light years when I came to recognize and nurture and honor the God within me. The God within me is part of the divine self we all have.

I spent so much time focusing on an external Higher Power that I neglected and rejected my own inner Higher Power, my higher self, my God within, my Christ consciousness, whatever one may call it.

217

My journey toward wholeness was not complete until I journeyed within to find God and saw that I beheld God within me. I actually had within me a completely overlooked source of power and wisdom that held the answers to my most complex spiritual dilemmas. I found that the God within me was genderless and was more of a consciousness than an actual entity, a consciousness of pure love, and light, and divinity. This consciousness had been patiently residing within me all along. And it was now ready to help me and heal me. I had access to this consciousness simply by tuning in to it. I saw how my looking around searchingly for God was like a fish looking around for water. I had been living and breathing in the pure consciousness of love, of God, all along.

As I nurtured this newfound relationship, I noticed that the struggle that had been going on inside me for so long was starting to abate. I had forever been trying to force myself into the box of someone else's belief, but came to realize that this was not what God intended. The more I tried to pigeonhole my beliefs into those of some religion or twelve-step group, the more I denied myself and my own inherent power and the worse my addiction became.

It may sound a bit arrogant to say that WE are our own Higher Power. Nevertheless, the kingdom of heaven lies within us. Jesus lies within us. Buddha, Krishna, Mohammed, Allah lies within us. The personae we fix on as all powerful, wise, loving, and forgiving are actually aspects of ourselves that we can connect with and draw power from. We have our salvation right within ourselves, and have all along. Fear is terrified of our knowing this, so fear tells us our natures are sinful and distrustful and addictive. By keeping our focus on outward manifestations of a Higher Power, fear effectively keeps us from ever connecting with the *inner* version of our Higher Power, which many refer to as the Higher Self.

But our *true* natures are not sinful. Our true nature is simply God's nature. Joel Goldsmith writes further that "God is the substance of which man is formed and the substance in which he lives and moves and has his being. The qualities of man are the qualities of God. . . . All that God is, we are. This is different from thinking of ourselves as separate and apart from God, having to ask God or attempting to influence Him; this is the difference between successful spiritual living and unsuccessful living of any type." He describes finding God as "relaxing into the Invisible."

The search for God is one of the most important journeys we will ever embark on. It is at the heart of our healing, because it is the spiritual hole within us that we misinterpreted as a physical or emotional hunger that has been causing our addiction. When we satisfy the spiritual longing, we finally satisfy the addictive hunger that has been plaguing us. So, A.A. had it right when they decided that a spiritual solution was vital to recovery. However, to search outside myself never empowered me. I finally found the peace and the wholeness and the power I had been searching for for so long as soon as I looked inside instead of outside myself in someone else's definition of God.

Every person's journey within will be different because each person is different. I believe that is why organized religion did so little for me. My needs were treated with disregard. Instead, I was taught how to act and how to pray, in order to receive God's love, making it all seem very conditional and making God seem very whimsical. He might decide on a whim to heal me and he might not. And who knew what the true requirements were? Everybody seemed to have a slightly different version.

Recognizing that we have a Higher Self, beyond the ego self, which has all the same rights, privileges, and power that we normally affix to a Higher Power outside ourselves, is a weighty responsibility. Not only does it mean we can no longer blame the outside world or a vengeful God for our problems, it also means we can actually direct and guide our own lives, we can find authority in our own experiences, we can establish new, workable beliefs that integrate our deepest wisdom with our highest good.

Finding our Higher Self means thinking for ourselves, letting go of being victims, and establishing our own internal belief systems based on trusting our intuition and letting our intuition guide us as to what is best for us personally. Finding our Higher Self also means allowing others to have their way of doing things, recognizing that each person is entitled to pursue his or her own road to enlightenment. We need not judge another for following his or her own path. As we pursue the path that feels right for us, we must give others the right to pursue their own paths as well.

It is important to distinguish between the Higher Self and the ego self and understand how to honor both and not deny either. The Higher Self is beyond the ego self. A good analogy is one given by author Gary Zukav in his book *The Seat of the Soul.* Imagine the ocean as being the vastness of the Universe, and then imagine someone dipping a cup into the ocean. The water in the cup comes from the ocean and contains all the properties of the ocean, yet in a smaller physical amount. We are the equivalent of the water in the cup, yet we contain all the properties within us of the ocean (the Universe) from which we come. As a wise Sufi said: "As the drop from the ocean merges into the ocean so does the ocean merge into the drop."

The ego self generally operates from a place of fear and seeks gratification in things outside itself whereas the Higher Self operates from a place of love and can see how all things work together for good. Many self-help books today portray the ego self as the bad guy, as a part of ourselves to be distrusted if we are seeking higher awareness. However, the Higher Self is able to constructively utilize the services of the ego in order to serve the highest good. The ego's need for recognition and approval can be put to good use by the Higher Self. Our truest dreams for ourselves are always the Universe's will for us. It is the *Higher Self* that knows what we can accomplish and gives us the inspiration to achieve certain goals in life. It is the *ego self* that follows through on accomplishing these goals. By gaining a healthy sense of accomplishment and working in harmony with the Higher Self, the ego self can stay in balance. An ego that is balanced will experience few or no addictive cravings.

When we deny the ego self and sublimate our wishes and desires in our drive to avoid being selfish, then the ego self, in its need for recognition, will switch tacks and try to get our attention through cravings, addictive impulses, and other "negative" behaviors. Honoring our Higher Self therefore includes honoring, in a healthy manner, our ego self's needs as well.

Each person should decide for him or herself who or what his or her personal God is. And each person should seek inwardly and outwardly to find the answers. This is where intuition and "listening to the heartbeat of the soul" is vital. And you can update and monitor your search by your experiences in the outside world.

There are many ways for you personally to find and connect with your Higher Self, especially in today's world. The number of self-help books and alternative resources is at an all-time high. There are books by traditional medical doctors, such as Bernie Siegel and Deepak Chopra, books examining the search for soul and meaning, such as those by Thomas Moore (*The Care of the Soul*) and Joseph Campbell's wonderful books such as *The Power of Myth*, as well as a host of New Age authors who explore every topic from Native American wisdom and practices to channeled teaching to shamanic journeys. Books by long-time, well-known authors such as Richard Bach and Dr. Wayne W. Dyer will appeal to many. Many people are turning to alternative health resource centers that may offer such things as chiropractic, homeopathy, meditation groups, kinesiology, nutrition counseling, reiki/energy work, inner child work, and hypnotherapy. In most urban cities you can find publications that have pages of advertisements for shamanic journeys, treks to power places such as Sedona, Arizona, and Nepal, past-life regression therapy, crystal work, and sweat-lodge ceremonies. Psychotherapists today offer many approaches instead of sticking to the old Freudian/Jungian models. Some churches are becoming attuned to the layperson's demand for less rigidity and formality. Unity churches are a good example. Their bookstores contain all sorts of healthy alternative resources and offer courses in everything from tai chi to creating treasure maps that visually contain all your highest goals and aspirations. Meditation centers are springing up left and right. The list goes on and on. All of this is in response to people's insistent need to find purpose and meaning in their lives beyond the rigid rules and expectations of our traditional institutions. Conforming and living in fear doesn't serve our souls.

People are dying to connect inwardly and their inability to find that connection is part of the reason we have such a violent, addictive society. Forcing a person's spirituality into a box is a sure way to ensure that it will come out in some other, perhaps less desirable way. However, the rise in alternative forms of spirituality is one way in which people's search for meaning and validation is coming out in a positive, loving way.*

James Redfield, author of the bestselling book *The Celestine Prophecy*, describes finding your Higher Self as being a transcendent experience; "This transcendent experience happens through meditation, prayer, dance, tai ch'i, martial arts, or being in 'the zone' through sports." He echoes my sentiment that there are many different ways in which to gain access to your Higher Self.

Many people describe finding their Higher Self as gaining access to that quiet place deep within. This is why many people can find their Higher Selves through meditation. However, what works for one may not work for another. As a dancer once said, "The fastest way to still the mind is to move the body." She obviously needs to *move* her body in order to experience the quiet within.

Finding the way that works best for you is a completely unique journey and your intuition can serve as your strongest guide if you can begin to honor it and trust it. One particular method may work for you for a short while, and then another may hold your interest. Or you may be one who examines every method put before you and takes a small piece of each. "Take what you want and leave the rest," as the saying goes.

---

*I would like to point out that New Age is not a strategy by Satan to divert us from God, as Pat Robertson and the 700 Channel would have us believe. The New Age movement is simply a desire on the part of people to have different ways to define their spirituality other than those being force-fed them by society. Most New Age people are seeking some way to break free from being told how they are to be, act, and feel. I personally gained a great deal of enlightenment by examining every avenue I came to, whether it was labeled New Age or not. Moreover, interestingly enough, when Pat Robertson does his attack on the "New Age movement" he defines it *very* narrowly and focuses on such practices as astrology and psychics, which because of the proliferation of 900 numbers and obvious scams is an easy target to pick on. He says nothing of established, reputable authors such as Dr. Deepak Chopra, Joseph Campbell, and Dr. Wayne W. Dyer, or such traditional practices as meditation, all of which could be categorized as "New Age."

The key is to be true to yourself and trust that you know what is best for you. The Higher Self knows that all you've done before was the result of your doing the best you could with the limited understanding you had. The Higher Self honors you on your journey, and asks that you trust as you move forward. Expect fear to dog your every step in the beginning, but trust that time and wisdom will make the journey much more joyful and pleasurable as you go along. As you find your Higher Self, you will find your internal power place, a place of love, forgiveness, and understanding.

Connecting with my inner God was a very profound step in my healing journey and one which clarified so many things for me. For instance, I began to see how God's will for us is the same as *our* will for us. This was a hard one to accept at first. You mean, I can do whatever I please? I can design my own life according to my will and my desire? "That's the only way it can be," God seemed to respond. "I created a free-will universe and outfitted you with the finest tools imaginable so that you might create as you wish." Even negativity has a place, for it offers great opportunities for learning about what you *don't* want to create. Seen in this light, it no longer becomes necessary to judge and blame others because everything has a place and a purpose although we often can't see the bigger picture. Addiction had an especially useful place in my own life because it showed me what I was really made of—beauty and power and divinity.

I was always taught that God's will was separate from my own. The implication I got from religion was that I was a sinner, and left to my own devices would do nothing but sin over and over again. The remedy was to turn my lowly, sinning will over to God and seek only to do His will. I felt demeaned. How could I ever be expected to develop healthy self-esteem when I was being told what a sinner I was?

When I joined A.A., I got the same sort of philosophy—I was a hopeless alcoholic, powerless over my disease, and my one choice was to turn my will and my life over to God as I understood Him. The implication to me was the same: God's will was separate from my own.

As I developed a personal relationship with my internal-dwelling God, I saw that God wanted for me what I wanted for me, and as I followed my self-will out as far as it would take me and let go of all judgments on my behavior I came to a startling realization. My true nature was not that of a sinner or a hopeless alcoholic. My true nature was divinity and love. My true nature was not that of an addict. I discovered that I truly cared about people, and life, and myself, and that I wasn't nearly as selfish as I had been taught I would be. It was when I was in tune with this aspect of myself that I began living my will and God's will. I truly began to learn who I was. I also learned that God does not judge me. If I choose to destroy myself, that is my God-given right just as much as it's my right to do healthy, positive things. The vengeful, judgmental aspect of God held sway over me no more as I deepened my internal connection with God.

But I'm rambling. These are some of the truths I have found for myself personally. They relate to all the limitations placed on me as I was growing up. I was taught limitation and learned to live limitation. My spiritual journey taught me the folly of limitation. I believe each person's truths will be different and unique.

I read the book *Conversations with God*, which, incidentally, became a bestseller, and I thought it should have been titled *Conversations with Myself*. Although there were many things in the book that I found to be true for me, there were other things that I thought were part of the author's own truths and not necessarily universal truths. It's always dangerous when speaking of spiritual matters to say "my way is the only way," or "my interpretation is the one true interpretation." Were this the case, there wouldn't be 114 different religions in the world and a fast-growing spirituality– "no religion" movement.

While the God within us has a place, we are all too willing to play God where we shouldn't by judging and labeling other people's behavior and actions. The wisest sages of all time know that it is not appropriate to judge another's life because you never know what is being worked out. A recent example of how little I know about another person's bigger picture happened the other day. A friend accompanied me to the mall one morning. Because it was the holiday season, we were taking our children to get their pictures taken with Santa Claus. My friend stopped in three or four high-end stores and bought very expensive items. She wanted to lunch at the most expensive restaurant in the mall. I thought to myself, "Boy, she's really a spendaholic," and I naively judged her behavior as negative. What I didn't know was that she came from a very hard background. Her family had very little money and she often had to go without basic necessities. She had worked hard all of her life and had finally attained financial independence after much toil and struggle. Her expensive tastes were her way of rewarding herself for all her hard work. She took great pleasure in buying things not only for herself but for others. She had the means to enjoy the finer things in life and let herself do just that, without guilt and without remorse. She was to be admired. My judgments simply showed my own shortsightedness.

While we are too happy to play God where we have no business playing God, we refuse to play God precisely where we should, in the area of personal power and spirituality. We are all too eager to give our power away and ask others to show us the way.

Our inner powerfulness is our God within. But far too few of us are willing to assume this vast responsibility. By letting others define our path for us, and by following only the external aspect of God, we are let off the hook of having to decide for ourselves. When we connect with our inner powerfulness, we have to give up the notion of powerlessness, which is a very scary proposition.

But our personal development will forever remain stymied and our wings will remain clipped if we don't go within. The wholeness and healing we seek is more extraordinary than we can ever imagine. I thought I knew a little about life and about myself. But then I discovered the true secrets to healing and entered an entirely different dimension. A dimension of working in harmony with God. And in harmony with myself.

29

Trust

ON TRUST, Sarah B. Breathnach writes in her book *Simple Abundance:* "Each time you experience the new, you become receptive to inspiration. Each time you try something different, you let the Universe know you are listening. Trust your instincts. Believe your yearnings are blessings. Respect your creative urges. If you are willing to step out in faith and take a leap in the dark, you will discover that your choices are as authentic as you are. What is more, you will discover that your life is all it was meant to be: a joyous sonnet of thanksgiving."

Trust means that we have faith in the Universe to work all things for our highest good. Trust means that once we find and connect with our Higher Self, we try to honor that Higher Self with our actions. Trust means listening to our intuition and having the courage to follow its guidance. Trust means leaving behind our fearful way of doing things and moving into a place of love and peace.

We can do all the inner work in the world, know precisely what our intuition would lead us to do, feel the guidance of our Higher Self working through us. However, all of this counts for nothing if we don't move forward and trust that we are following the right path. It takes trust if the path we are being called to tread is far different than that of others. It takes courage to be different. It also takes courage to enter the unknown, which is what trust asks us to do.

Trust comes to us from a place of love. Fear doesn't want us to trust. Fear wants to keep us forever dependent in the "tried and true" way. Fear is afraid of change, so fear asks us to repeat the same dull routines over and over again. We may not grow this way, but at least we know what to expect, which is the way fear prefers things. Fear tells us that what has worked for everyone else should work for us.

Love tells us to trust what feels right for us. Love validates whatever we need to do to honor ourselves, knowing love would never have us do something that would harm ourselves or others. Love gives us trust that whichever path we choose, if our intention is for the highest good, our highest good will result.

Love asks us to trust in many ways. Love may ask us to trust our inner convictions even when we see no evidence to support them. Many times we cannot see the bigger picture and we may label a particular experience as negative or harmful. If we can but trust love to see us through we will eventually see how all the things in our life work together for the good. Love would ask the abused woman or the laid-off factory worker to trust that a higher good can come from these negative situations.

We need to trust that life has many more infinite variations than we could ever imagine. Our limited minds may be able to see only three or four or maybe a few more ways in which a circumstance, situation, or behavior can be interpreted. However, love always sees the bigger picture. Love knows that if we can trust, we offer ourselves up to many more of the variations than we can see with our eyes or understand with our rational minds.

Trust opens us up to be able to take responsibility for our lives and stop playing the victim. For instance, the abused woman in the earlier chapter, being unable to trust, sees herself as being a victim and continually blames her husband for his physical attacks. If she could trust life she could see that she attracted this situation to herself just as much as her husband did in order to awaken and heal herself, heal her inner drama of blame and her need to play the role of victim. She could then take responsibility for having an inner need to attract abusive people into her life. With the intention to heal and create a better life for herself, she could then trust that the Universe will honor that intention and offer her many different ways to build a better life. She may notice an ad for a job that she is perfectly qualified for, and on the bus ride to the interview, she sees a cute apartment for rent within walking distance of the job. She will probably receive many unexpected offers for assistance in many areas of her life if she opens herself up to receiving them. And the way to open up to receive life's bounty is to trust.

Without trust we remain fearful, closed, and rigid. Trust allows us to slowly, at our own pace, open up to love. And with love all things are possible. Trust is also about believing in yourself. Again, love may ask us to trust our inner convictions when we can see no evidence to support them.

Trust often means looking past other people's behavior in order to see *our own* lessons. When we encounter problems with others, they are our teachers and what bothers us is our lesson. When I allow myself to become irritated or frustrated with my husband, I can now trust that it's not *him* I'm mad at. Trust allows me to see that it is my "script" for him that is making me upset. Because I have decided on a certain predetermined way in which I want him to carry out certain family duties, I set myself up for upset when he does things his own way and in his own time. Trust helps me to see this deeper drama by helping me to go to a place of love, and it is love that helps me see past his behavior and into my dynamic at work, my need to control. The dynamic in this case, a need to control, is fear-based. Fear says that things aren't being run in the best way they could because not everyone is following *my* script. Trust allows me to see that things run fine or even better without my need to control them precisely and fearfully. And it is trust that allows me to see past the teacher and focus on the lesson; I thus stop blaming the teacher.

Trust can most often be demonstrated from a position of vulner-ability. Vulnerability means that our defenses are down, that we are in a position of trusting that whatever comes our way, whether bad or good, contains the seeds of our greatest good. Another way to view trust, then, is as a surrender to a higher plan and a greater good than we are able to perceive. Before, when I was told to turn my will and my life over to a Higher Power it was with the *expectation* that He would relieve my suffering. But more often than not my suffering was *not* relieved. I often suffered long and hard in the midst of my turning my will over again and again. I no longer surrender myself to a higher plan while having expectations. Life has taught me over and over that I will get the very best response when I am completely open and trusting as to what comes my way, for everything can serve our greater good if we allow it to. Famous author and lecturer Louise Hay had one of her best affirmations printed on bookmarks that I now have scattered throughout my house to remind me of its truth: "Whenever there is a problem, repeat over and over: All is well. Everything is working out for my highest good. Out of this situation only good will come. I am safe." This is more than an empty promise. It's a very powerful truth if you believe in it and recite it. Trust that the things in your life that are negative or disheartening *always* have something in them for you.

We are offered many opportunities in life every day in which to practice trust. One day quite a few years ago, I had a very important interview. I was dressed and ready in time, but got snarled in post–lunch hour traffic. Instead of trusting that it would be okay to be a few minutes late, I let myself get upset and sat in my car fuming and fretting. I walked into the office of my interview barely five minutes late, just as the secretary was hanging up the phone. "That was Bruce," she said to me (Bruce was the man I had the interview with). "He called from his car to say he'd be a few minutes late." Life had been offering me a perfect opportunity to trust that even as I was sitting in traffic, things were being taken care of and everything was fine without my rushing and fretting and fuming. But instead I allowed my need for control to overshadow my ability to trust. Trust means giving up control.

We are created by God in His/Her image, so when we do not trust ourselves, we are essentially not trusting God. I believe that we are given free will, not to then see if we will turn it over to Him or anything else outside us, but to learn how wise and knowing and grand we truly are. Our bodies, our physical, emotional, mental, and spiritual bodies, represent the most wondrous, magical, fully-functioning systems in the entire Universe. No other being in this world has the talents, the gifts, and the capabilities that we as humans do. Our physical bodies carry out our desires, our emotional bodies use feelings to connect us with our internal wisdom, our mental bodies complement and enhance our emotional bodies, and our spiritual bodies represent our timeless, eternal, God-selves within. Just the fact that we possess these four separate yet connected bodies makes us wealthier than we could ever imagine. And yet we shackle ourselves to the limitations of past experiences, we cling to fear and doubt instead of risking life, and we imprison ourselves and our capabilities. Trust asks us to throw off our shackles, to walk confidently into the unknown, to risk failure or success, and to believe that everything we experience can be used for good. When we really believe that every life experience has something in it for us, we will walk fearlessly through life. Trust opens the doors to the abundance of the Universe. When we walk fearfully through life, we are telling the Universe, "Don't notice me. Don't give me any real responsibility. I'm having a hard enough time as it is." But walking through life with a trusting stance says, "I am open to all experiences. I prefer light, joyous ones, but I know negative situations will come from time to time and they are only here to be transformed into magical opportunities for growth." This kind of attitude allows greater and more wonderful experiences to come our way. Because as long as we are fearful, we will tend to draw negative, draining situations to us.

So do we keep feeding our fears or do we trust and step forward with faith? It is easy to get stuck by waiting for the fear to be gone before acting. But those who have made the leap of faith know that no amount of patient waiting will completely rid us of fear's presence. Trust means acting in the face of fear. Trust requires courage.

I had lunch one day with the editor of a local newspaper. He was telling me of his experience starting a neighborhood newspaper from scratch. He had no formula, no money, no advertisers, just a desire. He said that if he had waited around for the fear to go away, he never would have acted. Starting the paper, in his words, "required a leap of faith and courage." He has gone on to start another newspaper in an adjoining neighborhood and a third is in the works. I liked his response when someone initially approached him about starting the second paper. He felt overwhelmed by the prospect. He already had a lot on his plate and had done no research on whether this second paper would even work. But he told the person, "If I get green lights, I'll do it. But if I get red lights, I won't." He then told me, "Well, I got nothing but green lights all the way." That's sort of how it is when stepping forward in trust. We take one small step and everything works out and we receive a green light. Then we take another small step and get another green light to proceed farther. And before we know it, we've overcome all our precious limitations and accomplished a miracle.

Trust gives us the certainty that there is a broader picture than what we can see with our eyes, touch with our hands, or think with our minds. Love is the healing, miraculous balm that appears in our life as we open up with trust.

On trust, Ralph Waldo Emerson wrote: "Trust men and they will make it their business to trust you, treat them greatly and they will show themselves to be great." I would substitute "life" for "men." Trust life and life will make it its business to trust you. Trust life greatly and life will show itself to be great!

30

Acceptance

ACCEPTANCE IS the cornerstone of change. We all
have so many things we'd like to change: ourselves, other people, our
careers, our pasts, our unhealed issues. However, we will remain stuck
and stagnant within until we can begin to accept things just as they
are. Even the first step of the twelve-step model has you admit that
you are an alcoholic. This is to encourage you to *accept* the fact that
you have a problem with alcohol instead of denying it or running
away from it.

How does acceptance relate to healing from addiction? Addiction
offers us a surefire way in which to reject ourselves, to push others
away from us, and to reject love. As an active addict, I was so filled
with self-loathing and disgust I would have found it impossible to
accept myself. I found myself and my actions despicable. But, as irony
would have it, acceptance was precisely the healing agent necessary
for my change to more positive, healthy behavior.

My addictive thinking said that I would only become worthy of
love when I was sober and had achieved food abstinence. As a drunk
and a bulimic, I was unworthy of love, or so I thought. But, even in
sobriety, I found ways to withhold love from myself. I wasn't going
to enough meetings. I didn't share enough. I wasn't humble enough.
Other people were always better than I was. These were some of the
rejecting thoughts that went through my mind in sobriety. So, the

behavior that I thought would make me worthy of love only brought with it more expectations and greater requirements for love.

It wasn't until I began to love and accept myself in the midst of active addiction that the noose of nonacceptance was loosened from my neck. And it was when I realized that my addiction was about something, a reaction to my painful life rather than a statement of how unworthy I was, that the first few rays of acceptance started shining into the darkness of my addiction. For so many years I bought into the self-created belief that I must be an incredibly worthless person to be so addicted to drugs and alcohol and food. I watched as other people were able to hold down jobs, pay their bills, raise families, and meet all the untold obligations that come with being an adult. In the throes of my addiction I felt as if I were unable to do even the most minimal of tasks. The idea of living a responsible life overwhelmed me. And yet it was what I wanted to do more than anything else. I saw that my inability to be true to myself and follow my own dreams was part of the problem. And I saw that the pain this caused me was part of the reason for my addiction. I saw how my negative beliefs in my guilt and shame contributed to my disease. As I began to understand that there were real reasons at the root of my addiction, I was able to let myself off the hook. I became able to stop telling myself I was unworthy of love simply because I couldn't quit using. This was the beginning of my self-acceptance and my self-love. And the beginning of healing. As we learn to accept ourselves, we can more easily accept the reasons for our addictive behavior, our wounds, our negative beliefs, and our fears.

As we go within to heal our inner feelings of guilt, rage, resentments, blame, abandonment, shame, or whatever they may be, we need to practice accepting that these messages are what they are. Struggling to deny them or trying to convince ourselves that they haven't been as destructive as they have been will only increase the time it takes us to heal. Accepting ourselves just the way we are is the first step toward healing. Simple acceptance serves to give us clarity as to how we originally adopted these negative messages about ourselves in order to protect ourselves. Acceptance doesn't find fault.

Acceptance says, "Okay, I have a tendency to play the role of victim," or, "I have a tendency to attract situations that cause me to feel shame," without needing to blame others or ourselves.

As I accepted that shame was one of the negative beliefs I had about myself, I could see how I attracted shaming situations to me in order to validate my inner message. With acceptance I no longer had to flee from the pain I inflicted on myself by one shaming incident after another. Acceptance gave me the ability to face the issue straight-forwardly and then do the inner work necessary to change the message of shame to one of love and wholeness.

You can accept a situation without having to like it. One of the reasons we become addicted in the first place is because of our desire to flee from the underlying guilt and pain we hold inside. When we stop running and can face the pain with trust, love, and acceptance, we no longer feel the need to seek addictive escapes. We heal the pain. As we go within to deal with this pain, we usually steel ourselves for what we anticipate will be an awful and agonizing encounter with our inner demons. However, we discover that the pain of running from ourselves is much greater than the pain of facing and accepting ourselves. With acceptance we discover that we aren't really bad people after all, much to our relief.

Wherever you feel fear, you have some sort of emotional blockage within that will be mirrored by a physical blockage of some sort. The same can be said for nonacceptance. Wherever you feel nonaccept-ance, whether toward a person, situation, or circumstance, that is where you need to go. You need to go to the hidden meaning be-neath the feelings of nonacceptance. What are you not accepting about yourself that is being projected on to another person or situa-tion? Acceptance of the outer problem helps us to heal the inner problem. Acceptance goes hand in hand with love to heal our most painful parts.

I recently watched a very telling incident at the Dallas airport. While I sat waiting for my plane to arrive, I noticed a couple, with a young child who was maybe a year and a half old, walking through the concourse. The child noticed a rope condoning off a gate station from the traffic of the people in the concourse. She was entranced by the rope. She stopped to touch it and stroke it. The parents stopped walking and stood patiently beside her until her fascination waned. Then the child spotted a big fluorescent sign across the walkway with a bright picture of a tiger (an ad for the Dallas Zoo) and she tottered over to it. Once she got to the sign, she gleefully patted her hands on it and squealed with delight. The parents again stood by patiently, shielding her on either side from the passing traffic of people. She then went over to a row of luggage carts and played with them for a few minutes. I was completely mesmerized and awed witnessing this scene. The parents were so lovingly allowing their child to explore. They didn't stifle her, or try to rush her, or even try to guide her and point things out to her. They just allowed her innate curiosity to bubble forth. By standing next to her, patiently and lovingly, they no doubt gave her a sense of comfort and protection. But most important, the actions of the parents seemed to send a very strong message to the child that her needs and desires were just as important and vital as their own. They didn't try to fit her actions into their schedule of needs. Instead, they gave her the freedom and the validation to explore her own world at her own pace. I thought, if they keep this up, that child will never have a problem with self-esteem. She was receiving complete love and acceptance of who she was. Unfortunately very few of us grew up with such loving acceptance. Our needs were instead squeezed into the needs and desires of our parents and if our needs were different from theirs, it was often *our* needs that had to go, not theirs. The implicit message I got growing up was that I was loved and accepted if I was being good and that I was not lovable or worthy if I was being bad. I slowly began to believe that *I* was unacceptable, not just my behavior.

Our society is geared toward judging certain behavior as unacceptable and then casting judgment on the *person* as unacceptable. But, in truth, it's two separate things. Our behavior can be unacceptable without being a testament to our worth as a person. For myself, I had to learn how to let even my *behavior* be completely okay before I made any real progress toward changing it. My self-worth was so tied to my actions that I continually deemed myself unacceptable if my behavior was unacceptable. So as I learned to let even my worst behavior be okay, I went a long way toward validating myself as a person.

Feelings of nonacceptance can cause stress and irritation and wind up hurting only ourselves. Nonacceptance can cause a return of cravings as well. The two ways in which we are often the most nonaccepting are in our *expectations* about others and our *assumptions* about reality.

Almost all of us have scripts for the major areas of our lives. For our families, for our bosses, for our in-laws, for our lives. We expect them to live up to our roles for them, and when they don't, we allow ourselves to feel hurt and angry. However, it is *our own* expectations that are the cause of the hurt and anger, not the other person's behavior. As long as we hold fast to our scripts for others, we will needlessly experience conflict and struggle. When others don't live out our scripts for them, we further tighten the noose of unhappiness around ourselves by trying to cajole, manipulate, or downright dominate them into coming around to our way of doing things. Our *fear* of not getting our way causes us to exert this need to control other people and situations. Acceptance offers us freedom from this vicious cycle. Acceptance allows us to give the gift of love to the others in our life.

One of the miracles of acceptance is that as you allow others freedom from your scripts you will often find that they will do exactly what you wished them to do in the first place. One of the reasons for that is because we can all subconsciously sense energy dynamics that are at play beneath the surface. When you sense that someone is attempting to get you to do something, the automatic response is to resist. However, when you sense that the pressure is off and you can do as you wish, then you often feel pleased to do for another. Moreover, as long as we remain unhappy until others do or act in a certain way, we are still putting the responsibility for our lives outside ourselves.

We are solely responsible for our own happiness. If I am blaming my husband for my unhappiness, then I am irresponsibly placing control for my life in his hands. *I* determine my own happiness by acceptance and love and by making peace of mind a major priority in my life. Beware, however, that acceptance in this regard doesn't mean condoning harmful or destructive behavior. Acceptance means taking responsibility for *your* life and *your* happiness by not making it dependent on another's actions. It also means accepting the responsibility of leaving a situation that is potentially harmful to you or to a family member.

The second way in which we are the most nonaccepting is in our assumptions about reality. We all have assumptions about the way things "should" be. Life should be fair, hard work should always be recognized and rewarded, diets should work, a high moral code should make us a better person, criminals should not get off through failures of the justice system, homes should be sacred and safe from attack, people shouldn't die young, bad things shouldn't happen to good people. But as we all know, all of these things do let us down and for many of us they let us down every day. We get passed over for a promotion, a teenager smokes pot even though his parents struggled to raise him responsibly, homes get burglarized, criminals go free, children die suddenly, and bad things happen to good people. There is no escaping the absolute unpredictability of the world.

However, we do have choices. We can choose to become upset by every whim of reality that doesn't go according to our personal assumptions. If we do this, however, we live in fear of life constantly letting us down and experience unhappiness and upset. Or we can choose love and say, "It is the way it is. I don't like it, but it doesn't have to ruin my day or my life." Acceptance gives us the ability to move beyond our personal ego-driven assumptions about how life should treat us. Acceptance allows us to be proactive instead of passive. Passivity serves no one when it is couched in fear and rigid nonacceptance. Acceptance gives us the key to allow love to show us how each and every situation in our life is working for our highest good if we will simply allow it to.

So acceptance is the bridge that takes us from where we are to where we want to be. It is active, not passive. But if we are to be expected to accept the "negative" traits about ourselves, we must also learn to accept the positive, like the fact that we are divine and whole and complete just the way we are. And the fact that our imperfection is our perfection. Accepting imperfection helps us to see through to our perfection. On the other hand, *striving* for perfection will always lead to feelings of lack. Striving for perfection is like a dog chasing its tail. He never quite gets there. Like the dog, you might get there for a moment, but then you see someone prettier or more talented or more driven and you are again back to striving. Seeking perfection in a world full of vastly overblown images of what we are supposed to look like, eat, work at, play at, spend, or make is a losing game. But accepting imperfections is the key to our wholeness, for as we accept the parts we don't like, we move toward true wholeness. Accepting imperfections gives us permission to like ourselves just the way we are.

31

Becoming the Power Center in Your Life

THE FIRST FIVE COMPONENTS of freedom—healing your pain, honoring your intuition, finding your inner God, learning to trust, and acceptance—are all about taking full responsibility for your addictions, taking full responsibility for your healing, and learning to become powerful.

Becoming the power center in your life is about using the skills and insights in this book to be powerful in every area of your life, not just in the area of healing addiction.

I had been so indoctrinated in the need for powerlessness, I was never taught how to be empowered or anything about being powerful. Men were powerful, institutions were powerful, churches were powerful. I was just an addict. And my only solution was to turn what very little power I did have over to someone else. Leaving me with what? An empty shell. It was no wonder that I remained addicted.

Last weekend I attended a seminar for women in Atlanta entitled "Empowering Women." It was led by Louise Hay, author of *You Can Heal Your Life* and many other books about how to seize your inner healing potential and inner power. The seminar was little advertised but drew over three thousand women and many men. I was fifteen minutes late and barely found a seat in the large auditorium. I was amazed by the turnout.

Everywhere I look today I see a rising tide of consciousness that wants to teach us how to be powerful. Dr. Wayne Dyer, Dr. Deepak Chopra, and Shakti Gawain are only a few of the many authors today who write about how we can become the best we can be and be powerful in our lives. Many of their words saved my life.

However, it was primarily the seven components I have listed in this section, along with the belief in myself and a burning desire to be healthy and finally free from my addiction, that healed me. But if I had to single out the most important component of my ability to break the chains of my addiction, it would be this component, learning to become empowered, learning to connect with my inner power. Recognizing that I wasn't powerless but was, in fact, powerful was one of the most defining moments in my journey toward healing. Later, I saw how debilitating my insistence on powerlessness was and I also understood exactly why I had struggled for so long!

Becoming the power center in my life taught me to love myself just as I was, encouraged me to listen to my inner voice, encouraged me to find spiritual meaning from within by recognizing the God within me, showed me that life can be trusted, in all its randomness, and helped me to create the healing that I had been seeking for so long. So, in many ways, becoming the power center in our lives is a conglomeration of the other six components.

But it is also about understanding the difference between real power and illusory power. Real power comes from within and is not dictated by how much we have, who we can manipulate, how pretty or smart we are, or whether or not we are sober. Illusory power is just that, an illusion. Illusory power believes that the smarter, richer, or prettier we are, the more we can bend people to our will, the faster our cars, the bigger our houses, and the longer we have been sober, the more powerful we are.

Real power is authentic power. Illusory power is external power. Becoming the power center in our lives is about achieving authentic power, not external power. External power is superficial and doesn't serve the needs of the soul. External power keeps us addicted by always beckoning us to seek satisfaction and fulfillment in things outside ourselves. External power keeps us always grasping for more and has us search outside ourselves for the solutions to our problems. External power is grounded in fear—fear of not being enough, fear of being taken advantage of, fear that our inner messages of guilt, shame, etc. are true, fear of ourselves and our true natures. External power keeps us weak, powerless, addicted, and victimized.

Authentic power is within each and every one of us. Authentic power leads to empowerment, love, compassion, forgiveness, and healing. Authentic power is about going within and viewing our life and our experiences as being created solely by us. Authentic power lets us accept full responsibility for everything in our lives without our assigning blame to ourselves or others. Authentic power lovingly encourages us to heal our inner erroneous messages and discover the joy and beauty that lie within each of us. Authentic power lets us not be bullied by the circumstances in our lives but instead gives us a peaceful, calm center amid turmoil.

Authentic power lets us see how every situation in our life was created by us in order to be healed. Angry people around us represent our need to heal our anger. Being shamed by others indicates that we have shame issues. Ongoing feelings of guilt or unworthiness indicate that we have patterns of guilt that need healing. Continually feeling victimized means that we have feelings of blame and resentment that need healing.

Authentic power allows us to see these negative beliefs, not as judgments on us, but rather as areas that need to be cleansed and healed. If your child came home one day with a bloody, dirty scrape on his knee, you wouldn't judge the knee for having wounded itself. You would simply cleanse the wound, apply some ointment and a fresh bandage, and then probably hug and kiss your child to reassure him that he's okay.

It's the same principle for our negative beliefs. Judging ourselves for having them does no good. It only leads to more pain. Authentic power lets us accept the beliefs (our wounds) just as they are and apply the healing balm of love and forgiveness to them.

As we heal our painful parts, authentic power also encourages us to begin to lead lives of purpose and meaning, to give ourselves the gift of following our hearts and pursuing things we have dreamed of all our lives.

Authentic power knows that we aren't bad, and never have been, no matter how dastardly our deeds seem. Authentic power recognizes that we were each just seeking love in the only ways we knew how. Authentic power isn't concerned so much with our defects of character, wrongs, and shortcomings. Authentic power recognizes our beauty, our wholeness, and the things that are right about us.

Authentic power sees only two choices, ever: love or fear. Author Gary Zukav writes, in *The Seat of the Soul*, "There is no power in fear, or in any activities that are generated by fear. There is no power in a thought form of fear, even if it is supported by armies. The armies of Rome disappeared more than a millennia ago, but the force of the life of a single human that Roman soldiers put to death continues to shape the development of our species. Who had the power? . . . you lose power whenever you fear."

Becoming the power center in our lives means choosing love instead of fear as often as we can. It means choosing authentic power over external power. It also means becoming aware of when we are acting from fear. Becoming powerful means that we allow ourselves to be weak and fearful without condemning ourselves. We do not expect ourselves always to be able to choose love. We allow ourselves all the time we need to learn our lessons. Many need to continually learn through fear and doubt before being able to learn the way of love.

Love is all powerful. Love allows everything to exist without judgment for love knows that where love is not, there is only a cry for love, not a need to be judged. By accepting all things, all experiences as valid, those situations that we deem negative and destructive will no longer be drawn to us. Fear, on the other hand, attracts the things we fear. To fear a thing gives it energy and the power to manifest itself in our lives.

By viewing all things without judgment, love brings forth the good from the situations we deem negative. These situations will be shown to contain elements of beauty and rightness if we can view them without judgment, with a detached eye. Fear prevents us from seeing this truth.

Love allows us to be okay just the way we are, for love knows that as we let go of trying to control ourselves or others, we are magically transformed. Love allows our weaknesses to be okay and acceptable. Just as a healed bone becomes strongest at the point where it was broken, so do we. We become stronger in our weakest places. We no longer need to live weak, powerless lives that are run on fear and nonacceptance.

Love views all things as being equally worthy of love. Love views sobriety and drunkenness as equally worthy of love.

Becoming powerful means that we accept that life mirrors to us what is going on inside us, and as we move forward with love, we slowly release our need to judge or blame others. We can see that these are simply projections of our inner selves, projecting parts of us that desire love, acceptance, and healing.

We begin to learn forgiveness, and as we forgive others we ourselves are forgiven. As we release others from our blame and judgment, we watch in awe as they are freed to become the beautiful, loving people they really are. Releasing our blame and judgment of ourselves and others allows the true spark of divinity to emerge from within each of us. Then we can experience how truly powerful we are.

Becoming powerful means allowing the inner wisdom within each of us to be the primary authority for our lives. We are each able to honor our personal development by charting our own path, freed from the need for rigidity, conformance, and fear.

As we grow, we are better able to challenge our fears as they arise. Gary Zukav writes in *The Seat of the Soul:*

> Fear of growing and of transformation of self is what causes you to want to disengage from the present situation and reach for another. When you feel that you are in a pattern of wanting what you do not have instead of what you do have, of seeing the grass in the other pasture as greener because it is in the other pasture, confront it.

Challenge it each time that it comes up by literally realizing that when it comes up you are not in the present moment, you are not engaged in your present energy dynamic but, rather you are letting energy leak to a future that does not exist.

Becoming powerful is about accepting the present moment as perfect. The present is the Universe's gift to us and contains magic and beauty and transformation if we allow it to. The present moment contains everything we need to meet all of our *authentic* needs. Being present in the moment allows us to create lives of purpose, meaning, and fulfillment based on the greatest desire of our hearts.

As we open up and connect with the wisdom within each of us, we are actually cocreating and joining with our Higher Self in becoming the worthwhile, loving, whole person who was inside us all along. We become healed.

32

Creating a Meaningful Life

LIFE IS OUR CANVAS. *Your* life is *your* canvas. Create what you want. As you create exactly what you want in the way you want it, you will probably be challenged to face everything about yourself you wished to keep hidden. That's one reason I believe that addicts are luckier than the average person. We are forced either to live miserable, addictive lives or to choose to face our inner demons, discover that our demons are really angels, and realize that we have the power within us to do anything we choose. Most people, those without addictions, are never really put in a similar "do-or-die" type of situation. If we addicts can rise to the occasion, go deep within to the root cause of the addiction, we will discover we are really the beautiful, successful people we dreamed we were. Those dreams weren't alcoholic delusions. We really can create anything we choose. And as we do, we face more and more challenges, grow more and more confident, and put more and more distance between ourselves and our addictions.

However, back in my mid-twenties, when I was struggling to get sober, I didn't know this. I didn't know I could create anything I wanted to. I didn't know that life was just one big old marble block waiting for me to carve out my dreams on it. Back then, all I felt was a big void in my life. For the longest time I had assumed this void would go away if and when I quit drinking, using drugs, and eating addictively. I had naively assumed that the void was because of my addictions and that curing the addictions would cure the void. But, as irony would have it, I did get sober and abstinent and the void was still there. For a while after I achieved sobriety, I wasn't even aware that my life felt meaningless and unfulfilling. I had great camaraderie with the other members of the twelve-step groups I attended, and felt as if I had a bunch of wonderful new friends. But as the "honeymoon" wore off and the novelty of newfound sobriety became a little less novel, I began to sense vague stirrings of discontent within. I ignored this for a while. After all, I had started graduate school, so I had goals and ambitions. But I didn't achieve any real satisfaction from school. In fact, I didn't have anything that *really* satisfied me. The void loomed large. I eventually drank again, and used drugs again, and it wasn't until much later that I realized how far a meaningful life can go toward pulling you out of the depths of addiction. Because, as it turned out, the void existed because I lacked meaning and purpose in my life. The void represented meaninglessness, but I didn't know that yet.

When at twenty-nine I broke my engagement and moved into my own apartment, I didn't have to answer to anybody; for the first time in my life I could create anything I wanted to create. And I didn't have to look very far to figure out what it was I wanted to create. More than anything in the world, I wanted to create a healthy, successful life and a healthy, healed body. And so I began to do just that.

I pursued only those things that had meaning for me and as I did so, I felt a new freedom, a new happiness, and a new confidence I'd never before felt in my life. I had a friend who was on his own spiritual journey and we talked often and shared books and insights. Many people on the same search began to appear in my life. In fact, the person in the very apartment next to mine gave workshops on realizing your potential and finding meaning in your life. My life was taking on a meaning that was unique to *me*. And the urge to use was rapidly disappearing. I felt as if I were being healed from the inside out. A true healing, not a superficial one. I tested old limits and found them to be erroneous.

This new life I was creating was filled with what *I* wanted. My soul was beginning to feel as if a healing balm were being placed on it. Progress was slow sometimes and I would still beat myself up for not reaching my goals in the way I had envisioned. But I began using a mantra that helped me to open to receiving the Universe's gifts and lessons with equal acceptance. It was "the highest and best for all concerned." This mantra helped me to trust and to let go of trying to control how everything was supposed to unfold in my life. It also helped me to notice where I was still living out someone else's script for my life. It was necessary to occasionally update what I wanted, so I began by using my intuition. Does this feel right for you? Does thinking about doing this make you feel light and joyful (and maybe a little guilty for indulging yourself), or does it make you feel heavy and sad? Often, especially in the beginning, doing what I really wanted made me feel very guilty and the guilt of it almost convinced me to stop doing what I felt I needed to do. I can see now that the guilt was because I had never felt worthy of receiving, even if it was receiving the gift to follow my intuitions. I broke a few dates when I simply didn't feel like going out. I kept people at arm's length because I felt very afraid and vulnerable. Without my realizing it, all of this was creating meaning in my life. I was determining what the words "my life" meant for me personally.

It is a journey every addict should be encouraged to take. You need not move into your own apartment in order to take the journey. It is an inner journey, a journey to find what is really meaningful to you personally and giving yourself the freedom and the courage to pursue it.

Finding meaning in your life can cure even the most vicious of addictions. Deepak Chopra writes, in *Overcoming Addictions,* "Once an addict gains access to a deeper form of satisfaction than is possible through self-destructive behavior, the path away from addiction will naturally open up." Finding meaning in our lives means getting involved in something bigger than ourselves. Finding meaning in your life means cocreating with the Universe exactly the life you've always dreamed of. It means pursuing that favorite hobby or that pet project. But it's also much more than that. It's about giving yourself the freedom to do what your soul is beckoning you to do. It's about following your bliss and allowing miracles to happen in your life. And it's about filling the void.

It's also about Love. As we allow Love to unfold in our life, we can feel ourselves being drawn by some mysterious force to certain activities, secret wishes, or desires. It can be simple and about other people: volunteering at a nursing home or a meals on wheels, helping homeless people, or sending cheer to others in some way. Or it could be about doing more for *ourselves*, stopping co-dependently taking care of others, and instead doing what *we* want to do.

We have to be aware in the beginning, especially if we have feelings of guilt or unworthiness. It's easy to subconsciously undermine ourselves if we still carry around guilt. One mother described how she was finally pursuing her dream of painting now that the children were in school, but her guilt over doing something so intensely pleasurable just for herself showed up in her husband's insistence that she start doing his books at the office now that she had the time. Even though he had been managing without her for years, and could easily afford a bookkeeper, her guilt caused her to give in and let go of the one activity that was so nurturing to her soul.

So simply allow the feelings of guilt and ask for "the highest and best for all concerned." If you are doing what you need to do to take care of yourself, then those around you will be given what they need to take care of themselves. Asking for your Higher Self's guidance and care is also helpful. Trust the process even when it seems to make no sense. Remember how I described my desire to spend entire mornings in a bookstore? I now know why, and even though I felt guilty every time I did it, I'm glad now that I did it.

The first thing many addicts want to create is a healthy, addiction-free life. Envision that for yourself and envision what it feels like. Now imagine that you can have it. And you can have it by following your heart's desire. What an added bonus it is that by following our hearts, we heal ourselves. Quite a change from having someone dictate rigid models of expectations to us.

As we follow our hearts, we fill up the empty places in our souls, and if we continue to follow our hearts, we'll probably bump up against every area we have that causes us pain. Reminding ourselves that our goal is to create a healthy, addiction-free body, we can choose either love or fear with each problem that arises in our lives. The solution to our problems is not in something outside ourselves. Love says to go within and trust yourself. Find what works best for you. Honor your need for a twelve-step meeting if that is what you need. Read a self-help book that resonates with where you are at. Talk to someone. Pray. Meditate. Or just go to a movie. Hold fast to the idea that you are whole and complete just as you are and allow love to rush in.

In order to create a life with purpose, we must first choose an intention. The intention may be simply a commitment to follow our heart. Or we may decide our intention is to create a healthy, addiction-free body. Whatever your intention, it should be something that resonates with you internally, something that makes you feel joyful and vital when you think about pursuing and achieving it. It is from our commitment to an intention that we can begin. There may be a pet project that you've always wanted to pursue but never let yourself do so. Now would be a good time to pursue it. Even if it doesn't turn out exactly as you envisioned it (and it probably won't), you will have learned some things along the way and can build on the newfound confidence you now have.

Gary Zukav, in his wonderful book *The Seat of the Soul*, writes eloquently on how we each have a specific purpose or task whose fulfillment satisfies our deepest hunger, which is our spiritual hunger.

> Each soul takes upon itself a particular task. It may be the task of raising a family, or communicating ideas through writing, or transforming the consciousness of a community, such as the business community. It may be the task of awakening the awareness of the power of love at the level of nations, or even contributing directly

to the evolution of consciousness on a global level. Whatever the task that your soul has agreed to, whatever its contract with the Universe, all of the experiences of your life serve to awaken within you the memory of that contract, and to prepare you to fulfill it . . . Gratifying needs that are based upon fears will not bring you to the touchstone of purpose . . . Only when the personality begins to walk the path that its soul has chosen will it satisfy its hunger.

After you have decided on your intention, you need to surround it and back it up fully with belief, belief, belief. The very first self-help books ever written talked about how important belief is to achieving anything. And today's modern self-help books echo the same theme. As Napoleon Hill said so long ago in his book *Grow Rich with Peace of Mind,* "*Anything* the mind of man can *conceive* and *believe*, he can achieve." It may sound corny, but it's true.

The secret to creating a meaningful life is to use all of your God-given talents and abilities to the fullest, *all the while* enlisting the help of your Higher Self, the Universe, and all the unseen forces of the spiritual world such as angels and other guides. The twelve-step model seems to put the entire burden for our sobriety outside us and in an external, male God. The truth is that we have the power *within ourselves* to not only achieve sobriety but to achieve *any worthwhile thing* we choose. Choose your intention with love and not fear and you will be amazed by how high you can go.

I would like to quote from Napoleon Hill's book *Grow Rich with Peace of Mind,* which was written in the 1960s but is still very relevant today:

Belief is the key to basic mind power which turns concepts into realities. Goals can be attained in ways which seem miraculous, yet we use only natural forces available to everyone. *Even physical changes in the body* can be caused by deeply implanted belief . . . A true deep belief can change your glandular secretions and the content of your bloodstream, and work other physical changes beyond the power of

medical science to explain. . . . Concentrate on precisely what you
want, and you will see signposts that point the way. The forces of
human evolution now have been brought under human control, and
you can control your own evolution as a better, more successful
person.

We need only decide upon a thing, back it with belief, and then
allow our Higher Self working in conjunction with our intuition, to
guide our way. Because the path we are led to tread will probably be
different from our logical interpretation of it, it's best to remain open
and flexible to your inner wisdom and suggestions.

Many times what our intuition is guiding us to do will be what
appeals to us the most, so it is easy to follow its path. However, often
logic will get in the way of our intuition. Just when we think we are
ready to pursue a particular course of action, all sorts of doubts will
begin to creep in. Am I really up to doing things in a new way, one
I've never tried before? What will others think? What if I fail? I'm
sure I'll fail and look like an idiot. Best not to tell anyone what I'm
doing, we tell ourselves. When I first decided to achieve abstinence
from my food addiction *without* Overeaters Anonymous, I didn't tell
my sponsor. I wasn't ready to withstand her negative, rigid stance—
she'd seen others try it without O.A. and they'd always failed.

Logic will throw one curve ball after another at us in the beginning
in order to get us to stray from our course. Listen to your heart, and
follow it. Logic is often just the *conscious* aspect of subconscious fears.
And fear's goal is safety, the status quo, and conformity. Fear means
well, but fear doesn't want us to risk anything, *ever.* And if we are to
go to higher and higher levels of awareness, we *have* to risk. We have
to become aware of the limitations our old, outdated beliefs place on
us and risk trying things the way our heart tells us to do. The more
we do, the more the Universe will back us in amazing and miraculous
ways.

In our first steps toward creating with purpose, we will also knock
up against guilt. Remember guilt? Guilt is the little voice that tells us

we're not worthy, that good things always happen to other people, that to accept good in any form we have to sweat and toil and suffer and earn it. Guilt is also another conscious version of a subconscious fear.

I realized I still had guilt messages when good things began happening in my life and I had a hard time accepting them. When my husband and I really began to have an open, honest, trusting relationship, something we had striven for years to achieve, it felt very uncomfortable and awkward at first. I had wanted for so long to feel truly close to him and when we really started achieving that, my fear of intimacy kicked in along with some guilt feelings. I had to consciously allow the good things in. I noticed that when things would go smoothly between us for a while, I would be tempted to pick a fight for no reason. It was as if I couldn't take all this wonderfulness. I had to consciously allow wonderful things to happen to me. Having internalized the message that life is toil and struggle, I had come to accept that as a matter of course. Creating a life with purpose meant that I was achieving the dreams I had sought for so long, and achieving my dreams was in direct contrast to my internalized message of toil and struggle.

Allow good things to happen. Allow yourself to be worthy of love, no matter how bad a person you feel you've been. Allow yourself to pursue your dreams, and allow yourself to receive many wonderful, miraculous gifts along the way. Allow your life to run smoothly.

Nothing in nature experiences stress the way man does. We seem to have built-in mechanisms that cause us to worry, wring our hands, and keep success at arm's length. Success is right inside us, for every dream we hold dear. We just have to claim it.

In achieving the dreams and intentions you hold dear, use all the tools and assistance you have available to you: your Higher Self, your inner sense of empowerment, your intuition, and a sense of trust that all things are working together for good.

You can cocreate your destiny and shape your life with all the power of the Universe at your disposal. Remember, our fondest dreams for ourselves are God's will for us. Paint the canvas of life the way that suits you and appeals to you. I have often had little wishes about certain things, and have thought, "I wish things were *this* way instead of *that* way." I discovered that often it was only my *belief* that a certain thing was *that* way that made it so. If I could suspend logic (and guilt) and allow things to be *this* way, they usually were this way.

Achieve what you want to achieve, believe it and do it. The tools and forces of the Universe lay ready for you to use them. Suppose you had a child who had an obvious delight in and talent for art and you bought that child all sorts of art tools: crayons, paper, watercolors, colored pencils, charcoal. You became excited at the store when buying the tools, thinking, "Oh, he'll love this. And think what he can do with this, and this, and this." Money was no object, so you purchased the finest of everything and even secured the unlimited services of the best local artists in order to guide your son and instruct him along the way. Laying it all before him, you waited for him to seize all the tools with gusto. But, much to your disappointment, he simply sat in the corner and said, "No thanks, Mom, I'm really not worthy. Give them all to someone more deserving than I am. Besides, even though I feel really alive when I create art, I'm really just a child and I shouldn't be able to create such wonderful things anyway. Better just take it all back."

Having made the finest of everything available to him, only to see him shun it because he felt as if he did not deserve it made you want to cry. You just couldn't understand. That's a little bit how the Universe feels when we choose to live humdrum, stifled lives of fear and conformity when the world offers us the finest and most powerful tools in the Universe with which to fashion our own personal creations.

Our Higher Self, which is simply our Higher Power within us, our intuition, our spiritual guides and aides, our sense of wonder and trust, our imagination, all of these are the tools of the Universe. They are lying at our feet simply waiting for us to use them.

What does it feel like when we are creating with purpose? In *Seat of the Soul*, Author Gary Zukav sums it up nicely:

When the deepest part of you becomes engaged in what you are doing, when your activities and actions become gratifying and purposeful, when what you do serves both yourself and others, when you do not tire within but seek the sweet satisfaction of your life and your work, you are doing what you were meant to be doing. The personality that is engaged in the work of its soul is buoyant. It is not burdened with negativity. It does not fear. It experiences purposefulness and meaning. It delights in its work and in others. It is fulfilled and fulfilling.

Allow love to guide you. Let yourself be worthy of being taken care of by yourself. Remember, our fondest dreams for ourselves are God's will for us. As we create a life with meaning and purpose, we clear away all the debris of our past and begin to live fully in the present. We begin to live with purpose and conviction instead of fear and dependence. We become who we were meant to become, not necessarily who others want us to be. In doing so, we find we are more alive and vital and are thus more available to those around us. We are able to serve others better after we first learn to serve ourselves.

CONCLUSION

And let us now live our lives . . .

33

Going It Alone

THIS BOOK HAS BEEN all about providing you with the guidance and encouragement to carve your own path, a path that is unique to *your* needs and experiences, a path that encourages you to go within to recognize and honor your inner wisdom. This path, in encouraging you to go within, will lead to your healing and release you from the destructive aspects of addiction. By recognizing that addiction is simply a signpost that something is going unhealed within us and needs our loving attention, we can free ourselves from its clutches.

It would seem that by my pointing out the drawbacks of the twelve-step model, I am encouraging people to stop attending A.A. meetings. That is not what I wish to do, and it is not the message I wish to convey. A.A. meetings and other twelve-step programs have been instrumental in helping thousands of people find abstinence and sobriety from their addictions. However, sobriety is only part of the process. If we are to truly heal, we must learn to acknowledge and work on our inner erroneous messages of guilt, shame, rage, blame, condemnation, abandonment, and unworthiness. We learn to accept and heal those messages and replace them with the truth of our being— the truth that we are powerful and wise beyond our imaginings.

As we become our own internal authority, it means leaving behind the fear-based models of behavior and belief systems and carving out our own path, which is directed by our soul. As we learn to follow our heart, we grow up and move beyond the need for parent-child-type relationships. We essentially become our own parent.

Fear tells us there is only one way to achieve sobriety. Love knows there are many different, varied, individualistic paths to recovery, and love honors them all. Going it alone means finding what works best for you and honoring it. Honoring your own path may mean more A.A. meetings, it may mean trying out different meetings, like Native American A.A. meetings. Honoring your path may mean no meetings and a good therapist. It may mean meditation and self-help books. Going it alone may mean adopting a new religion altogether. Or it may mean charting your own path as you go, using what works for now and living spontaneously.

Going it alone always means honoring your Higher Self by doing what feels right, and letting go of having fear run your life. It means taking control of your life and cocreating your destiny with the Universe, letting love be your guide always.

The phrase "going it alone" is actually not accurate. Treading the path of fear and dependence is actually going it more alone than is honoring your own path. Letting fear and dependency direct your life keeps you more alone because it keeps you from actually getting to know the person you've been running from all of your life, which is yourself. Honoring our own path requires us to go within and merge with ourselves. It asks us to dare go where no one has gone before, and lovingly asks us to dissect the very issues that keep us sick.

If you went to a doctor with a large cancerous tumor under your skin and he treated you by only applying a superficial lotion to your skin, you'd think he was crazy. The doctor has to go within your body and cut out the cancer to make you well again.

The same goes for us. The cancers of our unhealed emotional pain from the past keep us sick, and our inability to feel powerful and creative keeps us from living up to our potential.

As we dare venture to go within ourselves, we joyfully discover that our inner messages of guilt, shame, lack of forgiveness, blame, and unworthiness are erroneous. We are not all those things. Early experiences, from this lifetime or previous lifetimes, only convinced us we were, and we choose to identify ourselves with those fearful messages. Therefore, internalizing these incorrect messages left us with feelings of inadequacy, which we covered with fear and control. Fearing our inner inadequacies, we tried to control and manipulate them with rigid, formal belief systems. We all participated as part of the collective unconscious in creating these rigid systems of belief in order to protect ourselves from what we thought were our own sinful, addictive natures. We then willingly gave our power away to these external institutions to keep ourselves from realizing the truth. The truth is that we are powerful, wise, creative, vital, abundant, and loving beings. We are forgiven by the Universe and by our Higher Selves for simply not knowing any better. We were all asleep to our own power and beauty. Each of us awakens in our own time and in our own way. Love honors all ways, for love knows each person has to find his own way home. We can, however, all assist and guide and encourage one another. But I can't tell a person what is right for his own soul.

Ironically, by daring to go it alone and assume full responsibility for our own journey, we are less alone than ever before. We have the vast, unlimited support of the Universe and our Higher Selves backing us up every step of the way. We have help from our unseen guides and aides, and our inner wisdom and intuition. We are given a choice every moment to choose love or fear. And we are not judged by the Universe if, in our unconsciousness, we choose fear. We can choose fear as long as we need to in order to learn our lesson. As we begin choosing love more and more often, we can see how it always offers us the easiest, most harmonious path.

Love has always offered us the easiest, most harmonious path but in our fear we didn't always believe that. Even today, when I'm struggling with a particularly tough issue, I am tempted to choose fear because at least I'm familiar with it. Love often wants us to go into that unknown where outcomes are always uncertain until the last moment. Then, at the last moment, when we can finally see clearly, we exclaim, "Oh, that's how it all works. I see now. How silly of me not to have trusted all along."

Going it alone means having the courage to tread a path no one has tread before, *or* it may mean following others if that is what feels right to you. Be aware that what feels right to you doesn't necessarily mean it's the comfortable way. Often, honoring our highest path means taking the hard, tough road. But if our Higher Selves are guiding us, we can be certain that, along the way, we will be provided with everything we need.

Going it alone also means being flexible and knowing that what works now may not be what works next year or even next month. Honoring our own path means forever adapting and expanding who we are and what works for us.

By going it alone we allow love and intuition to guide us and we open ourselves us to help and assistance from all the forces of the Universe. By no longer having one limited, fear-based set of beliefs to direct us, we can receive wisdom and experience from any religion, practice, book, group, or network that we choose.

We are no longer forced to fit what feels right for us into one or more of the boxes of a rigid belief system.

So we are not actually going it alone at all. We will have help from our unseen spiritual guides, our Higher Selves, and all the accumulated wisdom of the ages, but without the parts that don't feel right for us personally. Instead of doing exactly what everyone else has done, going it alone means going it uniquely and individually.

Fear tells us to follow the tried and true. Love tells us to follow our hearts.

34

About Moderation

I MENTIONED SEVERAL TIMES throughout this book that I can have an occasional glass of beer or wine without it leading to harmful addictive behavior. I would like to explain that I do not think this is possible for many alcoholics and should not be hoped for at all. In my case, I had over three and a half years of sobriety before I decided I could drink champagne on my wedding day. I had felt many times before that day that I could drink moderately, but I didn't dare try because the fear-based A.A. message of "If you drink again, you'll die" was echoing in my ears. I had also heard many people in meetings say "That's just your -ism talking" in response to other people saying they felt they were cured.

The A.A. notion is one of recovery, not recovered, for life. They view alcoholism as a progressive disease that we will have for the remainder of our lives. I personally feel that this is a limited *belief* that we do not necessarily have to adopt. However, the progressive disease view will probably be true for many of those who do not move past limiting expectations. I also think there are people who should abstain completely for life. For those persons, alcohol in any form and in any amount is too much of a lure and moderate drinking will probably never be an option.

However, a word of caution here. We should not have as our *objective* in healing the ability to one day drink again in moderation.

263

If this is our goal, then we are still addicted to thinking that our fulfillment and satisfaction lies in things outside ourselves. The search for satisfaction in external things is one of the major components of addiction.

The magical part about going within, healing our souls, and discovering our inner happiness is that it provides such an overwhelming sense of fulfillment from inside us that we no longer have the *urge* to use anymore. The twelve-step model has your sobriety as its goal. The recommendations in this book go much deeper than sobriety. By going straight to the core of what causes us to use in the first place, we cure the need to use.

This book has shown you ways in which fear-based thinking keeps us sick, and how a move toward love-based thinking and acting will heal us. Just as many people have been cured, or cured themselves, of terminal illnesses and have gone on to live illness-free lives with no return of the original disease, so can we become completely free of the need to be addicted.

I wouldn't encourage anyone to give even a thought as to whether they could drink again or not until they have achieved sobriety for a substantial length of time and have done a great deal of inner work. If you are one of those who after a period of sobriety truly feel you can drink again in moderation, let your intuition be your guide.

If you have truly worked on the seven components to healing given in this book, your life should be relatively balanced. You probably have meaningful work, you are able to see where you still cling to fear, and you are able to choose love more and more often in your life. You let your heart, your intuition, and your Higher Self guide you, and you are free from addictive impulses. If this is the case, and you feel an inner prompting to have an occasional drink, trust your intuition. *You* know *you* better than anyone else.

Check with yourself to be certain that the desire to drink doesn't arise from an impulse to escape some part of your life you are not dealing with. Today, I usually only drink on special occasions, such as celebrations, or on vacation. But I also do not forbid myself to have a beer whenever I may feel like it, which is not often and does not stem from a desire to escape some aspect of my life. I find that one drink is usually enough and is all I really wanted. There have been times when the desire to overindulge has been strong, and a couple of times I felt I had too much to drink and questioned the validity of drinking at all. However, my overindulgences ran to only two or three drinks more than I had anticipated and not a week-long binge that would have included cocaine and food. Also, the next day I found I had no desire to drink (when before it would have been the first thing I wanted to do).

I think the important thing is to be absolutely true (and truthful) with yourself. You will know if you are okay with drinking in moderation. A nice glass of wine with dinner when going out with friends helps me, personally, to feel like a normal person instead of a diseased person who has to fear alcohol all of her life. I have spent a great deal of time trying to *resolve* my fears and move past my limitations. I saw no reason why alcohol and the beliefs surrounding it weren't *perpetuated by all of our beliefs about it.* The more power we give a belief, the more truth it will hold for us. So if we hold the belief that *alcohol* and *disease* are the bad guys, that is what we will experience.

If we hold intentions of love and healing, that is what we will experience. Love itself has no limitations. Love doesn't view one aspect of us as worthy of healing and another aspect as not worthy of healing. That is what *we* do to ourselves. We set the limitations within our bodies and then get upset when someone challenges those limitations. Argue for your limitations and what do you get? Limitations! What a prize!

We tend to mold ourselves around our belief systems *instead* of molding our belief systems to suit us and our needs and capabilities. We take a belief system and use its parameters as rigid, unbreakable boundaries. But food and the area of food addiction is a good example of how we can make a belief system suit us instead of the other way around. With alcohol, because of its addictive qualities and the out-of-control behavior it evokes in an alcoholic, we think that full recovery from alcoholism is not possible and drinking again in moderation is impossible and foolish. But food has just as many addictive qualities. In fact, in many ways it was much more alluring and addictive for me than alcohol. And food addicts exhibit all the same traits and behaviors as alcoholics do with alcohol. I had much less control over food than I did over alcohol. Whereas I could put off drinking any alcohol until later in the day after I had accomplished a few things, food thoughts invaded me anytime and anywhere. Food cravings pulled me out of class, made me leave meetings, break dates, lie. My food cravings always seemed much more insistent that my alcohol cravings. And my battle for food abstinence was much more difficult than my trying to achieve sobriety. And yet, it never occurs to us that we *can't* one day eat food in moderation. Because of the basic necessity of our bodies for food, complete abstinence from food is not a possibility. Therefore, to achieve freedom from food addiction, *moderation is a must.* We do not have a choice about it. We can't *not* eat. But we also can't continue to eat addictively if we want to be happy. So, here, we learn to adapt our belief system ("I can learn to eat moderately") to suit our needs (the body's need for food). Why can't we mold our belief system regarding alcohol in the same way? Is alcohol more addictive than food? Absolutely not. Does sugar cause a similar chemical reaction in our brains as alcohol does? Medical researchers says unequivocally that yes, it does. Then who is to say that an alcoholic can never drink again but that a food addict can learn to eat moderately? For myself, I really have no desire to *learn* to drink moderately as if it were a rigorous discipline I needed to embark on in order to achieve success. I would just like to be able to have an occasional beer or glass of wine with my meal or at a social function. Nothing more than that. And I have a belief system, along with my intuition, that says this is okay. It's no big deal. It can be as simple as that if we allow it to be.

You can fill up your life with limitation and limiting thoughts. You can live your life by using other people's experiences and achievements as barriers to your own. Or you can set your beliefs according to what you want to accomplish. Think of all the great people throughout history, people like Abraham Lincoln, Benjamin Franklin, Albert Einstein, Andrew Carnegie, Henry Ford, Franklin

Roosevelt, Margaret Thatcher. These were not people who blindly accepted the beliefs of those around them. Instead, they let their dreams and ambitions dictate their beliefs. You will become more like the Universe created you as you learn to do the same. We lead much more stifled lives than we need to. Let your heart's desires be the basis of your beliefs, and prove the fallibility of believing in limitation. Dictate what you want, what your heart truly desires, and then use all your resources to achieve it.

In doing so, be faithful to what feels right to you. Many people, being relieved of an addiction, see no reason to tempt fate; I honor their choice. Every person is free to choose the path that feels right for him or her. If you feel you are okay enough to have an occasional drink or two, but find on trying it that it still holds too much addictive appeal for you, then honor that. Don't beat yourself up for not knowing better. This was simply your way of finding out what worked best for you and what didn't.

If your life is free from addictive impulses, which is what this book will hopefully help you achieve, you have come a long way. If you have truly healed your soul, you may feel "normal" enough to have alcohol in moderation. The key always is to do what feels right for you. Honor your highest path and keep love as your intention.

35

Alternatives to
Twelve-Step Programs

WHEN I LEFT twelve-step programs for good and began my own journey of healing, I didn't know that many people before me had done the same thing. Each had tried A.A., found that their real needs were not being addressed, and left the twelve-step model behind to chart a course of healing that did work for them.

I was surprised to find that I had never heard of any of these authors or their programs until I began my research for this book. Each of the different alternatives to twelve-step programs was very sound and useful. So why did I not know anything about them? Perhaps because A.A. and its proponents fiercely claim it to be the only true recovery program by telling those who decline to subscribe to its belief system that they are either in denial about the severity of their powerlessness or are in denial about their ability to help themselves. Whenever I let my attendance at meetings slip, I was always reminded by a loyal A.A. member to remember that without A.A. my only options were "jails, institutions, or death," the implication being, "Remember, Marianne, you can't do it without us." I believe this is another area in which A.A. members simply spout A.A. slogans without stopping to evaluate whether they are really true for everyone. Perhaps I had just assumed that A.A. was the only game in town because of its very high profile; courts routinely sentence drunk-driving offenders to A.A. in lieu of jail time, the military routinely enforces A.A. attendance for its alcohol abusers, and social welfare agencies throughout the country send their alcohol-dependent clients to A.A. without mentioning that there may be alternatives. Furthermore, A.A. is the foundation of the majority of treatment centers in the United States today. It has become an institution. A.A. seemed to have eclipsed any and every other treatment option in my mind. I had never heard of any alternatives to A.A. and it therefore simply did not occur to me that any existed.

A.A.'s presence as the most well-known solution to alcoholism, along with all the twelve-step groups that have been spawned from A.A., had also led me to assume that it is the most successful treatment program for alcoholism. However, many fine studies, especially those documented by Dr. Stanton Peele in his books *The Diseasing of America* and *The Truth About Addiction & Recovery*, show that A.A. is no more successful than any other treatment option and that the most successful treatment for alcoholism occurs when people simply stop on their own *without any treatment at all*. Perhaps 30 to 40 percent of those who achieve long-term sobriety do so without treatment, whereas A.A. helps perhaps 3 percent of the drinking population achieve long-term sobriety. These are not the numbers shown in the media or talked about by the high-profile celebrities who attend the Betty Ford treatment center and are interviewed by *People* magazine. It is not very sensational to write about people achieving sobriety on their own.

These reasons could explain why I had never heard of these other programs. In fact, if I hadn't been doing the research for this book, I wonder if I ever would have stumbled upon these alternatives to A.A. We need to know these other programs exist so that we can decide for ourselves what works best for us and what doesn't. By having A.A.'s catchy slogans forced down my throat, I felt that I had no right to feel that the steps just didn't have what I needed. I was so thrilled to discover that others had felt the same way. The five programs I outline below, interestingly enough, were each born, in part, from the founders' personal dissatisfaction with A.A. As you read ahead, bear in mind the following quote from Jack Trimpey's (the founder of Rational Recovery) *The Small Book*, where he gives his own version of step one: "Step One—We made a fearless evaluation of our most personal beliefs and chose the recovery program that made the most sense."

WOMEN FOR SOBRIETY

Founded by Jeane Kirkpatrick in 1976, W.F.S. is dedicated to helping women achieve sobriety outside the domain of A.A. Through her own struggles, Dr. Kirkpatrick realized that the needs of women alcoholics were different from those of men. She found that A.A. "just did not meet my needs" and felt that women needed a separate arena in which their particular reasons for drinking could be addressed.

The W.F.S. program centers around thirteen statements, "The Thirteen Statements of Acceptance," that are not rigid steps. The statements are designed to empower women, encourage them to move past negative, self-deprecating ways of thinking, release shame and guilt, and build up fragile egos. No one is expected to adhere rigidly to the statements and disagreements are accepted.

Author and therapist Charlotte Kasl gives high praise to the W.F.S. program in her book *Many Roads, One Journey*. "Kirkpatrick understands the needs for women to have groups of their own that stress choices, the positive power of the mind, imaging, broadening one's perspective, the ability to love, and physical healing."

There is now a program for men entitled Men for Sobriety (M.F.S.) patterned after W.F.S. and with a similar emphasis on empowering men, uncovering their reasons for drinking, and encouraging new, positive ways of thinking, and taking responsibility for their lives.

To obtain information on W.F.S. or M.F.S. write or call:

W.F.S. (or M.F.S.)
P.O. Box 618
Quakertown, PA 18951
Tel: 215-536-8026
Website: www.womenforsobriety.org

RATIONAL RECOVERY

The R.R. program was founded by Jack Trimpey, another A.A. dropout. In response to his dissatisfaction with A.A., Trimpey wrote a book entitled *The Small Book*, a rebuttal to the Big Book. At the time it was published, *The Small Book* was very controversial and was seen as "A.A.-bashing" by many. However, his program has gone on to help thousands recover from the insidious effects of alcoholism. R.R. does not depend on a Higher Power or any spiritual power. Trimpey places complete reliance in the power of one's rational mind to overcome addiction. He uses a process called Addictive Voice Recognition Training (A.V.R.T.) to strengthen the rational mind and to help alcoholics identify and overcome the influences of the addictive mind.

In both *The Small Book* and his follow-up book, *Rational Recovery*, Trimpey debunks many of the senseless theories of A.A. as being "irrational." He writes in *The Small Book* that, "The difficulty in getting stopped stems, in large part, from the extremely popular, irrational alcoholic belief that alcoholic people cannot choose to become non-addicted. The truth is that many do it and do it every day."

Additional information on Rational Recovery can be obtained from:

R.R. Systems
P.O. Box 800
Lotus, CA 95651
Tel: 530-621-4374
Website: www.rational.org/recovery

Secular Organization for Sobriety/ Save Our Selves (S.O.S.)

This organization was founded by James Christopher, who believes that you can obtain sobriety no matter what you believe about God. The core of his approach lies in his "sobriety priority" statement: "I don't drink, no matter what." This program encourages people to think for themselves, determine their own sets of values, and run groups based on preferences instead of formal guidelines.

His organization has received a very favorable response from the public and currently has meetings worldwide. S.O.S. believes in support groups that offer "support without dogma." Members do not include just alcoholics. All types of addiction or dependency problem are addressed.

His book, *How to Stay Sober in Recovery Without Religion,* is a very helpful treatise on the S.O.S. program and offers guidelines for organizing secular sobriety groups.

For additional information:

S.O.S. International Clearinghouse
5521 Grosvenor Boulevard
Los Angeles, CA 90066
Tel: 310-821-8430
Fax: 310-821-2610
Website: www.unhooked.com

Empowerment Groups

Charlotte Davis Kasl, author, psychologist, and lecturer, has founded a sixteen-step empowerment model that is outlined in her book *Many Roads, One Journey: Moving Beyond the Twelve Steps.* Ms. Kasl's book is a wonderfully inspiring, very thoroughly researched book that looks at the various aspects of addiction, the drawbacks of the A.A. model, the role society and patriarchy play, the special needs of women and minorities, and states that the best way to recover is in whatever way works for you, a far cry from the A.A. dictum to "thoroughly follow our path." Her approach is that each person needs to access their inner wisdom to find their healing path. She writes, "True healing occurs through empowerment and love, not fear."

Ms. Kasl encourages those who are dissatisfied with A.A. to start their own support groups. To that end, she has published a book entitled *Yes, You Can—A Guide to Empowerment Groups*. The book serves as a guide for starting and maintaining a sixteen-step group in your community. It also includes a resource guide on how to find out if there is an existing sixteen-step group in your area. The book gives specific hints for having a successful group and gives a detailed treatise on each step. Ms. Kasl stresses that the steps can and should be modified to suit the differing needs of the group. She encourages each group to find its own voice, and to honor what feels right without making the twelve-step model wrong.

Her sixteen steps are a wonderful affirmation of a "life-loving/creative spirituality" approach to addiction. Ms. Kasl understands that recovering from addiction is about healing and uncovering our negative beliefs. She also knows that there is no one way of recovery that is right for everyone. Her model of empowerment gently encourages members to move past limiting, oppressive beliefs from the past, understand where they originated from, and create more positive, uplifting beliefs for the future.

She encourages treatment programs to inform clients of alternative models of healing. "To help find a program that is right for them would probably save countless people from relapse and pain because they would be free to put their energy into uncovery and discovery rather than adapting a program that doesn't feel right."

The sixteen steps have been met with a great deal of enthusiasm within the recovery community. Many people who have felt alienated by the twelve-step model are finding a home in the sixteen-step empowerment model. As one member says, "I want empowerment, not powerlessness."

Ms. Kasl leads workshops, is available for consultations. and has a list of tapes and books available for furthering recovery. She can be contacted at:

Ms. Charlotte Kasl
P.O. Box 1302
Lolo, MT 59847
Website: http://members.aol.com/empower16/steps.htm

If anyone is interested in finding a group or listing one in a national directory, they can contact Adam White, 362 Cleveland Ave. #1, St. Paul, MN 55104. Tel: 651-645-5782. E-mail: empower16@aol.com.

MODERATION MANAGEMENT

Moderation Management is a self-help organization for people who want to reduce their drinking. The program promotes balance, moderation, self-management, and personal responsibility.

According to their Website on the Internet, "Moderation Management is a recovery program and national support group network for people who have made the healthy decision to reduce their drinking and make other positive lifestyle changes. M.M. empowers individuals to accept personal responsibility for choosing and maintaining their own recovery path, whether moderation or abstinence. Individuals who are not able to successfully reduce their drinking either find a local abstinence-only program to attend or remain in M.M. and choose abstinence as their goal."

Moderation Management, founded by Audrey Kishlin, has come under fire from many proponents of A.A. as offering false hope to alcoholics that they may one day drink again in moderation. However, Moderation Management is very adamant that its program is not for everyone. It is geared more toward the problem drinker and away from the true alcoholic. One of the things I find encouraging about the program, along with the others listed in this section, is that they do not contend that they are the only solution (besides jails, institutions, or death) for the problem drinker or even the alcoholic. M.M. makes a distinction between the alcoholic and the problem drinker, the latter being much more prevalent and in need of different treatment than simple abstinence. M.M. not only steers alcoholics toward abstinence-based programs but informs them of their options, such as A.A., Rational Recovery, SOS, Women for Sobriety, and SMART. M.M. tries to help problem drinkers at the earliest stage at which their drinking becomes harmful.

The program consists of "nine steps toward moderation and balance," which encourage members to examine how drinking has affected their life, determine under what cicumstances they drink, learn the M.M. guidelines for moderate drinking, abstain for thirty days, and make positive lifestyle changes.

If you are interested in M.M., a good starting point is to read Audrey Kishlin's book, *Moderate Drinking* (Crown, $14). It can be ordered directly at 800-726-0600 or your local bookstore. Their Website also offers a M.M. guidebook, a list of support groups, a chat room, along with suggested guidelines and limits for moderate drinking and other useful information.

Their address is:

Moderation Management, Inc.
P.O. Box 1752
Woodinville, WA 98072
Tel: 888-561-9834
Website: www.moderation.org

SMART Recovery

Recovery from alcohol addiction, drug addiction and dependence, family problems, legal issues, court-mandated recovery program attendance, non-twelve-step groups, meeting directory, non-twelve-step recovery links, overeating, compulsive disorders, stopping an addiction. SMART is not affiliated with Alcoholics Anonymous.

SMART Recovery
24000 Mercantile Rd.
Suite 11
Beachwood, OH 44122
Tel: 216-292-0220
Fax: 216-831-3776
Website: www.smartrecovery.org

ADDITIONAL RESOURCES

Aside from these support-group–type programs, there are several excellent self-help therapies available to help addicts. They are outlined in the following books.

The Truth About Addiction and Recovery, by Dr. Stanton Peele and Archie Brodsky (Simon & Schuster, available in bookstores). Dr. Peele draws upon the resources used by countless addicts he has observed who helped cure themselves of addiction. The Life Process Program focuses on using the personal strengths and resources of the addicts to effect their own sobriety. Peele emphasizes coping skills, problem-solving strategies, and life-management skills that are a natural part of a person's development. He believes it is possible to encourage and promote these skills to effect change. Peele describes addiction as occurring along a continuum from severely debilitating to mild abuse and believes that a person's place on the continuum determines the degree of treatment needed. The Life Process Program is a very life-affirming program that deemphasizes the disease theory and instead places the responsibility on the addict. It helps him to examine where personal problems lie and encourages the addict to get involved in other things that are bigger than the addiction.

Dr. Peele outlines ways to set goals, find positive activities to replace the addiction, and recommends that you define and recognize "high risk" situations that trigger addictive episodes. Peele states that "getting better is not a matter of believing a dogma" and that the addict must find and develop his own power if he is to get better.

With its emphasis on identifying underlying problems, the Life Process Program is an excellent tool for those seeking to better understand the reason for their addiction. "[Healing] addiction is part of an intergrated life change," Peele says in his book, and the Life Process Program is designed as a tool to instigate that change.

The best resource guide to understanding addiction and the various approaches to recovery can be found at Stanton Peele's internet site: www.peele.net.

When AA Doesn't Work for You: Rational Steps to Quitting Alcohol, by Albert Ellis and Emmett Velten (Barricade Books). Dr. Ellis is the founder of Rational Emotive Therapy (R.E.T.), which is the basis for Jack Trimpey's Rational Recovery. In this book, Ellis outlines the ways in which people can stop drinking or can stop any self-defeating behavior by getting a handle on their own beliefs and thinking processes. He states in his book that he designed R.E.T. to "empower you and increase your self-acceptance and freedom . . . We will teach you how to direct your own therapy and become an effective self-helper." One of the cornerstones of R.E.T. is the notion that you make yourself "needlessly miserable when you take your preferences and desires for healthy goals and turn them into strong, rigid shoulds, oughts, musts, and commands." Ellis teaches that the way to break out of this trap of rigid thinking is to change the self-defeating thought system from one of irrational beliefs, such as the belief that something outside you is responsible for your behavior, into more rational lines of thinking. Ellis's program encourages unconditional self-acceptance rather than highly conditional self-esteem. He shows in his book that our behavior has causes, and he then shows you how to identify those causes. More information is available from:

The Institute of Rational Emotive Therapy
45 East 65th St.
New York, NY 10021
Tel: 212-535-0822
Material orders: 1-800-323-IRET

Help Yourself, A Revolutionary Alternative Recovery Program, by Dr. Joel C. Robertson, Robertson Institute, Limited (Nelson Books). According to Dr. Robertson, most addicts can recover without hospitalization or outside therapy. His book discusses the mistruths about addiction and explains what an individual needs to know to successfully treat his or her own addictive behavior. Dr. Robertson's plan includes how to understand the body-mind-spirit connection, how to identify the stages of recovery, and how to find the support system that is right for you. He explains how addicted persons need to identify their self-defeating behavior and then need to work on changing their thoughts. He stresses the importance of tailoring recovery techniques to fit the personality, the importance of finding positive rewards, trusting our emotions, and proper diet and exercise.

Additional information is available from:

Robertson Institute
3555 Pierce Rd.
Saginaw, MI 48604
Tel: 517-799-8720

Beyond A.A.—Dealing Responsibly with Alcohol, by Clarence Barrett, J.D. (Positive Attitudes). In his book, Clarence Barrett explains how the sole responsibility for the alcoholic's behavior rests squarely on his shoulders—not on disease theories, outside conditions, or character defects and how willpower and determination can be used to achieve sobriety. He summarizes the various treatment approaches and introduces the concept of Reality Therapy: "All the alcoholic is doing is trying to satisfy certain of his basic needs, needs that are shared by all human beings, but is doing so irresponsibly and needs to be taught more responsible ways. This book undertakes to teach those ways."

The book is available from:

Positive Attitudes, Publishers
91060 Nelson Mountain Rd.
Greenleaf, OR 97430
Tel: 503-964-3731

All of these various recovery programs and books offer different things for the different treatment needs of alcoholics. It is interesting that so many components of the different programs overlap, such as accepting full responsibility for our alcoholic behavior, changing our negative, self-defeating belief systems, and finding positive expressions for ourselves. I believe that the best recovery program of all is the one that addresses our own particular needs, validates us, and uplifts us. One that encourages us to take the tragedy of our addictive behavior and use it to construct a healthy, powerful, responsible life. In conclusion, I would like to leave you with the words of Charlotte Kasl: "And simply presenting people with choices to explore is empowering." May your own journey be one of empowerment.

HOW TO CONTACT THE AUTHOR

Please feel free to write to me with your own stories and suggestions.

Marianne Gilliam
P.O. Drawer R
Acworth, GA 30101
E-mail: mgilliam@mindspring.com
Website: www.mariannegilliam.com

Check this Website often for updates and interaction with people who are achieving sobriety and freedom from addiction.